# SAMS
# Teach Yourself

## Microsoft® Office
# FrontPage® 2003

# in 24 Hours

Rogers Cadenhead

**SAMS**   800 East 96th St., Indianapolis, Indiana, 46240 USA

# Sams Teach Yourself Microsoft® Office FrontPage® 2003 in 24 Hours

## Copyright © 2004 by Sams Publishing

International Standard Book Number: 0-672-32552-7

Library of Congress Catalog Card Number: 2003103643

Printed in the United States of America

First Printing: November 2003

06   05   04   03          4   3   2   1

## Trademarks

## Warning and Disclaimer

## Bulk Sales

Sams Publishing offers excellent discounts on this book when ordered in quantity for bulk purchases or special sales. For more information, please contact

**U.S. Corporate and Government Sales**
**1-800-382-3419**
**corpsales@pearsontechgroup.com**

For sales outside of the U.S., please contact

**International Sales**
**1-317-428-3341**
**international@pearsontechgroup.com**

**ASSOCIATE PUBLISHER**
Greg Wiegand

**ACQUISITIONS EDITOR**
Michelle Newcomb

**DEVELOPMENT EDITOR**
Laura Norman

**MANAGING EDITOR**
Charlotte Clapp

**PROJECT EDITOR**
Dan Knott

**COPY EDITOR**
Krista Hansing

**INDEXER**
Kelly Castell

**PROOFREADER**
Suzanne Thomas

**TECHNICAL EDITOR**
Bill Bruns

**TEAM COORDINATOR**
Sharry Lee Gregory

**INTERIOR DESIGNER**
Gary Adair

**COVER DESIGNER**
Alan Clements

**PAGE LAYOUT**
Eric S. Miller
Michelle Mitchell

**GRAPHICS**
Tammy Graham
Tara Lipscomb

# Contents at a Glance

Introduction     1

**PART I Creating Your First Web Pages**     **5**

Hour 1   Create a Web Page     7

2   Organize a Page with Links, Lists, and Tables     21

3   Display Graphics and Photos on a Page     35

4   Lay Out a Page with Tables     53

**PART II Designing an Entire Web Site**     **65**

Hour 5   Create a New Web Site     67

6   Develop a Site Quickly with Templates     77

7   Make Your Site Look Great with Themes     89

8   Let FrontPage Create a Site for You     105

**PART III Improving Your Site's Appeal**     **121**

Hour 9   Collect Information from Your Visitors     123

10   Make a Site Look Great with Graphics     137

11   Offer Animation, Video, and Games     151

12   Use Web Components to Jazz Up a Site     167

**PART IV Making Your New Site a Success**     **185**

Hour 13   Publish Your Site     187

14   Attract the Widest Possible Audience     199

15   Promote a New Site     211

16   Learn More About Your Site's Audience     225

**PART V Enhancing Your Site**     **239**

Hour 17   Add a Search Engine to Your Site     241

18   Turn Your Site into a Community     253

19   Connect a Database to Your Site     265

20   Use Your Site to Gather Information     279

**PART VI  Creating Web Sites Like a Pro**                                    **299**

Hour 21    Create and Edit Pages Using HTML                                    301

    22    Format Your Site with Cascading Style Sheets                     315

    23    Share Information with XML                                        331

    24    Divide a Page into Separate Frames                               345

**PART VII  Appendices**                                                       **361**

Appendix A    FrontPage Internet Resources                                     363

        Glossary                                                          367

        Index                                                             387

# Contents

**Introduction** 1

**Part I  Creating Your First Web Pages** 5

**HOUR 1  Create a Web Page** 7

Start Using FrontPage 2003 ........................................................................7

Create a Page from a Template ...................................................................9

Create and Save a New Page .....................................................................10

Add Text to a Page .....................................................................................12

Create a Headline .......................................................................................14

Choose a Font and Color ...........................................................................15

Summary .....................................................................................................18

Q&A .............................................................................................................18

**HOUR 2  Organize a Page with Links, Lists, and Tables** 21

Add a Hyperlink to a Web Page ...............................................................22

Create a List ...............................................................................................24

Create a Collapsible Outline ...............................................................25

Organize a Page with Tables .....................................................................26

Line Up Text in a Table ............................................................................27

Add a Table to a Page ..........................................................................27

Add Data to a Table .............................................................................30

Remove Rows or Columns from a Table ............................................31

Change the Size of a Table ..................................................................31

Summary .....................................................................................................32

Q&A .............................................................................................................33

**HOUR 3  Display Graphics and Photos on a Page** 35

Work with Graphics in Different Formats ...............................................36

GIF Graphics ........................................................................................36

JPEG Graphics .....................................................................................37

PNG Graphics ......................................................................................37

Selecting the Right Format .................................................................38

Add a Graphic to a Page ...........................................................................38

Layout Graphics with Text .......................................................................40

Add a Hyperlink .........................................................................................42

Add a Caption .............................................................................................43

Add Clip Art to a Page .............................................................................45

Change the Size of a Graphic ...................................................................47

Save a Page with New Graphics ...............................................................49

Find More Clip Art to Use ...................................................................50

Summary ...............................................................................................50

Q&A ......................................................................................................51

**HOUR 4 Lay Out a Page with Tables                                     53**

Arrange Elements of a Page .................................................................54

Add a Layout Table to a Page ..............................................................55

Add and Remove Table Rows and Columns ........................................58

Make Adjustments to Page Layout ......................................................60

    Change the Margins of a Table ......................................................61

    Format a Layout Table Cell ...........................................................61

Summary ...............................................................................................63

Q&A ......................................................................................................63

**Part II  Designing an Entire Web Site                                  65**

**HOUR 5 Create a New Web Site                                          67**

Build a New Web Site ..........................................................................67

Explore the New Site ...........................................................................69

Add a New Page to a Site ....................................................................70

Import Files into a Site ........................................................................71

Delete a Site .........................................................................................72

Use Word Documents on the Web .......................................................74

Summary ...............................................................................................75

Q&A ......................................................................................................76

**HOUR 6 Develop a Site Quickly with Templates                         77**

Select a Web Site Template ..................................................................78

Create a New Web Site ........................................................................78

Customize Your New Web Site ............................................................80

    Add and Remove Comments .........................................................81

    Making Changes to a Shared Border .............................................82

Explore the Personal Web Site Template ..............................................84

    Add a Timestamp to a Web Page ..................................................86

    Save Changes to a Site ..................................................................87

Summary ...............................................................................................88

Q&A ......................................................................................................88

**HOUR 7 Make Your Site Look Great with Themes                         89**

Give a Site Personality ........................................................................90

Select a Theme .....................................................................................90

    Using Animated Graphics in a Theme ...........................................93

    Testing a Theme in Different Browsers ..........................................94

Change to a New Theme ......................................................................94

Create a Custom Theme .............................................................95
    Select a Color Scheme .......................................................96
    Select Fonts for a Theme ....................................................98
    Select Graphics Used By a Theme ...........................................100
    Save the New Theme .........................................................102
Delete a Theme ...................................................................102
Summary ..........................................................................102
Q&A ..............................................................................103

HOUR 8  Let FrontPage Create a Site for You                                     105

Open a Site-Creation Wizard .....................................................105
Import an Existing Site into FrontPage ..........................................107
    Choose an Import Method ....................................................108
    Choose Where to Save the Site ..............................................111
    Choose How Much to Import ..................................................112
    Import the Site's Files .....................................................113
    Work on the Imported Site ..................................................114
Create a Corporate Web Site .....................................................115
    Choose Pages for the Site ..................................................116
Summary ..........................................................................118
Q&A ..............................................................................119

Part III  Improving Your Site's Appeal                                          121

HOUR 9  Collect Information from Your Visitors                                   123

Collect Feedback from Your Visitors .............................................123
    Save Visitor Feedback to a File ............................................126
    Receive Visitor Feedback in Email ..........................................127
Call on the Form Page Wizard ....................................................129
    Set Up Questions on a Form .................................................130
    Using the Form Page Wizard .................................................133
Summary ..........................................................................135
Q&A ..............................................................................135

HOUR 10  Make a Site Look Great with Graphics                                   137

Edit an Existing Graphic ........................................................137
Reshape a Graphic ...............................................................138
    Resize a Graphic ...........................................................138
    Crop a Graphic .............................................................140
Add Text to a Graphic ...........................................................141
Make Part of a Graphic Transparent ..............................................143
Share Your Digital Photos in a Photo Gallery ....................................145
Summary ..........................................................................148
Q&A ..............................................................................148

**Hour 11  Offer Animation, Video, and Games**                                    **151**

   Add a Scrolling Marquee ...................................................................................151
   Use Animation and Other Special Effects to a Page .......................................153
   Create Page Transition Effects ........................................................................154
   Animate Page Elements with Dynamic HTML ...............................................156
      Apply a DHTML Effect to Text ................................................................156
      Create a Mouseover Graphic ....................................................................158
   Copy Formatting from One Place to Another .................................................159
   Add Video to a Page .......................................................................................160
   Add Flash and Java Content ...........................................................................161
   Summary ..........................................................................................................165
   Q&A .................................................................................................................165

**Hour 12  Use Web Components to Jazz Up a Site**                                 **167**

   Add Components to a Web Site ........................................................................168
   Put MSNBC Features on a Page .....................................................................169
   Link to Maps on Expedia ................................................................................171
   Add a Link Bar ................................................................................................172
      Add a Navigational Link Bar ....................................................................173
      Add a Back/Next or Custom Link Bar ......................................................176
   Put a Banner on a Page ....................................................................................178
   Create Dynamic Web Templates .....................................................................179
   Summary ..........................................................................................................182
   Q&A .................................................................................................................182

**Part IV  Making Your New Site a Success**                                       **185**

**Hour 13  Publish Your Site**                                                    **187**

   Find a Server to Host Your Site .......................................................................187
   Publish Your Site for the First Time ...............................................................190
      Solve Any Publishing Problems ...............................................................193
      Prevent Something from Being Published .................................................194
      Keep a Web Site Synchronized .................................................................194
   Summary ..........................................................................................................196
   Q&A .................................................................................................................196

**Hour 14  Attract the Widest Possible Audience**                                 **199**

   Cope with a Diverse Audience ........................................................................200
   Make Your Web Compatible with Multiple Browsers .....................................201
      Choose Your Target Audience ..................................................................203
      Restrict Specific Technology on a Web Site .............................................205
      Handle Differences Between Web Browsers ..............................................207
   Preview a Page with Different Browsers ..........................................................208

Summary .................................................................................................................210
Q&A ......................................................................................................................210

**HOUR 15 Promote a New Site** **211**

Let Search Engines Know About a New Site ...............................................212
Submit the Site to Web Directories ...........................................................213
Exchange Links with Similar Sites .............................................................216
Join a Web Ring ..........................................................................................218
Add a Weblog to Your Site .........................................................................221
Summary .....................................................................................................223
Q&A ............................................................................................................224

**HOUR 16 Learn More About Your Site's Audience** **225**

Explore a Web Server's Logging Capability ...............................................226
See Usage Information for a Web Server ..............................................226
View the Usage Reports for Your Site .........................................................231
Add a Hit Counter to a Site .......................................................................234
Share Usage Reports with Your Visitors ....................................................235
Summary .....................................................................................................236
Q&A ............................................................................................................237

**Part V  Enhancing Your Site** **239**

**HOUR 17 Add a Search Engine to Your Site** **241**

Make Your Web Site Searchable .................................................................242
Customize How Results Are Displayed ......................................................244
Limit the Pages That Are Searched ......................................................246
Add a Search Form to an Existing Web Page .......................................246
Add an MSN Search ...................................................................................247
Add a Site Map ...........................................................................................248
Summary .....................................................................................................250
Q&A ............................................................................................................250

**HOUR 18 Turn Your Site into a Community** **253**

Create a Discussion Site with a Wizard ....................................................254
Choose the Pages to Include ................................................................255
Pick a Name and Folder ........................................................................256
Select a Format for Articles ..................................................................257
Establish a Membership Policy ............................................................258
Offer a Table of Contents .....................................................................259
Set Up Search Results ...........................................................................259
Choose a Layout ...................................................................................260
Complete the Discussion Site ..............................................................262

Maintain a Discussion Site ....................................................................263
Summary ..............................................................................................263
Q&A .....................................................................................................264

**HOUR 19  Connect a Database to Your Site                         265**

Make Use of Existing Database Files ......................................................266
Add an Existing Database to a Site ........................................................268
Display Database Records on a Page ......................................................269
Save Information to a New Database ......................................................275
Summary ..............................................................................................277
Q&A .....................................................................................................277

**HOUR 20  Use Your Site to Gather Information                     279**

Create a Form by Hand ..........................................................................280
Add Elements to a Form ........................................................................282
    Add a Text Box or Text Area ............................................................282
    Add a Label ......................................................................................285
    Add a Check Box or Option Button ..................................................286
    Add a Drop-Down Box ......................................................................287
    Add a Pushbutton ............................................................................289
    Add a Graphical Submit Button ........................................................290
Receive Information from a Form ............................................................291
    Save Form Responses to a File ........................................................291
    Send Form Responses via Email ......................................................294
    Sending Form Responses to a CGI Program ....................................296
Create a Confirmation Page ....................................................................297
Summary ..............................................................................................297
Q&A .....................................................................................................298

**Part VI  Creating Web Sites Like a Pro                           299**

**HOUR 21  Create and Edit Pages Using HTML                        301**

Get Started with HTML ..........................................................................302
    Using HTML Tags ............................................................................303
    Work with HTML Tags ......................................................................303
Tag a Page with HTML Commands ........................................................304
    Change a Page's Title ......................................................................306
Leave Existing HTML Untouched ............................................................307
Clean Up the HTML on a Page ..............................................................309
Add HTML to a Web Page ......................................................................311
Summary ..............................................................................................313
Q&A .....................................................................................................313

**Hour 22 Format Your Site with Cascading Style Sheets** 315

Use Styles to Design a Site ..................................................................316
Create a Style Sheet ............................................................................318
Edit a Style Sheet ................................................................................319
    Change the Appearance of Text ....................................................322
Apply a Style to a Web Page ..............................................................324
Match HTML Tags with FrontPage Features ......................................327
Summary ..............................................................................................328
Q&A ......................................................................................................329

**Hour 23 Share Information with XML** 331

View and Edit XML Files ....................................................................331
Save Forms as XML ............................................................................334
Display XML Data with a Data View ..................................................336
    Choose How Many Records to Display ..........................................339
    Filter Records on Different Criteria ..............................................340
    Format the Data View ....................................................................340
    Sort Records and Group Them Together ......................................341
Summary ..............................................................................................343
Q&A ......................................................................................................344

**Hour 24 Divide a Page into Separate Frames** 345

Create a Frame ....................................................................................346
    Add a Frames Page to a Site ..........................................................347
    Put a Page in a Frame ....................................................................348
Work on a Framed Page ......................................................................349
    Create an Alternative to Frames ....................................................353
    Save a Frames Page for the First Time ..........................................354
    Make Adjustments to a Frame ......................................................355
    Create a Frame of Changing Size ..................................................356
Add an Inline Frame ............................................................................357
Summary ..............................................................................................359
Q&A ......................................................................................................360

**Part VII Appendices** 361

**Appendix A FrontPage Internet Resources** 363

Web Sites and Discussion Groups ......................................................363
    Web Sites ........................................................................................364
    Discussion Groups ..........................................................................366

**Glossary** 367

**Index** 387

# About the Author

**Rogers Cadenhead** is a Web developer and *Linux Magazine* columnist. He has written 16 books on Internet-related topics, including *Sams Teach Yourself Java 2 in 21 Days* and *How to Use the Internet, Eighth Edition*. He's also a Web publisher whose sites receive more than seven million visits a year. He maintains this book's official World Wide Web site using FrontPage 2003 at `http://www.frontpage24.com`.

# Dedication

*To my wife, Mary Christine Moewe, for the first 15 years of forever. We'll always have Arlington, Denton, Fort Worth, Denver, Peoria, Dallas, Jacksonville, Palm Coast, and St. Augustine.*

# Acknowledgments

I'd like to thank the team at Sams Publishing, including Greg Wiegand, Michelle Newcomb, Laura Norman, Charlotte Clapp, Dan Knott, Bill Bruns, and Krista Hansing. With a group like this working on the book, I'm proud to have my name on the cover so I can claim a disproportionate share of the credit.

I also must thank my wife, Mary, and sons, Max, Eli, and Sam. You've given patience, support, humor, and love to someone who has spent enough time at a computer to qualify as a plug-and-play device. I love you at least 250% above the recommended daily allowance.

Finally, I'd like to thank Microsoft Bob.

# We Want to Hear from You!

As the reader of this book, *you* are our most important critic and commentator. We value your opinion and want to know what we're doing right, what we could do better, what areas you'd like to see us publish in, and any other words of wisdom you're willing to pass our way.

As an associate publisher, I welcome your comments. You can email or write me directly to let me know what you did or didn't like about this book—as well as what we can do to make our books better.

*Please note that I cannot help you with technical problems related to the topic of this book. We do have a User Services group, however, where I will forward specific technical questions related to the book.*

When you write, please be sure to include this book's title and author as well as your name, email address, and phone number. I will carefully review your comments and share them with the author and editors who worked on the book.

Email:     feedback@samspublishing.com

Mail:      Greg Wiegand
           Associate Publisher
           800 East 96th Street
           Indianapolis, IN 46240 USA

For more information about this book or another Sams Publishing title, visit our Web site at www.samspublishing. Type the ISBN (excluding hyphens) or the title of a book in the Search field to find the page you're looking for.

# Introduction

As a childhood fan of old-time radio shows like *The Shadow* and Orson Welles's infamous *War of the Worlds* broadcast, I often wondered what it must have been like to create a new mass medium from scratch. The creators of radio entertainment in the 1930s and 1940s were operating without a rulebook—the possibilities before them in the "theater of the mind" were limited only by their imaginations, actors, and the need for a good sound effects person.

When the World Wide Web came into our lives in the mid-1990s, I didn't have to wonder any longer. In the space of a few years, a quiet corner of the Internet grew into a mass medium to which millions of people turn for information.

People are using this amazing new medium to shop, learn, communicate, play, and teach. A network that once was occupied by a few thousand scholars, students, and military officials is now as ubiquitous as television. People who don't even own computers are familiar with Internet companies such as Amazon.com, Yahoo!, and eBay. Thousands of new Web sites are launched each day by a variety of publishers—corporations, small businesses, organizations, and individuals.

Millions of people are putting themselves and their companies on the Web, even if they don't consider themselves "computer geeks" by any stretch of the imagination, publishing interesting sites for people all over the world.

If you want to be one of those people, you've picked up the right book.

## What Is FrontPage 2003?

FrontPage 2003 is the brand-spanking-new version of Microsoft's Web site creation tool, one of the most popular and easy-to-use programs of its kind.

The best thing about the software is all the things it prevents you from learning.

That might sound like a knock, but it's a compliment: A person who uses FrontPage 2003 can publish on the World Wide Web without learning any of the following:

- Hypertext Markup Language (HTML)
- Cascading Style Sheets (CSS)
- Dynamic HTML
- JavaScript
- Common Gateway Interface (CGI) programming
- Active Server Pages (ASP)

You don't need to learn any of these Web design languages and technologies because FrontPage 2003 does all it for you. When you work on a Web site in FrontPage, you edit it in a visual point-and-click environment that's similar to Microsoft Word. Web design features that are the stock in trade of professional Web designers can be implemented in FrontPage with a few mouse clicks.

# Who Should Use FrontPage 2003?

FrontPage, now in its sixth major release from Microsoft, is also a tightly integrated part of Microsoft Office, the most popular productivity suite in the world.

You might be familiar with FrontPage 2002, FrontPage 98, or another older version of the software. FrontPage has always been one of the most popular Web-editing tools because it makes creating a Web page as easy as writing a letter in Microsoft Word.

Whether you are a business owner launching an online store, a high school student publishing fledgling literary efforts, or an armchair pundit seeking to share your political views on a weblog, you can benefit from FrontPage's sophisticated editing, publishing, and site-maintenance capabilities.

# Who Should Use This Book?

FrontPage 2003 makes it simple to master the complex tasks required of a Web publisher, but you must first learn a bit about the software itself.

The fastest way to do this is with *Sams Teach Yourself Microsoft FrontPage 2003 in 24 Hours*.

During 24 one-hour lessons, you'll develop hands-on skills with each feature of FrontPage 2003:

- Creating new Web sites quickly with templates, themes, and wizards
- Editing Web pages exactly as they will appear in a browser—a feature known as WYSIWYG, or "What You See Is What You Get"
- Turning on and off features of FrontPage 2003, depending on the Web browsers used by your audience
- Adding interactive capabilities such as discussion sites, surveys, and feedback pages
- Editing digital photos and other graphics within FrontPage instead of using an image-editing program

- Publishing your own weblog site and using XML data created by another Office program, two of more than a dozen new features introduced in FrontPage 2003 that are covered in this book
- Connecting your Web site to a Microsoft Access database
- Integrating your Web seamlessly with the other programs in the Office 2003 suite
- Bringing existing sites into FrontPage 2003 without altering their appearance
- Telling FrontPage 2003 what you want and letting the software figure out how to implement it through sophisticated Web technology such as Cascading Style Sheets, JavaScript, and Active Server Pages

Creating a FrontPage Web site has never been easier.

Whether you're using FrontPage 2003 at your office, home, or home office, *Sams Teach Yourself Microsoft FrontPage 2003* provides the skills you need to publish your own Web sites.

By the time you've completed the lessons in this book, you'll be taking part in the same publishing revolution that has spawned billions of pages, including well-known sites such as Yahoo! and ESPN.com, and more unusual fare such as Rocklopedia Fakebandica.

For several years, the writer T. Mike has been compiling the delightfully pointless Rocklopedia Fakebandica, an encyclopedia of musicians and musical groups that don't exist—fictional artists mentioned on TV shows and movies. If you'd like to know more about the Wonders and Cap'n Geech and the Shrimp Shack Shooters (from *That Thing You Do*), or Johnny Bravo and the Silver Platters (from *The Brady Bunch*), visit the encyclopedia at http://www.vgg.com/tp/tp_080700_fakeband.html.

As you read this book, you'll also become well acquainted with one of the first Web sites created with FrontPage 2003: this book's site, at http://www.frontpage24.com. My site for the book contains the following features:

- Updates to the material covered in the book
- Links for any Web site mentioned in the book that has moved
- Answers to questions commonly asked by other readers
- A way to contact author Rogers Cadenhead with your own questions, comments, and corrections

You will also find information on this book at http://www.samspublishing.com.

By the time you finish *Sams Teach Yourself Microsoft FrontPage 2003 in 24 Hours*, you'll be equally surprised by how much FrontPage 2003 can do for you. It can make Web sites much easier to create and manage, letting you focus on the content you want to publish and the audience you want to reach.

# How to Use This Book

Each lesson of this book should take you approximately an hour to learn. The book is designed to get you productively working in FrontPage 2003 as quickly as possible. There are numerous figures to illustrate the lessons in the book.

Each lesson begins with an overview and a list of topics. The lesson ends with questions and answers and a summary of the hour. Within the lessons, you'll find the following elements, which provide additional information:

Notes provide extra information on the current topic.

Tips offer a particularly useful technique for using FrontPage 2003.

Cautions put up a "danger" sign for potential problems, giving you advice about how to avoid or repair them.

You will also find a helpful Summary section at the end of the chapter that will give you a concise review of what you learned in that lesson. Following the Summary is a Q&A section where you can find answers to some common questions regarding the content of that lesson.

"New to 2003" notes point out something that's new in this version of FrontPage.

Code listings will be in this style of font:

```
Hello World!
```

Text that you are to type into a page or dialog box will appear in this style of font to help you pick it out of the surrounding text: **Hello World!**

# PART I

# Creating Your First Web Pages

## Hour

1 Create a Web Page

2 Organize a Page with Links, Lists, and Tables

3 Display Graphics and Photos on a Page

4 Layout a Page with Tables

# HOUR 1

# Create a Web Page

Even if you've never created a Web site before, you probably have most of the skills you need to start using Microsoft FrontPage 2003.

How is this possible? Because FrontPage is a lot like Microsoft Word, the popular word-processing software that's also part of the Office suite.

Although Word has hundreds of different features, the basic mechanics of creating and editing a document are fairly simple. You type text into a window, click a few buttons or menu commands to format the text, and save your work. You can start using Word long before you have mastered its more sophisticated features.

You can learn to use FrontPage the same way.

In this hour, you will learn

- How to create and save a Web page
- How to add text to a page
- How to turn text into an attention-grabbing heading
- How to change the font, size, and color of text

## Start Using FrontPage 2003

FrontPage 2003 contains all the tools you need to create, publish, and manage a professional, eye-catching, and entertaining World Wide Web site.

After you install the program, it is added to your Start menu. Run the program, and you'll see the program's graphical user interface, which looks a lot like a word processor with a few extra buttons, toolbars, and menus.

When you run FrontPage for the first time, the program helpfully creates a new Web page that you can begin working on immediately.

Before you can do that, here's a quick rundown on the four most important features of the interface.

Figure 1.1 shows FrontPage being used to work on a new Web page.

**FIGURE 1.1**

*Using FrontPage to create a Web page.*

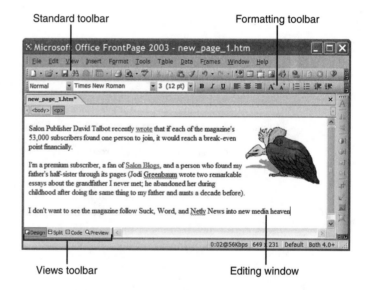

Standard toolbar · Formatting toolbar · Views toolbar · Editing window

In Figure 1.1, I wrote an essay by typing text in the editing window. While I was typing, I was able to change the appearance of the text using the Formatting toolbar, which includes buttons to apply boldface or italics, change the font, and add other special effects.

The picture of a vulture is a piece of clip art I picked from a library of thousands of free graphics, videos, and sound files included with FrontPage. I also turned a few words on the page into hyperlinks, which can be clicked to visit different Web sites.

To add the picture and hyperlinks, I used buttons on the Standard toolbar, which can open and save files, load the page in my favorite Web browser, and handle other essential tasks.

As I worked, I could see exactly how the Web page will look when someone views the page with a Web browser. This is usually the case in FrontPage; it's one of the real selling points of the program. Software companies call this WYSIWYG (pronounced "wizzy-wig"), an acronym for "what you see is what you get."

If I want to see how Internet Explorer will display the page, I don't have to load that program separately—instead, I can click the Preview button on the Views toolbar, which replaces the editing window with a mini-browser.

FrontPage does this often—the user interface changes in appearance based on what you are working on. To close the mini-browser and get back to work on my page, I can click the Design button on the same toolbar.

# Create a Page from a Template

Now that you've learned a bit about the toolbars and the editing window, you're ready to create your own Web page:

1. Open the **Start** menu, then find and run FrontPage 2003.

   FrontPage 2003 opens, displaying the last thing you were working on when the program was closed. If this is your first time to run it, a blank Web page is created for you.

 In case you're wondering, you don't need to be connected to the Internet as you work on a page. Later when you test a page's hyperlinks, you will need to connect to your Internet service provider.

2. To create a new Web page, choose the menu command **File, New**. The New pane opens to the right side of the editing window, as shown in Figure 1.2.

3. Click the **More Page Templates** hyperlink in the New Page section.

   The Page Templates dialog box opens, listing all of the templates you can use when creating your new Web page.

4. To find out more about a template, click it once and read the Description section of the dialog box. Every Web page in FrontPage must be based on a template.

5. To start with a completely empty page, choose the **Normal Page** icon; otherwise, choose one of the other icons.

FIGURE **1.2**

*Choosing the kind of Web page to create.*

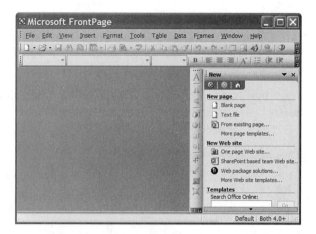

 Some of the page templates, such as the feedback form and the photo gallery, are fairly sophisticated. They are discussed in later hours.

6. Click the **OK** button. The Page Templates dialog box closes. FrontPage creates your new Web page and opens it in the editing window. You can begin working on it immediately.

The newly created page is initially given a unique filename, such as `new_page_1. htm` or `new_page_2.htm`, and a bland title, such as New Page 1.

The last part of a Web page's filename is important—it ends with `.htm`, which is short for Hypertext Markup Language (HTML), the language used to format Web pages. When a file ends with `.htm`, FrontPage and Web browsers recognize that the file is a Web page.

## Create and Save a New Page

When you save a page for the first time, you have the chance to pick something better than the existing name and title.

Choosing a succinct, descriptive title is important for two reasons: It helps people use your page, and it helps others find it.

The title of a page is displayed in the Web browser's title bar. It also is used by search engines. For example, when you search for something on Google at `http://www. google.com`, each Web page that turns up is listed by its title.

You give your page a new name and title when you save it the first time:

1.  Click the **Save** button on the Standard toolbar. The Save As dialog box appears (see Figure 1.3).

**FIGURE 1.3**

*Saving a Web page on your computer.*

2.  Using this dialog box, find and open the folder where you will be saving the Web pages that you create.
3.  In the **File Name** text field, give the file a new name, making sure it still ends with `.htm`.
4.  The Page Title section displays the current title. To pick a new title, click the **Change Title** button. The Set Page Title dialog box opens.
5.  A page's title should be descriptive and reasonably succinct. Type a new one in the Page Title field, and click **OK**. You are returned to the Save As dialog box.
6.  Click **Save**.

After you have named and saved a Web page, you can save it again quickly by clicking the Save button on the Standard toolbar. The filename you chose previously will be used again automatically.

> If you forget to give a page a good title when saving it, there's another way to do it: Right-click the page in the editing window. A context menu appears—choose the menu command Page Properties.
>
> This opens the Page Properties dialog box, which has a Title text field. Type a new title in this field, and click OK.

To open a Web page that you saved earlier, choose the menu command File, Open. The File Open dialog box opens—use it to find and click the page.

## Add Text to a Page

Even though audio, video, games, and animation are common on the World Wide Web, the Web is primarily a written medium. Most of your time in FrontPage will be spent creating and editing text.

After you have opened a Web page in the editing window or created a new one, here's how to add text to it:

1. Click anywhere on the page. A cursor blinks at that spot. The next text you type will appear there.

2. Start typing.

When you are adding text to a Web page, you should let text wrap around the right margin at all times and press the Enter key only when you finish a paragraph.

The main reason you shouldn't worry about the right margin is that it varies depending on the Web browser and system being used to view a page.

On most Web browsers, this causes the text to be displayed in block style, with each paragraph beginning at the left margin and a blank line separating paragraphs.

If you'd like to end a line with something shorter than a paragraph break, hold down the **Shift** key when you press **Enter**. A line break is inserted. Line breaks separate text with single-line spacing instead of double-line spacing.

You can apply most word-processor techniques to the text on a page: Drag your mouse over text to select it, move text around, use **Ctrl+V** to copy and **Ctrl+C** to paste, and so on.

The easiest way to apply formatting is to select text and use the buttons on the Formatting toolbar.

To find out what a button does in FrontPage, hover your mouse over it for a few seconds. FrontPage displays a ScreenTip containing the name of the button.

**1**

When you are working with text on a Web page, pressing the Enter key causes a paragraph break to appear, even when you're arranging graphics and other page elements along with text.

As you work on Web pages, it's important to recognize that people will view your pages in many different ways, some of which are entirely outside of your control.

Unlike a medium such as print, where a page looks exactly as the designer intended it to look, the Web site is a fluid medium in which, depending on the viewer's browser, pages can rearrange themselves to fit the space they have available to them.

Someone with the monitor resolution set to 800×600 will see much more text per line than someone with the monitor set to 640×480. A person who has enabled large text for easier reading will greatly reduce the number of characters that appear on a line. These are just two examples of the variability of Web presentation.

To see this in action, connect to the Internet, load your favorite Web site, and resize your browser window so that it takes up a portion of your desktop instead of the whole thing. Keep changing the size of the window, and you will probably see parts of the page moving around.

Figure 1.4 shows the same Web page—my personal home page at `http://www.cadenhead.org/workbench`—in two different browser windows.

**FIGURE 1.4**

*Viewing Web pages in different ways.*

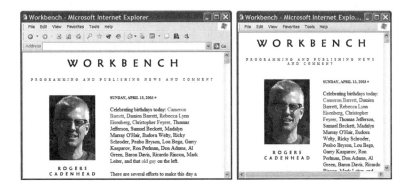

As shown in Figure 1.4, the text of the page wraps differently depending on the space that's available to it.

Every paragraph break on a Web page causes a blank line to appear between paragraphs (or other elements on the page) in all of the popular Web browsers. To begin text at the left margin without a paragraph break, you can insert a line break instead.

Line breaks can be used to ensure that text appears on different lines without a paragraph break separating them. They're also useful when you're aligning images and other page elements.

The Formatting toolbar includes a few other buttons that work exactly like their counterparts in a word processor such as Microsoft Word:

- The Align Left, Align Right, Center, and Justify buttons line up paragraphs of text using the chosen style.
- The Decrease Indent and Increase Indent buttons move the margins of paragraphs accordingly.
- The Bold, Italic, and Underline buttons apply those styles to text.

> Underlined text looks like a hyperlink in many Web browsers, so anything you underline on a page could be a source of confusion for some of your audience. For this reason, you might want to avoid using that particular button on the Formatting toolbar.

## Create a Headline

Text on a Web page can be set apart from other text by turning it into a *heading*, an eye-catching headline that stands out from surrounding text.

Headings range in size from 1 (largest) to 6 (smallest), and they can be used for the same purpose as a headline in a newspaper—a title for the text that follows. They also can be used as subheads with a larger article, as enlarged quotations, and for other attention-grabbing purposes.

To turn text into a heading, follow these steps:

1. Select the text by dragging your mouse over it. The text is highlighted.
2. Open the **Style** pull-down menu on the Formatting toolbar to pick one of the six heading sizes, as shown in Figure 1.5.

   The selected text (and any text within the same paragraph) becomes a heading.

The display size of a heading depends on the Web browser used by a visitor to your site and how it has been configured. But as a general rule, you can rely on the 1-to-6 ranking system.

**FIGURE 1.5**

*Creating a text heading.*

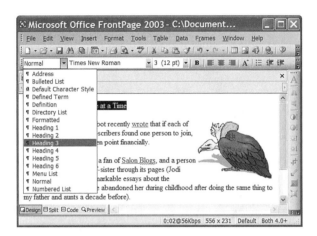

Figure 1.6 displays the same heading at all six sizes on a Web page from 1 to 6. The last paragraph on the page is body text, demonstrating that some heading sizes might be smaller than the surrounding text.

**FIGURE 1.6**

*Creating a text heading.*

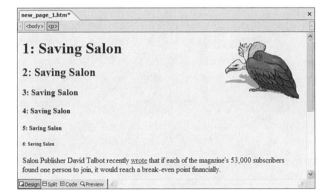

Headings can be used in most ways as if they were text. One exception is that a heading must occupy its own paragraph.

To see this in action, highlight a single word in a paragraph and turn it into a heading. Everything in the paragraph becomes a heading.

# Choose a Font and Color

At this point, the text you have added to a Web page is displayed using the same default color and font as in Internet Explorer: black 12-point Times New Roman.

You can change each of these aspects of the text (and others).

A font can be chosen for all of the text on a page, specific paragraphs, or even part of a paragraph.

Any font that's present on your computer can be used and will look great when you view the Web page on that computer.

However, the visitors to your Web site will not be viewing the page on your computer. This brings us back to the biggest lesson of Web design: The pages that you create will look different to different people.

When you are creating pages, the fonts you select should be ones that likely will be available to as many of your visitors as possible. Many fonts will be specific to a particular operating system—Windows, Mac, and Linux users do not share many fonts in common.

If a font isn't present, a default font, such as Arial, Helvetica, Times Roman, or Verdana, will be used in its place.

> The following fonts are installed with Internet Explorer on both Windows and Mac OS systems: Arial, Comic Sans, Courier New, Georgia, Impact, Times New Roman, Trebuchet, and Verdana.
>
> This means that they can be viewed by more than 95% of the people using the World Wide Web—even if they have chosen to use another Web browser, the fonts are installed on the computer and will work in that program.
>
> All of these fonts look best on large headings and text that are 12 points or larger in size. For smaller text, Georgia, Verdana, and Trebuchet are designed to be readable fonts at small sizes.

One way to hedge your bets when using fonts is to specify a list of fonts, such as Times Roman, Times, serif or Courier New, Courier, monospace. When a Web browser displays the page, it will pick the first available font in the list. Step 6 in the steps that follow explains how to list more than one font for the selected text.

The size of a font can be designated as a point size or on a scale from 1 (smallest) to 7 (largest).

To format a font on a Web page you are editing, follow these steps:

1. Select the text that should be changed.
2. On the Formatting toolbar, use the **Font** drop-down menu to select a specific font.

   The text is immediately displayed in the new font. You can pick only one font with this menu (see step 6 for a way to specify more than one font).
3. On the same toolbar, use the **Size** drop-down menu to specify a font size.
4. To pick a different text color and make other changes, choose the menu command **Format, Font**.

   The Font dialog box opens (see Figure 1.7).

**FIGURE 1.7**

*Formatting a font on a Web page.*

5. Use the **Color** drop-down menu to select a color for the text.

   If you select Automatic instead of a color, the default color is used.
6. To specify a list of fonts, type them in the **Font** list box, separated by commas.

   Other formatting effects and spacing can be applied using this dialog box.
7. To see what a particular effect does, enable its check box in the **Effects** pane.

   The Preview pane displays how sample text looks with the selected formatting—including the chosen effect.
8. When you're happy with how the text looks, click the **OK** button.

Because FrontPage shows you how a page is turning out while it is being edited, you see the chosen font and style immediately.

If you want to see how a line of text has been formatted, click it. The Formatting toolbar is updated to show what you've applied to that text.

# Summary

Text and headings make up the largest part of the World Wide Web. By combining them, you can create lots of pages and put them on the Web for an audience of millions.

Of course, that audience is going to wonder why you're not using any feature of the Web that was introduced more recently than 1994.

You'll get a chance to correct this perception in the next several hours as you work with hyperlinks, lists, and tables.

# Q&A

**Q  I'm not a computer programmer. Why would I want to use text effects such as Variable, Code, and Keyboard?**

**A**  You probably wouldn't. Those effects aren't used on many pages today—even when things such as variables and source code are displayed on a page. Most Web browsers display these effects simply as boldface, italicized, or underlined text, so the Bold, Italic, and Underline buttons on the Formatting toolbar can be used instead.

FrontPage includes these effects primarily for long-time Web designers who are accustomed to them. You can probably avoid them entirely, especially if none of your own pages is on a technical subject.

**Q  I want to make one word of a paragraph into a heading, but FrontPage won't let me do this. Why not?**

**A**  One of the rules of HTML, the formatting language of the World Wide Web, is that a heading must occupy its own paragraph. For this reason, when you select part of a paragraph and use the Formatting toolbar to turn it into a heading, FrontPage applies the change to the entire paragraph. As a workaround, font size changes can be applied to a word (or words) in a paragraph using the Size drop-down menu on the Formatting toolbar.

**Q** **During this hour, the serif and monospace fonts were mentioned. I've never encountered these when selecting a font. Are they new?**

**A** Those fonts are generic, catch-all fonts that a Web browser matches to a real font that's present on the system. There are five of these: serif, sans serif, cursive, monospace, and fantasy. The Web browser chooses the default font for each of these styles, which is most commonly a Times font for serif, Helvetica for sans serif, Courier for monospace, something like Zapf-Chancery for cursive, and Western for fantasy. A good way to use these fonts is to put them last in a comma-separated list of fonts—such as Verdana, Helvetica, sans serif. That way, if the reader doesn't have any of the other fonts you have specified for your text, the page will still come out looking reasonably close to the desired appearance.

**Q** **My FrontPage menus are different than the ones mentioned in this chapter— for instance, I can't find Format, Font. How can I turn these menu commands on?**

**A** FrontPage and the other Office programs hide menu commands that you use infrequently. Since you're just starting to use the program, you won't see some menu commands. To see all of the commands on a menu, click the double-down arrow at the bottom of that menu.

To turn off the menu-hiding feature completely, choose Tools, Customize. The Customize dialog box opens with the Options tab on top. Enable the Always Show Full Menus check box and click Close.

# Hour 2

# Organize a Page with Links, Lists, and Tables

Now that you're comfortable adding text to a Web page, you're ready to take the next step and organize the contents of the page for presentation in several different ways.

*Lists* are groups of related information set apart by bullets, numbers, or other symbols.

*Tables* are boxes that hold text, graphics, or even smaller tables.

*Hyperlinks* are clickable links that can be used to load a new page in a Web browser.

In this hour, you will learn

- How to organize text into lists
- How to put one list inside another
- How to turn a list into a collapsible outline
- How to create tables and use them to hold text
- How to connect Web pages together with hyperlinks

# Add a Hyperlink to a Web Page

Documents on the World Wide Web are connected to each other by hyperlinks—clickable areas of a Web page that cause a new page or another kind of file to be opened in a Web browser.

Hyperlinks usually are associated with text, but that's not a requirement. You can place a link on any part of a Web page: photos, buttons, Java applets, QuickTime movies, MP3 sound files—you name it.

Text hyperlinks are displayed in a way that sets them apart from other text on a page. The most common way that hyperlinks are presented in a Web browser is by underlining the linked text. Figure 2.1 shows a Web page that contains two hyperlinks that are identified by underlines: the text "Joshua Redman" and "Tony Bennett."

Underlining other text that isn't a hyperlink is frowned upon. Users will click the underlined text and wonder why it isn't functioning as a hyperlink.

**FIGURE 2.1**

*Viewing text hyperlinks on a Web page.*

A hyperlink contains a URL, which is short for Uniform Resource Locator, but there's a much simpler way to describe them: a URL is an address to something on the Web.

Web browsers usually display the address of the page you're viewing in the browser's Address bar. Some sample URLs include the Sams Publishing home page at `http://www.samspublishing.com`, Google's U.S. government search engine at `http://www.google.com/unclesam`, and Microsoft's Knowledge Base FTP server at `ftp://ftp.microsoft.com`.

A hyperlink can also be used to send a new email—these addresses begin with `mailto:` and are followed by an email address. For example, U.S. Rep. Bernie Sanders can be reached through the URL `mailto:bernie@mail.house.gov`.

To create a hyperlink, follow these steps:

1. On a Web page that's open in the editing window, drag your mouse over the part of the page that should be associated with the link. That part of the page will be highlighted to show that it has been selected.

2. Choose **Insert, Hyperlink** (or click the Insert Hyperlink button on the Standard toolbar).

   The Insert Hyperlink dialog box is displayed (see Figure 2.2).

**FIGURE 2.2**

*Adding a hyperlink to a page.*

Hyperlinks can be associated with files on your computer or any address on the World Wide Web:

- If you are linking to a file on your computer, use the dialog box to find and select it.

- If you are linking to a Web address, type it in the **Address** text field (or paste it from the Windows Clipboard, if it has been copied there from the Web browser). Then click **OK**.

The Insert Hyperlink dialog box closes, returning you to the editing window.

If the hyperlink is associated with text, it will be underlined on the Web page.

After adding a hyperlink to a page, you can change it by right-clicking the link. Then on the context menu that appears, select Hyperlink Properties.

The Edit Hyperlink dialog box opens. To remove a link entirely, click the Remove Link button.

# Create a List

In most Web browsers, paragraphs of text are separated by blank lines and displayed flush left with no indentation. Another way to organize text is to turn it into a list.

On a Web page, lists are groups of related items set off from the rest of the page by numbers, bullets, or similar symbols. You can use two kinds of lists:

- Numbered lists, with each item prefaced by a unique number
- Unnumbered lists, with each item prefaced by a bullet, a circle, or another character

The preceding text is a two-item unnumbered list. The "•" character is similar to the bullets commonly displayed on Web pages.

To turn lines of text into a list, follow these steps:

1. Select the text that should be turned into a list.
2. Click either the **Unnumbered List** button or the **Numbered List** button on the Formatting toolbar.
3. As a list is being edited, press the Enter key to add a new item. A bullet or number appears on a new line.
4. To change how a list is presented, place your cursor on a list item, right-click, and select List Properties from the shortcut menu that appears. The List Properties dialog box is displayed (see Figure 2.3).

**FIGURE 2.3**

*Configuring a list.*

This dialog box can be used to specify a different starting number for a numbered list and the appearance of bullets in an unnumbered list.

Lists can be placed inside other lists. Figure 2.4 shows several lists nested within each other.

**FIGURE 2.4**

*Displaying lists inside other lists.*

```
┌─────────────────────────────────────┐
│ EVENTS CALENDAR                      │
│                                      │
│   • Jacksonville Jazz Fest           │
│        ○ 4/11/2003                   │
│        ○ Jacksonville, FL            │
│        ○ Performers                  │
│             ▪ Tony Bennett,          │
│             ▪ Joshua Redman          │
│             ▪ Boney James            │
│   • Great Hawaiian Jazz BlowOut      │
│        ○ 5/3/2003                    │
│        ○ Honolulu, HI                │
│        ○ Performers                  │
│             ▪ Local jazz musicians   │
└─────────────────────────────────────┘
```

**2**

As shown in Figure 2.4, bullets that are displayed next to items in an unnumbered list provide a visual clue about the list to which they belong. If an unnumbered list is placed inside another, the two lists have different styles of bullets.

To place a list item inside another list, highlight the item and click the Increase Indent button twice.

To take an item out of another list, highlight it and click the Decrease Indent button twice.

You can put one list inside another as many levels deep as needed.

## Create a Collapsible Outline

Sites designed for recent versions of Internet Explorer, Mozilla, and other popular Web browsers can use *collapsible outlines*—lists in which items can be hidden or displayed by people visiting the page. Items in a collapsible list can be clicked to show or hide any of the lists that they contain.

The collapsible outlines feature should be selected in FrontPage only if the people who will view the Web page will be using version 4.0 or later of Netscape Navigator, Microsoft Internet Explorer, or another popular browser released in the last several years. (This is a pretty safe bet—less than five percent of all Web users are using browsers as old as Navigator 4.0.)

To make all or part of a list collapsible:

1. Place your cursor on a list item, right-click, and select **List Properties** from the context menu that appears.

The List Properties dialog box is displayed.

2. Select the **Enable Collapsible Outlines** check box.

   The Initially Collapsed check box becomes active.

3. If the entire list should be hidden when the Web page first loads, enable the **Initially Collapsed** check box.

As you'll learn in Hour 14, "Attract the Widest Possible Audience," anticipating the Web browsers used to view your Web pages is an important element of Web design.

FrontPage can be set up to target specific versions of Web browsers. As part of this browser compatibility support, features such as collapsible outlines might be deactivated as you use the software because it has been set up with a target audience that can't use them.

When you run into a menu command, check box, or another part of FrontPage that is inactive and cannot be used, the cause is often the way browser compatibility has been set up.

## Organize a Page with Tables

One of the things that befuddles first-time Web page designers is the fluid state of a Web page. Text, graphics, and other parts of a Web page move around depending on the way they're presented. The same page can look remarkably different in two different browsers on different computers. It can even vary in appearance on a single computer if the browser window is resized.

Web designers can achieve more control over the appearance of page elements by placing them in tables.

Tables are rectangular grids that are divided into individual cells. Information can be placed into each of these cells to line it up vertically or horizontally with the information in other cells.

If you're having trouble conceptualizing a table as it relates to a Web page, think of a wall calendar:

| SUN | MON | TUE | WED | THU | FRI | SAT |
|-----|-----|-----|-----|-----|-----|-----|
|     |     | 1   | 2   | 3   | 4   | 5   |
| 6   | 7   | 8   | 9   | 10  | 11  | 12  |
| 13  | 14  | 15  | 16  | 17  | 18  | 19  |
| 20  | 21  | 22  | 23  | 24  | 25  | 26  |
| 27  | 28  | 29  | 30  |     |     |     |

A calendar like this is a rectangular table containing a bunch of cells.

On a wall calendar, each day takes up its own cell in the table. The name of each day, from SUN to SAT, also occupies its own cell.

Tables are divided into vertical columns and horizontal rows. The wall calendar shown has seven columns and six rows.

The primary purpose of tables is to organize information that must line up into straight rows and columns. You can use tables to display data such as an expense report in easy-to-read columns.

 Tables also are useful when structuring the content of a Web page. Anything that can be put on a Web page can be placed inside a table cell—even another table. FrontPage 2003 includes a new table layout feature that can be used to organize the contents of a page, as you'll see in Hour 4, "Lay Out a Page with Tables."

# Line Up Text in a Table

Although tables are useful for page layout, they're also an effective way to present text in tabular rows and columns.

Before you create a table with FrontPage, you must decide how many rows and columns it will contain. Columns are counted from left to right, and rows are counted from top to bottom.

Tables are displayed as an empty grid when they are added to a Web page. Figure 2.5 shows a newly created table that contains two columns and four rows.

The number of rows and columns in a table determines the initial number of cells that it contains. The table in Figure 2.5 contains eight cells.

## Add a Table to a Page

A table is empty when it is created on a Web page. Then you fill its individual cells.

**FIGURE 2.5**

*Viewing a new table on a Web page.*

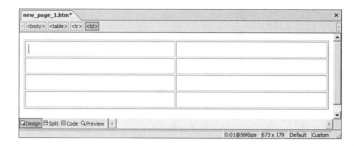

To add a table to a page, follow these steps:

1. With the page open in the editing window, click the spot where the table should be inserted.

2. Choose **Table, Insert, Table**. The Insert Table dialog box opens, as shown in Figure 2.6.

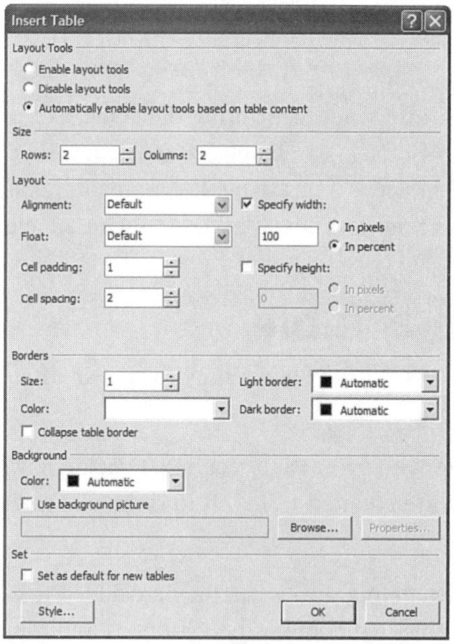

**FIGURE 2.6**

*This dialog box is used to define the size and spacing of your table.*

3. In the Size section, use the Rows and Columns list boxes to set up the dimensions of the table.

   The choice you make doesn't have to be permanent. You can easily add and sub-tract rows and columns from a table as you work on it, so the initial values are not important.

The Size section sets up the rows, columns, and number of cells in the table, but it doesn't determine how much space the table takes up on the Web page when it is displayed. A table normally occupies as much of the page as needed to display the contents of the cells (and no more space than necessary).

4. To establish the amount of space a table should occupy, enable the **Specify Width** check box and choose a unit of measure:

   • For a specific width, select the **In Pixels** option and then type the desired width in the adjacent text field.

   • To set the width as a percentage of the available space on the page (measured from side to side), select the **In Percent** option and then type a percentage from 1 to 100 in the adjacent text field.

   If you choose a width of 100%, the table will take up all the space it can.

5. To set the table's height, repeat step 4 with the Height field.

It's uncommon to set the height of a table—Web pages usually take up a fixed amount of space from side to side and as much space as they need from top to bottom.

Three more ways to fine-tune a table are to set its border, cell padding, and cell spacing measurements.

The *border* determines the size of the border that surrounds the table. If it is set to 0, the border and all of its grid lines will disappear. The cells of the table will still line up correctly, but it won't be as apparent that a table is being used on the page.

*Cell padding* is the amount of empty space that surrounds the contents of each cell. If you increase padding from the default value of 1, cells will grow bigger, while their contents will stay the same size.

*Cell spacing* is the amount of space in the grid border between each cell. This makes the height and width of the grid lines bigger, if the border is visible. When spacing is increased, the table grows while cells remain the same size.

1. In the Insert Table dialog box, use the Border, Cell Padding, and Cell Spacing list boxes to set these values as desired.

2. When you're done setting up the table, click the **OK** button.

The new table is added to the Web page as an empty grid of cells. The next step is to add text to the cells or adjust the size of cells or entire rows and columns.

## Add Data to a Table

When you have a table on a page, you can add text to any of its cells: Click your cursor within a cell and begin typing. You also can use cut, copy, and paste or drag and drop to fill out a cell.

Tables begin with all cells and rows the same size, and FrontPage attempts to keep them the same size as you add text. Words wrap around the right edge of a cell as if it were the right margin of a page.

When you're filling out a table, press the Tab key to jump to the next cell on the right (or the next row) or press the Shift and Tab keys simultaneously to move in the opposite direction.

An unusual thing happens if you press Tab when you're in the last cell in the table (the one on the bottom row and the far-right column): FrontPage creates a new row and moves the cursor into the first cell on this row.

This enables you to keep adding new data to a table even if you underestimated the number of rows you needed when it was created.

> When working with tables, if you don't know how many rows you will need, simply start with a few and add more as you are entering data.

To add one or more columns or rows to a table, follow these steps:

1. Click a cell adjacent to where the new cells should be inserted.
2. Choose **Table, Insert, Rows or Columns**. The Insert Rows or Columns dialog box opens (see Figure 2.7).

**FIGURE 2.7**

*Adding rows or columns to a new table.*

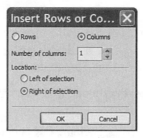

3. Select either the **Columns** or **Rows** options.

4. Choose the number of columns or rows to insert in the **Number Of** list box. They are added next to the cell selected in step 1.

5. In the **Position** section, choose an option to determine exactly where the new columns or rows will be placed.

6. Click **OK**.

The table makes room for the new cells you've added, adjusting the size of the existing cells as necessary.

## Remove Rows or Columns from a Table

Rows and columns can also be deleted after you have selected them:

1. Place your cursor over the outside table border of a row or column that you want to delete. Move the cursor around that border until it changes to a small black arrow that points at the table.

2. Click once. The row or column in the direction of the arrow is highlighted.

3. To delete it, press the Delete key or right-click the highlighted area and choose **Delete Rows or Delete Columns** from the context menu that appears.

## Change the Size of a Table

As a general rule, FrontPage sizes a table so that all cells take up the same amount of space, unless some of them contain text that's too big for this to be possible.

An easy way to format a table so that it occupies less space is to make it shrink so that it takes up the minimum amount of space needed: Click anywhere on the table and choose Table, AutoFit to Contents.

You also can resize a table so that particular rows and columns have specific pixel or percentage widths:

1. Right-click one of the cells in that row or column.

2. In the context menu that opens, choose the **Cell Properties** menu command.

   The Cell Properties dialog box appears, which can be used to set a cell's width in the same manner as a table is configured.

3. To set the width of that cell, enable the **Specify Width** check box, choose either **In Pixels** or **In Percent**, and then enter a measurement value in the adjacent text field.

4. For the height, enable **Specify Height** and repeat the instructions in step 3.

5. If you want to remove a height or width measurement for a cell, remove the check from the **Specify Height** box or the **Specify Width** box.

   If no other cells in that row or column have measurements set, all cells are displayed in the same size.

6. Click **OK**.

FrontPage can use the new dimensions of the cell to determine how the other cells in the same row and column will be sized.

The following rule of thumb applies: If the cell is the biggest one in its row or column, the other cells will grow to be the same size.

> Setting specific pixel dimensions for a table cell (or an entire table) can easily detract from the presentation of a Web page, especially if you're making it larger than 800 pixels wide or 600 pixels tall. Those dimensions match the monitor resolution for many Web users, so bigger tables will require scrolling to be seen in full.

When you set the dimensions for a specific table cell, you shouldn't use Table, AutoFit to Contents again or you'll wipe out your changes.

## Summary

You now have three new places to put text in your sites:

- **Pages**—Separate Web documents linked with hyperlinks
- **Lists**—Groups of related items set apart by bullets, symbols, or numbers
- **Tables**—Rectangular grids of cells that can hold anything Web pages can hold

Hyperlinks connect the Web pages you create and go even further, connecting your work to the billions of documents created by others on the World Wide Web.

Lists are primarily useful as a way to organize text within a larger document.

Tables are useful for presenting tabular data and organizing the layout of a Web page.

# Q&A

**Q** I've been deleting cells by right-clicking a cell and choosing the Delete Cells command. At times, the Delete Cells command can't be selected when I right-click the area. What's wrong?

**A** You can select a group of adjacent table cells in FrontPage in two ways. One is to drag your mouse over the cells to highlight them in the same way that text is highlighted and then press the Delete key.

If this selection method doesn't allow you to delete the cells, try the alternative: Hover your cursor at the outer border of the row or column you want to delete. The cursor changes to a thick arrow pointing at that row or column. Click once; the chosen area is highlighted, and you can use the Delete Cells command or the Delete key to remove that part of the table.

**2**

# HOUR 3

# Display Graphics and Photos on a Page

Although the World Wide Web is primarily a written medium, all of your well-chosen words will be for naught unless people stick around long enough to read them.

To entice visitors to your site and keep them coming back, you can surround your text with eye-catching graphics, digital photos, and other Web browser window dressing. FrontPage 2003 makes it easy to add a graphical flair to your pages, even if you're not remotely artistic.

You don't even need your own graphics—FrontPage includes a clip art archive containing thousands of icons, drawings, and photographs that you can use on your own pages.

In this hour, you will learn

- How to place graphics and photos on a Web page
- When to use each of the popular graphics file formats: GIF, JPEG, and PNG
- How to arrange graphics alongside text
- How to add hyperlinks and captions to a graphic

# Work with Graphics in Different Formats

Before you start working with graphics, it's important to learn what kind of formats you should be using. Visual imagery can be represented on a computer in dozens of different formats, but the budding Web designer needs to be familiar with only three: GIF, JPEG, and PNG.

You probably have some of these files on your computer already: Look for anything with the file extensions .gif, .jpg, or .png.

Most images on the World Wide Web are in either *Graphics Interchange Format* (*GIF*) or *Joint Photographic Experts Group* (*JPEG*) format. A newer format that's becoming popular is *Portable Network Graphics* (*PNG*).

## GIF Graphics

The GIF format holds images that are limited to 256 colors. This is ideal for simple images with lots of solid color (menu buttons), small graphics (icons, ads), and other images that don't require much fine detail.

If a photo is to be displayed as a GIF, it must first be reduced so that no more than 256 different colors appear in the image.

> GIF files can become prohibitive to use on the Web if an image is large or complex. Even if a photo was reduced to 256 colors, it might still be too large for publication on your site—visitors wouldn't want to stick around until it finishes loading.

The GIF format supports two special effects that are popular on the Web: transparency and animation.

Transparency is a technique that makes a portion of a graphic blend in with the background of the page, which can be a solid color or a graphic. Transparency works by designating one color in a GIF graphic as the transparent color, which will not be displayed when the graphic is shown on a Web page. To see this in action, look at two GIF graphics on a page in Figure 3.1.

The Web page shown in Figure 3.1 has a striped background. The trumpet on the left does not have a transparent color, so you see the entire graphic, which includes a white square around the instrument. The trumpet on the right has been created with that particular shade of white chosen as its transparent color, so you can't see it—the stripes on the page show through.

**FIGURE 3.1**

*Viewing nontranspar-
ent and transparent
graphics.*

A GIF graphic can be animated by displaying several related GIF images in sequence. These images are stored together in a single file with information on how long to display each image, the order of display, and the number of times to loop through the sequence.

You've undoubtedly seen hundreds of animated GIF graphics as you browse the Web; they are a favorite technique of advertisers.

You'll learn how to select a background and create your own transparent and animated GIF graphics in Hour 10, "Make a Site Look Great with Graphics."

## JPEG Graphics

The JPEG format holds photo-quality graphics that may contain thousands of different colors. To make the file size reasonable, making the graphics faster to download on the Web or be transferred by other means, JPEG uses a data-compression technique that makes the file size smaller at the expense of image quality.

When a JPEG file is created by a digital camera, scanner, or software, a balance is struck between size and quality. The higher the clarity and color depth of the image are, the larger the size of the file is.

Because of compression, JPEG is usually the best choice for complex images with a large number of colors. JPEG files are good at displaying scanned photographs that don't have large areas of solid colors.

JPEG is often a poor choice for images with large areas of a single color. Because of how compression is handled, wavy lines (often called "jaggies") will appear along the edges of any solid blocks of color, making the image appear more blurry.

## PNG Graphics

The PNG format was introduced to be a replacement and enhancement for GIF and JPEG graphics. It can be used to display images with 256 or fewer colors, like a GIF (PNG-8 format), and images with thousands of colors, like a JPEG (PNG-24 format). PNG graphics also can support transparency and other special effects.

Web site designers have been slow to choose PNG because it wasn't always supported in Web browsers. Internet Explorer 4 and Netscape Navigator 4 were the first editions of either program that could display PNG graphics without the help of a plug-in (a program that extends the browser's capabilities).

Today, the current versions of the five most popular browsers—Internet Explorer, Netscape Navigator, Mozilla, Opera, and Safari—support PNG, although most do not support all of its features.

## Selecting the Right Format

Using FrontPage, you can add graphics to a site in several other formats with which you might be familiar: BMP (Windows bitmap), EPS (Encapsulated PostScript), RAS (Raster), TGA (Truevision Targa Graphics Adaptor), TIFF (Tagged Image File), and WMF (Windows Metafile).

When you add one of these graphics to a page and then save it, FrontPage converts it to GIF format if it contains 256 or fewer colors, or JPEG format if it contains more.

The software encourages you to use only GIF or JPEG, offering the following recommendations on one of its dialog boxes:

- "GIF: Best for line art and computer-generated drawings. Only 256 colors. Insufficient color for many photos."
- "JPEG: Best for photos. Accurate color and small file size. Bad for line art and computer-generated drawings."
- "PNG-8: Similar to GIF but with better color support. This format isn't very common and isn't supported by all browsers."
- "PNG-24: Similar to JPEG but with lossless compression and usually larger file size. This format isn't very common and isn't supported by all browsers."

My own rule of thumb is to use JPEG for photos and use GIF or PNG for everything else. When a GIF graphic is so visually complex or large that its file size is 30K or larger, I make the graphic simpler or replace it with something else. This keeps the graphic from taking an excessive amount of time to appear when a Web user on a dial-up modem connection views it on a page.

# Add a Graphic to a Page

Now that you know a bit about graphics, you're ready to start putting them on your own Web pages.

In FrontPage, graphics are added to a Web page as it is being edited. You can do this in lots of ways: You can drag a file from a folder or Windows Explorer; copy it to the Clipboard and paste it on the page; choose Insert, Picture, From File; or click a button.

The last option is the easiest, so it will be used in this section.

To add a graphic to a Web page, follow these steps:

1. Open the page you want to edit.

2. Place your cursor at the spot on the page where the graphic should be displayed.

3. Click the **Insert Picture from File** button on the standard toolbar.

   The Picture dialog box appears. Use this box to find the folder that contains the graphic. Can't remember the name of the graphic you want? Click the arrow to the right of the Views button and select Thumbnails from the pop-up menu that appears. Little thumbnail-size images of each graphic will be displayed, as shown in Figure 3.2.

**FIGURE 3.2**

*Choosing a graphic for a page.*

Views button

**3**

4. Choose the graphic and click **Insert**. The file is displayed as part of the page in the editing window, enabling you to see how it looks immediately.

When a graphic is placed on a page, the rest of the page content moves to make room. Text and other page elements flow around or below the image. To move the graphic, click and drag it to a new spot.

Although it appears that the graphic has been merged with the Web page, it remains in its own file—the one you selected with the Picture dialog box.

# Layout Graphics with Text

The first time you add a graphic to a section of text in FrontPage, you're likely to be disappointed in how it looks. Text flows awkwardly from the lower edge of the graphic, leaving a lot of whitespace around it.

Selecting a new wrapping style for the graphic corrects the problem. The wrapping style is a setting that determines how the graphic should be displayed in relation to adjacent text and other content on the page.

To choose a wrapping style for a graphic, follow these steps:

1. Double-click the graphic. The Picture Properties dialog box opens (see Figure 3.3).

**FIGURE 3.3**

*Change how a graphic is displayed.*

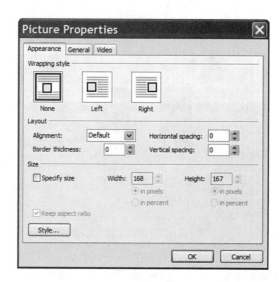

2. If the Appearance tab is not visible, click the tab's name to bring it to the front.

3. Choose one of the options under the **Wrapping Style** heading—click the icon above the labels **None, Left**, or **Right**. The icons show how the graphic will be placed in relation to text.

4. To add or reduce the amount of blank space between the sides of the graphic and the text, adjust the **Horizontal Spacing** setting.

5. To add or remove some space on the top and bottom, adjust the **Vertical Spacing** section.

6. Click **OK**. The Picture Properties dialog box closes, and you can see the results on your page.

Figure 3.4 shows two Web pages that are identical in every way but one: The photo of jazz artist Joshua Redman has been set to a different wrapping style.

**FIGURE 3.4**

*Two layouts of the same picture, one with left alignment and one with right alignment.*

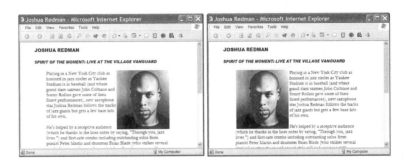

The wrapping style of a graphic determines only how it is displayed next to adjacent text.

To add a blank line before or after a graphic, place the cursor to the left or right of the graphic and press Enter to insert a paragraph break. To insert a smaller line break instead, press Shift+Enter.

Another way to customize the placement of a graphic is to use its alignment setting.

This setting, which is similar to the wrapping style, determines how a graphic will be lined up next to other graphics and text that are close to each other in height.

To set a graphic's alignment, follow these steps:

1. Double-click the graphic. The Picture Properties dialog box opens.

2. If the Appearance tab is not visible, click the tab's name to bring it to the front.

3. Under the Layout heading, choose one of the options of the Alignment list box:

   - Left and Right alignment cause the graphic to appear to the left or right of the surrounding text.

   - Top alignment lines up the top edges of the graphics and text.

   - Bottom alignment lines up the bottom edges of the graphics and text. This is also the default alignment for a new image.

   - Middle alignment lines up the middle of the graphics with the bottom of the text.

   - Absolute Middle alignment lines up the middle of the picture with the middle of the text.

More options exist, but all of them are pretty similar to these six. You can use alignment options with text, graphics, or anything else that is small enough to be displayed beside a picture.

   4. Click **OK**.

If using wrapping styles and alignment isn't sufficient to achieve the page layout you'd like, you'll learn how to accomplish more sophisticated positioning in the next hour, "Lay Out a Page with Tables."

# Add a Hyperlink

Any text or graphic on a Web page can have a hyperlink associated with it. The link can point to another page or file on the same Web site, a different site on the Web, or any other resource that has an Internet address.

To add a hyperlink to a picture, follow these steps:

   1. Click the picture.

      Small handles appear at the corners and sides of the picture to indicate that it has been selected for editing.

   2. Click the **Insert Hyperlink** button on the Standard toolbar.

      The Insert Hyperlink dialog box opens, as seen in Figure 3.5. This box can be used to select several kinds of links:

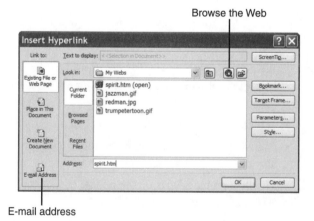

**FIGURE 3.5**

*Adding a hyperlink to a graphic.*

Browse the Web

E-mail address

- If the link is to a Web page or another file on your computer, use the dialog box to find and click that file. Its name appears in the Address field.
- If the link is to an email address, click the Email Address icon in the Link To pane. The dialog box displays Email Address and Subject fields. Fill these in.
- If the link is to another Web address, type it in the Address field (or copy the address from your Web browser's Address bar and paste it in the field).

3. To open your Web browser and look for the right address, click the **Browse the Web** button (see Figure 3.5).

4. Click **OK**.

You'll learn more about organizing sites in Part II of the book, "Designing an Entire Web Site."

# Add a Caption

One of the ways to make your Web pages more usable is to give each graphic a caption that describes the image.

As a page is being downloaded, some Web browsers show a graphic's caption in the area occupied by the graphic.

If the graphic is being used as a menu button or for some other kind of navigational purpose, the caption enables your users to make use of it before the picture is downloaded. People who are using a slow Internet connection (56.6K or less) will appreciate the courtesy, especially if the graphic is large.

Text descriptions are also the only way a text-only Web browser such as Lynx can make any sense of graphics. If a graphic must be clicked to navigate your Web, it should have text that describes its purpose.

By supplying this text, you provide more information about the page's contents that search engines can utilize. The Google Images search service at images.google.com, which displays images matching one or more keywords, makes use of captions.

You also provide information that's essential for people with disabilities to use your Web site, which increases its accessibility.

The goal of accessibility, which is one of the hottest topics among Web designers today, is to ensure that a Web site can be used with screen readers and other assistive technology. By providing captions for each graphic—especially those which have hyperlinks associated with them—you expand the prospective audience for a site. Figure 3.6 shows a good example of a Web site that makes use of captions: the home page for Poynter Online, a resource for professional journalists published by the Poynter Institute.

**FIGURE 3.6**

*Browsing without graphics.*

On the Poynter home page shown in Figure 3.6, each of the items along the left edge is a hyperlinked graphic to a part of the site. Because the designer was so diligent about providing captions, the site can be used by the widest audience possible.

To add a caption to a graphic or edit an existing caption, follow these steps:

1. Double-click the graphic.The Picture Properties dialog box opens.
2. Click the **General** tab to bring it to the front. This tab can be used to change or replace a graphic, choose a hyperlink, or provide a caption and other descriptive information.
3. Type a succinct caption for the graphic in the Text field (or replace the existing caption, if one exists), as shown in Figure 3.7.
4. Click **OK**.

To see what your page looks like without graphics, most Web browsers can be configured to stop displaying them. In Internet Explorer 6, do the following:

1. Choose **Tools, Internet Options**.

    The Internet Options dialog box opens.
2. Click the **Advanced** tab to bring it to the front.
3. Scroll down the **Settings** list until you find the Multimedia section.
4. Remove the check next to the **Show Pictures** check box.
5. Click **OK**.

Pictures will not be displayed for all Web pages that you load after that point, although some pages in your cache will still come up with graphics.

**FIGURE 3.7**
*Adding a caption to a graphic.*

You can turn picture display back on by selecting the Show Pictures check box.

The Web site Bobby at `bobby.watchfire.com` can test any page on the Web to see if it meets current standards for accessibility. If it doesn't, the site offers documentation and a frequently asked questions list for guidance on how to meet those standards.

# Add Clip Art to a Page

FrontPage 2003 includes a library containing thousands of clip art graphics, photos, and other multimedia files. These can be freely incorporated into your own Web pages.

Although some of the offerings are unspeakably hideous, if you comb through the library using FrontPage's search engine, you will probably find some suitable icons and other eye-catching imagery.

The clip art library includes graphics from FrontPage and any other Office products you have used, such as past versions of FrontPage. It also might include some graphics, digital photos, and other images on your computer—the Microsoft Clip Organizer included with Office searches your computer for graphics files and other multimedia.

To find and add clip art to a page, follow these steps:

1. Place your cursor at the spot where the art should be displayed.

2. Choose **Insert, Picture, Clip Art**. The Clip Art pane opens to the right of the editor (see Figure 3.8). You might also be asked whether the Clip Organizer should catalog the multimedia files on your system. This takes a lot of time and can be done at any time (I'll describe the process later this hour), so there's no need to do it immediately.

FIGURE **3.8**

*Searching for clip art.*

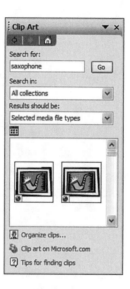

3. In the **Clip Art** pane, type one or more words in the Search For box that describe the kind of art you seek.

4. To narrow a search, use the **Search In** list box. FrontPage can search its own clip art collection, other Office art, clips you have organized, or all three at the same time.

5. To narrow it further, use the **Results Should Be** list box. The clip art library includes several types of multimedia: clip art drawings, photos, movies, and sounds. You can search for one type or all of them.

6. Click the **Go** button. Files matching your search are displayed in the pane. Thumbnail images of each clip art graphic and photo are displayed—use the scrollbar to view them. Figure 3.8 shows results from a search for saxophone images— to give you some idea of the size of the library, 107 different illustrations of a saxophone were found.

7. When you find a graphic you like, double-click it. The graphic appears on the page, often at a size much larger than you need. You'll be able to resize the graphic as needed.

Clip art from the library is usually much larger than you might expect. This is by design because it's easy to shrink a graphic to the desired size without losing its image quality. It is much more difficult (often impossible) to increase the size and maintain the same quality.

When you add clip art to a page, the original graphic remains in the library. None of the changes you make to the graphic will alter the original copy of the image.

# Change the Size of a Graphic

**3**

The size of any graphic on a Web page can be changed—increased to a larger size, shrunk to a smaller one, or even distorted so that the width is at a different scale than the height.

The size of a graphic can be changed in two ways in FrontPage. You can resize the actual graphic, which alters the file containing the image, or change the display size of the graphic.

Graphics presented on a Web page can be displayed at sizes larger or smaller than their actual size, making it possible for the same graphic to be presented at different sizes on two different pages of a Web site.

Because of this, it's important to note the difference between *resizing* a graphic— changing its actual dimensions—and simply displaying the graphic at a different size, which does not alter the original graphic file.

If you're never planning to display a graphic at the larger size, resizing the graphic is a better choice because it loads faster when a visitor views your page. (If the graphic isn't from the clip art library, save a copy of the larger graphic somewhere for safekeeping.)

Clip art graphics look better when they are permanently resized instead of displayed at a different size because FrontPage works some image-editing mojo on the file to smooth edges and sharpen details. This process is called *resampling* the graphic.

To resize a graphic, follow these steps:

1. Click the picture. Selection handles appear around the edges of the image, as shown in Figure 3.9. When you place your mouse over one of the handles, your cursor changes to an arrow, which indicates that you can drag the handle around.

**FIGURE 3.9**

*Resizing a graphic.*

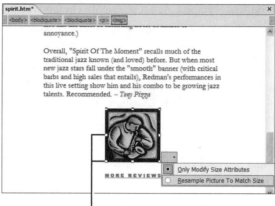

Selection handles

2.  To change the size of the graphic, drag a handle to a new location:

    -   To change the height, grab the handle at the middle of the top or bottom of the graphic.

    -   To change the width, grab the handle at the middle of the left or right.

    -   To change the size while keeping the height and width proportional to each other, grab any corner.

    The graphic changes in size as the handles are being moved around, enabling you to preview the change before it's finalized.

3.  Release the handle. A small box appears next to the graphic. Click this box to open a drop-down menu that determines how the graphic should be resized (see Figure 3.9):

    -   Choose Only Modify Size Attributes to change the display size of the graphic.

    -   Choose Resample Picture to Match Size to permanently resize the graphic.

To change the size, drag the box to a new location to make the picture larger or smaller.

Some of the clip art included with FrontPage retains its quality when enlarged or shrunken, but this isn't the case with most other graphics. With digital photos and other GIF and JPEG graphics, you will have much better results making them smaller than doing the opposite. Enlarged graphics often end up with jagged edges, a boxy appearance, and other unsightly visual glitches.

After clip art has been added to a page, it can be treated like any other graphic. You can move it around, add a caption, and make other changes.

# Save a Page with New Graphics

Whenever you add clip art to a page or resize another graphic, your work isn't permanent until the next time you save the page by clicking the Save button on the standard toolbar.

After you save the page, the Save Embedded Files dialog box opens, as shown in Figure 3.10.

**FIGURE 3.10**

*Saving new and edited graphics.*

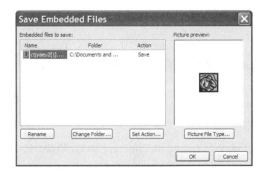

This dialog box contains a list of all new clip art and edited graphics.

Clip art is given a nonsensical name by FrontPage, so you should change it to something more descriptive, in case you need to find the graphic later.

To change a filename, select the file in the Embedded Files to Save list and click the Rename button. The name changes to a field that you can edit—type a new name and press Enter.

As described at the top of this hour, FrontPage chooses a format for new graphics based on how many colors they contain. Clip art with more than 256 colors is saved as a JPEG graphic, and art with 256 or less is saved as in GIF format.

To choose the format for a graphic, select it and click the Picture File Type button. The Picture File Type dialog box appears.

This dialog box lists the four possible formats for the graphic: GIF, JPEG, PNG-8, and PNG-24. One already will be selected—the format FrontPage was going to select for you.

FrontPage might recommend that a clip art illustration be saved as a JPEG, but this is usually a bad idea. The GIF format handles solid color much better than JPEG and reduces the size of the graphic considerably.

After selecting a format, click OK to close the Picture File Types dialog box.

After you have selected a filename and format for each graphic in the Save Embedded Files dialog box, click OK. The graphics and page are saved.

After clip art has been saved, you can make use of it on other Web pages like any other graphic on your computer.

## Find More Clip Art to Use

If you can't find suitable clip art in the library included with FrontPage 2003, more multimedia files for your Web pages are available on Microsoft's Office Online Web site. To go there, follow these steps:

1. If the Clip Art pane is not open, choose **Insert, Picture, Clip Art**.
2. Click the **Clip Art on Office Online** link at the bottom of the pane.

Your Web browser opens at the Microsoft Office Clip Art and Media site, where you can browse by category or search for specific keywords.

Files that you select from Office Online are imported automatically into the clip art library of FrontPage 2003.

To find the clip art that's available on your own computer, return to the Clip Art pane and click the Organize Clips link. Microsoft Clip Organizer opens and guides you through the process of finding and cataloguing graphics and other multimedia files on your computer. After your own files have been added, you can search for them from the Clip Art pane.

## Summary

The Web is a competitive place. A visitor could be looking at literally millions of things other than your Web site, so you must find a way to catch someone's eye before a short attention span and a quick mouse finger send him to another link at hyperspeed.

One way to accomplish this is to make your Web pages more visually compelling through the effective use of graphics: digital photos, icons, clip art, and other images.

In this hour, you learned how to choose the right format for a graphic—which is usually GIF for icons and simple colorful images, and JPEG for digital photos and other complex images.

You also learned how to find clip art and resize it by grabbing a selection handle around the graphic and dragging it to a new location.

Using the wrapping style and alignment features of the Picture Properties dialog box, you can lay out graphics above, below, and beside the other elements of a Web page.

This hour only scratched the surface of FrontPage's graphical features. You'll learn how to edit graphics, add backgrounds, and work with digital photos in Hour 10, "Make a Site Look Great with Graphics."

**3**

# Q&A

**Q** **Is there a limit to how much you can expand a graphic? I'd like to create a tiny, one-color GIF and stretch its display size to cover a large part of a page.**

**A** That's a pretty good idea: The graphic loads quickly because of its miniscule size and can be displayed at any desired size.

If the only color in a graphic is transparent, it can be used to open up space between other elements of a page. This technique is becoming less common because there are several other ways to accomplish the same thing. You can arrange page elements by placing them in a table, as you'll see in the next hour, "Lay Out a Page with Tables," or use Cascading Style Sheets to arrange a page, as described during Hour 22, "Format Your Site Through Cascading Style Sheets."

**Q** **Are there any restrictions to how I use pictures from FrontPage clip art and the Office Online Clip Art and Media in my own Web sites?**

**A** Microsoft's end-user license for Office Online is filled with lots of language that only a lawyer could love. However, it appears that owners of FrontPage 2003 or another Office 2003 product can use the clip art and other files in the gallery as part of your own Web sites, printed publications, and other works, as long as your material is not obscene or scandalous under U.S. law. There's only one big exception: You cannot use the files in a library of clip art offered to others.

The licensing terms for Microsoft's clip art might have changed by the time you read this, so you should check the license for FrontPage 2003 and the Office Online Web site.

# HOUR 4

# Lay Out a Page with Tables

Designing an eye-catching Web page requires more than attractive graphics, fonts, and colors. You must be able to arrange those elements to form an easy-to-read, well-organized layout.

Page layout is an exceptionally challenging task for new Web designers because of the fluid nature of the World Wide Web.

Unlike print and other media, Web pages are viewed in dramatically different ways by their audience. The appearance of your work varies depending on the Web browsers, screen resolution, and browser window size of each visitor to your site.

FrontPage 2003 includes a new feature to simplify page design: layout tables.

Like the tables you've used to organize text, layout tables organize an entire Web page.

In this hour, you will learn

- How to create a layout table and place elements of a Web page inside the table's cells
- How to change the size of a row or column in the table
- How to add and remove rows and columns
- How to change the margin between table cells

# Arrange Elements of a Page

In Hour 2, "Organize a Page with Links, Lists, and Tables," text was organized into rows and columns using tables, a grid of rectangular cells stacked on top of each other.

Tables are a feature of Web design that's useful for the presentation of tabular data such as a monthly calendar, an expense report, or the like.

One of the things you can do with a table is turn off its borders so that only the contents of the table are displayed. The table dictates the layout of text but isn't visible.

This has benefits elsewhere because the use of tables isn't limited to text. Anything that can be put on a Web page can be placed within a table cell.

Invisible tables are the most popular way to lay out Web pages. To see an example of this, take a look at the two images in Figure 4.1.

**FIGURE 4.1**

*Laying out a Web page with tables.*

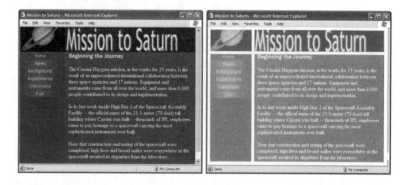

In Figure 4.1, the image on the left is a Web page that was designed using an invisible table that contains two rows and two columns (in other words, four cells). The image on the right shows the placement of the cells within the table.

In FrontPage 2003, layout tables are simply tables used to arrange elements on a page. The table is a framework into which the contents of a Web page can be placed.

The tables you learned about in Hour 2 can be used for page layout also—they're actually the same Web feature offered two different ways in FrontPage.

"Layout tables" is simply the term Microsoft uses to describe the new page layout feature in this version of its software.

# Add a Layout Table to a Page

Layout tables are added to a page as an empty framework of cells. When the framework is in place, you can fill each cell with text, graphics, and other contents. The Layout Tables and Cells pane is used to set up your table for layout (see Figure 4.2).

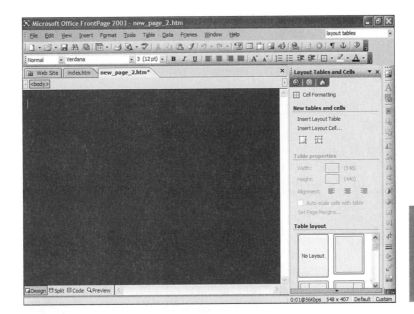

The Table Layout section at the bottom of the pane lists 11 different templates that can be used as the basis for your layout table. A graphical preview of each template shows the relative size and placement of cells within each table. Templates range from a simple two-by-two grid like the one shown earlier in Figure 4.1 to some complex tables with six or more cells in unusual arrangements.

To use one of these templates, click its preview graphic. The layout table is added to the page with several controls that you can use to resize the table:

- Green diamonds (which might look like triangles in some layouts) appear at the border of each row and column.
- A pair of matching Measurement drop-down menus are displayed alongside each row and column.

A table showing these controls is displayed in Figure 4.3.

FIGURE 4.3

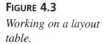
FIGURE 4.3

*Working on a layout table.*

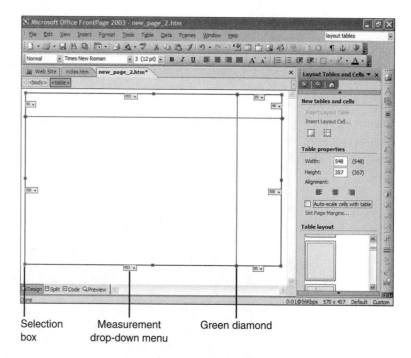

Selection box     Measurement drop-down menu     Green diamond

One of the first things you should do when setting up a layout table is identify any rows or columns that should expand to fill the space that's left over by the rest of the table. This capability is called *autostretch* by FrontPage, and it makes a layout table much more flexible in how it presents a page.

There's also another advantage: A table with exactly one autostretch row and one autostretch column will be much easier to design—as you resize the rest of the table, the autostretch cells will grow or shrink accordingly.

Here's how to create a new Web page that uses a layout table:

1. Click the **Create a New Normal Page** button on the Standard toolbar. A new empty page opens for editing with a name such as `new_page_1.htm` or `new_page_2.htm`.

2. Click anywhere on the page and choose **Table, Layout Tables and Cells**.

   The Layout Tables and Cells pane opens along the right side of the editing window, as shown previously in Figure 4.2.

3. Click a layout template's preview graphic to add a table based on that template.

   If the Layout Tables and Cells pane is not showing the templates, hover your mouse over the thin arrow button at the bottom of the pane.

4. On a layout table, green diamonds are used to adjust the size of rows or columns. To change the size of adjacent rows or columns, drag the green diamond between them to a new location.

When you move a diamond, the line attached to it moves, causing the rows or columns that it touches to be resized. The layout table and all measurement drop-down menus are updated with the new sizes.

The layout table feature of FrontPage is extremely picky about where you click your mouse. If you click inside a table cell, the green diamonds and Measurement drop-down menus disappear.

To get them back, hover your mouse over the outermost edge of the table until a green border appears around the entire table, and then click once. (For some undetermined reason, I'm having much better luck doing this over the bottom edge of a table than doing it over the top or the sides.)

5. To set a row or column to autostretch, click its **Measurement** drop-down menu and choose the **Make Autostretch** command.

6. To set a specific width or height for a row or column:

   • Click its **Measurement** drop-down menu and choose the menu commands **Change Column Width** or **Change Row Height**, respectively.

   A properties dialog box appears, as shown in Figure 4.4.

**FIGURE 4.4**

*Setting a column to a specific size.*

   • Use the **Width** (or **Height**) list box to set the size in pixels.

   • If other cells in the same column or row have different measurements, you can remove them: Enable the **Clear Contradicting** check box.

7. Click **OK**. The column or row is changed to the new dimensions. Unlike the movements of a green diamond, this does not cause anything else with a specific width or height to change size. The only other cells that are resized are ones in an autostretch column or row.

8. When you're done setting up the size of rows and columns, click inside any table cell.

   The green diamonds and Measurement drop-down menus disappear. You can bring them back at any time.

After the resize controls are gone, the table is displayed as a grid of dotted lines. You can place things in each cell as you would text in any other table—click once within a cell to place your cursor there, and then add text, graphics, and other contents normally.

> Although FrontPage 2003's new layout tables feature is extremely useful once you know how to make use of it, there are times when it gets in the way, especially when you're done laying out a table and ready to put text, graphics, and other Web content inside it.
>
> To turn the layout tables feature off while editing a page, choose Table, Layout Tables and Cells, then click the Show Layout Tool button on the Layout Tables and Cells pane. None of the layout table features will appear on that page until you click that button again.

# Add and Remove Table Rows and Columns

The layout table templates that are included with FrontPage take care of the most common page layouts, but you'll likely run into situations in which they don't suit your needs for a particular page design.

You can adjust an existing layout table by adding and deleting rows, columns, and cells. Click within any cell in the table to enter cell editing mode. The table is displayed using thin dotted lines, which indicates that you can add content to the cells of the table. You also can move, duplicate, and delete rows and columns while the table is in this mode.

To select several cells, click inside one cell and drag your mouse to another cell; then release your mouse. All of the cells between the two cells then are displayed with a black background, to indicate that they have been selected, as shown in Figure 4.5.

To edit an existing layout, follow these steps:

1. Use the click-and-drag technique to select an entire row or column (and no other table cells).

2. To delete the cells, press the **Delete** key.

3. To duplicate the cells in another part of the table, press **Ctrl+C** to copy them to the Clipboard and press **Ctrl+V** to paste them. The row or column then is duplicated next to the original cells.

4. To move the cells, drag them to the edge of the row or column where they should be relocated.

5. Click your mouse within any cell to enter the normal editing mode. Table cells are drawn as thin dotted lines.

6. Hover your mouse over an edge of a cell you'd like to modify. When a blue line appears over that cell, click the mouse. Blue selection boxes appear around the cell, and its dimensions are displayed, as shown in Figure 4.6.

**FIGURE 4.5**

*Selecting cells in a table.*

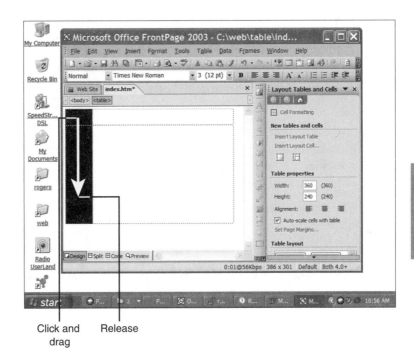

Click and drag    Release

7. To split one cell into two, hover your mouse over a selection box on an edge of the cell until the cursor becomes a small T square icon pointing away from the cell. While this cursor is visible, click and drag the selection box into the cell.

    As you drag the mouse, a dotted line shows where the cell will be split.

8. Release the mouse to split the cell at that line.

The biggest challenge when using the layout tables feature of FrontPage is to recognize each of the editing modes and how to switch between them.

If you're done with layout and are ready to begin filling the cells, click within any cell's borders to enter normal editing mode. The table's grid appears as thin dotted lines.

FIGURE **4.6**
*Editing an individual cell.*

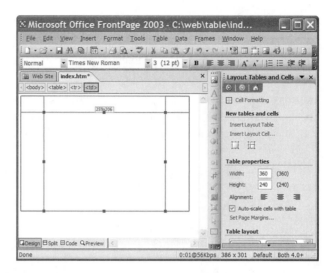

To make changes to the layout, hover your mouse over a table edge or cell edge. When the border is green and surrounds the entire table, click the mouse to enter layout table editing mode and resize rows and columns of the table.

When the border is blue and surrounds one cell, click to enter cell editing mode and modify that cell.

## Make Adjustments to Page Layout

With what you know thus far, you can begin using layout tables to arrange the elements of a Web page.

However, with a few more techniques, you can do a lot of fine-tuning to the table to enhance the presentation of the page.

The first thing you might want to do is to remove the margins around the table. When a layout table is added to a page, it uses the default margins of the page. These vary from browser to browser, but most of the popular browsers display a page with a default margin of 5–10 pixels on all edges. Even if your layout table is set up to occupy 100% of a page, the margin will still be present.

## Change the Margins of a Table

To eliminate (or expand) the margins, follow these steps:

1. If the Layout Tables and Cells pane is not visible, choose **Table, Layout Tables and Cells**. The Layout Tables and Cells pane opens.

2. Click anywhere within the table.

3. Click the **Set Page Margins** hyperlink.

   The Page Properties dialog box opens with the Advanced tab up front, as shown in Figure 4.7. The Margins section of the tab contains four Margin list boxes, which might contain a default value or be empty to indicate that there are no margins on the table.

**FIGURE 4.7**

*Setting the margins of a layout table.*

4. Change the value of **Top Margin** and the other list boxes below it to select a new margin for that edge of the page. Set a margin to **0** to eliminate it entirely.

5. Click **OK** to close the dialog box and see the effect of your changes.

## Format a Layout Table Cell

Another way to modify the presentation of a layout table is to give a cell its own background color, alignment, and other formatting.

Because a layout table is no different than any other table, you can right-click the table and choose **Table Properties** to make changes to the entire table.

For the purposes of layout, it's often easier to modify an individual cell:

1. The table should be in normal editing mode (a grid of thin dotted lines). If not, click anywhere inside a cell to switch into this mode.

2. Hover your mouse over the edge of the cell you want to modify, moving it around until you see a blue border around that cell; then click.

   Blue selection boxes and a size measurement appear around that cell.

3. Choose **Table, Cell Formatting**. The Cell Formatting pane opens alongside the editing window, as shown in Figure 4.8. There are fields that can be used to change the padding, background color, vertical alignment, and the like.

**FIGURE 4.8**

*Changing the formatting of a cell.*

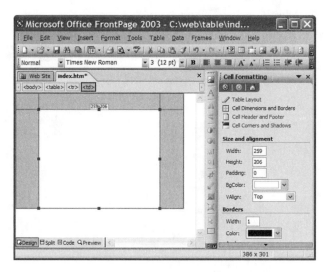

 *Padding* is the empty margin inside the cell's borders; it's comparable to a page margin and is useful when you want the text within a cell to be set off from other rows and columns in the table. Cells have no padding by default.

4. Change the value of the **Padding** field to give the cell a margin (in pixels).

5. Use the **BgColor** list box to give the cell its own background color.

   If you want to use the table's background color, choose **Automatic** instead of a particular color.

To give the entire table a background color, right-click any cell in the table and choose Table Properties. The Table Properties dialog box opens. In the Background section, use the Color list box to select a color or choose Automatic to use the page's background.

6. Use the **VAlign** list box to select a vertical alignment. The vertical alignment of a cell determines how its contents will be displayed within the cell. It can be Top to place contents near the top edge, Bottom for the bottom edge, and Middle to center them vertically.

## Summary

The World Wide Web is a challenging place for a page designer.

Print designers who come to the Web are often frustrated by the malleable nature of a page. They're not accustomed to having their work move around and appear differently for each member of their audience.

FrontPage 2003 reduces the complexity of Web design by offering layout tables.

The layout tables feature can be used to create tables, add and remove cells, and adjust the size of rows, columns, and margins. Once you become comfortable with the different layout table modes and how to switch between them, you can use this feature to achieve professional and flexible page designs.

## Q&A

**Q** **I'm working on a Web site that I created before using FrontPage 2003. It makes considerable use of tables. Can I change these tables into layout tables so I can work on them with FrontPage?**

**A** Layout tables are simply tables that are being used to arrange the contents of a Web page.

For this reason, there shouldn't be any need to change the existing tables to work on them using FrontPage's table layout features.

When you load one of the pages in FrontPage, you can choose Table, Layout Tables and Cells and make changes to it.

4

**Q  When I am specifying the size of a table using the Table Properties dialog, FrontPage offers the option to set it as pixels or a percentage. Which should I use?**

**A**  The choice of pixel values and percentages depends on how much control you want over the placement of elements within the table.

Percentages are calculated based upon the space available to the table within the Web page—if the page is displayed in a Web browser window 600 pixels wide and contains a layout table with width set to 90 percent, the table will be 540 pixels wide. If the browser window is resized to 500 pixels, the table will become 450 pixels wide. This can have dramatic effects on the contents of the page—think back to the Hour 1 example shown in Figure 1.4—but it's also the way to make a page flexible in dealing with the variety of screen resolutions and browser window sizes employed by Web users. When using percentages, there should be an Autostretch column or row to handle the variations in size.

Pixel values offer more precision in how elements are placed. Many Web designers use tables 600 pixels wide under the assumption that most Web users are viewing pages in a full-screen browser window on a monitor that's at least 800 by 600 in screen resolution.

# PART II

# Designing an Entire Web Site

## Hour

5   Create a New Web Site

6   Develop a Site Quickly with Templates

7   Make Your Site Look Great with Themes

8   Let FrontPage Create a Site for You

# HOUR 5

# Create a New Web Site

Now that you've spent a few hours creating Web pages, you're ready to learn how they can be brought together to form a Web site.

A *Web site* is a collection of Web pages and other files that are presented together as a unified work. It's comparable to how chapters are combined into a book.

In this hour, you will learn

- How to create a new Web site and add new pages to it
- How to import existing Web pages and graphics to a site
- How to delete a Web site
- How to make use of Word documents in a site

Importing files comes in especially handy if you have some material created with Microsoft Word or another program that you want to offer on the World Wide Web.

## Build a New Web Site

FrontPage offers numerous features that make it easy to create, manage, and publish Web sites.

Sites managed by FrontPage are organized with the use of your computer's file folders. A site occupies a main folder and several subfolders, each serving a different purpose.

When a folder has been designated as the main folder for a site, it cannot be used for any other site.

When FrontPage is installed, a My Web Sites folder is created inside the My Documents folder of your computer. This is a good place to keep the individual folders that will hold the sites that you create.

To create a new Web site from scratch, run FrontPage and follow these steps:

1. Choose the menu command **File, New**. The New pane opens along the right side of the FrontPage interface, next to the window where Web pages are edited.

2. Click the **More Web Site Templates** hyperlink.

   Web sites are created in FrontPage by using templates, stock versions of several Web sites that you can customize. You'll delve into them heavily in the next hour.

3. Select the icon of the **One-Page Web Site** template, which is used to create a simple, no-frills site that contains nothing but a single blank Web page.

Next, you can create a new folder on your computer where the site's files will be saved.

1. Click the **Browse** button. The New Web Site Location dialog box opens, as seen in Figure 5.1.

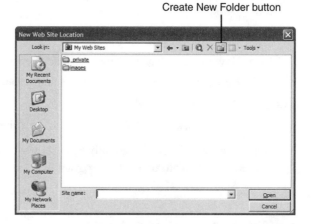

Create New Folder button

**FIGURE 5.1**

*Choosing a folder for a Web site.*

2. Each Web site managed by FrontPage must be given its own folder. Before you can do that, find and open the folder where you will be keeping this folder—a suitable location is the My Web Sites folder inside My Documents.

3. To create a folder for your new site, click the **Create New Folder** button, shown in Figure 5.1. The New Folder dialog box opens.

4. Provide a name for the folder in the **Name** field, and click the **OK** button. The folder is opened and displayed in the Look In drop-down menu of the New Web Site Location dialog box.

5. Click the **Open** button. Your newly created folder is displayed in the text field labeled Specify the Location of the New Web Site.

6. Click **OK**.

FrontPage creates all of the files and folders it needs to manage the Web site, storing them in the selected folder.

Because the One-Page Web Site template was chosen, the site includes a blank Web page called index.htm.

Every Web site created with FrontPage should have a page named index.htm. This serves as the site's home page, which is the first one visitors will see when they visit the main Web address of your site after it is published on the Internet.

In some places, FrontPage 2003 calls a Web site "a Web," a bit of terminology that was used frequently in older versions of the software but much less frequently now. You might be unclear about what the term means. "Web" simply refers to a Web site—all the pages, files, and folders that comprise the site.

# Explore the New Site

5

When you create a new Web site, FrontPage adds all of the necessary files and folders to the site's main folder.

To give you a clear picture of what the site contains, it is displayed in Folders view, which is shown in Figure 5.2. (You might not see the Folder List pane to the left of the Folders view; this will be described momentarily.)

As you might recall from Hour 1, "Create a Web Page," the user interface of FrontPage changes depending upon what you're using it to do. You can work on a page in the editing window in Design view and test it in a Web browser in Preview view.

To switch from one view to another, click the Views bar at the bottom edge of the interface.

Folders view works exactly like a file folder—you can drag and drop files to move them around, and you can rename or delete them (right-click the file and choose either Rename or Delete from the context menu that opens).

Web site tab

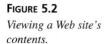

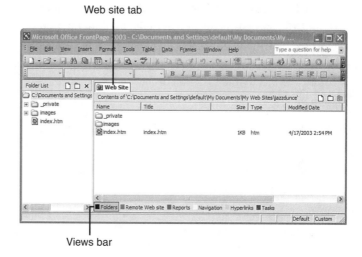

**FIGURE 5.2**
*Viewing a Web site's contents.*

Views bar

To open a Web page in the editing window, double-click the file. Double-click `index.htm` to open the home page of the newly created site for editing.

To get back to Folders view, click the Web Site tab atop the editing window or choose View, Folders.

> There's also a way to see the files in a Web site as you're editing a page: Click View, Folder List to open a smaller folders window along the left side of the interface (one is shown in Figure 5.2). To close it later, click View, Folder List again.

# Add a New Page to a Site

In the first four hours of this book, you learned that FrontPage can be used to create and edit Web pages that aren't part of any Web site.

These pages can be added to a site, as covered in the next section.

You also can create a new page that's added to the site you are currently editing:

1. Choose **File, New** to open the New pane if it is not already open.

2. Select the kind of page you are creating:

   - For a completely empty page, click the **Blank Page** hyperlink.
   - For other kinds of pages, click the **More Page Templates** link.

The Page Templates dialog box appears, listing the kinds of templates that the new page can be based upon. Select the desired template's icon and click the OK button.

In the main folder of the site, FrontPage creates a new page using the template and gives it a name such as new_page_1.htm or new_page_2.htm. The page name will be followed by an asterisk character ("*") when it contains changes that have not yet been saved.

Click the Save button in the Standard toolbar to save the file that's currently being displayed in the editing window. Choose File, Save All to save all the files that are open for editing.

To close a Web site, choose File, Close. If any modified pages have not been saved, a dialog box opens for each one asking whether to save that file. Click Yes to save the file or No to discard the changes permanently.

# Import Files into a Site

The World Wide Web can present other kinds of documents besides Web pages:

- Graphics files in GIF, JPEG, PNG, and other formats
- Sound files such as WAV, MIDI, and MP3 files
- Movie files in AVI, MOV, MPG, and QuickTime formats
- Macromedia Shockwave and Flash programs, and other interactive programs

When you create a new site, its folder will include an images subfolder in it where a site's graphics can all be stored. If you're working with other types of media, you might want to create folders for them as well—such as sounds for any sound files you're using.

One way to incorporate these media files and others into your site is to import them into the site:

1. With the site open for editing, choose **File, Import**.

   The Import dialog box opens, listing the files you have selected to import into the site. You haven't imported any yet, so the list is empty.

 If you can't find the Import command on the File menu, it's because FrontPage hides menu commands that you don't use frequently. To see all of the commands on a menu, click the double-down arrow at the bottom of that menu.

5

> You also can turn off this command-hiding feature entirely, causing full
> menus to be displayed at all times: Choose Tools, Customize. The Customize
> dialog box opens with the Options tab at the top. Enable the Always Show
> Full Menus check box and click the Close button.

2. Click the **Add File** button. The Add File to Import List dialog box opens.

3. Use the dialog box to find and open the folder that contains the file. Then click the file. The file is listed in the Import dialog box.

4. Click **Add File** to select another file to import, or click **OK** to import the selected files to your site.

Imported files become part of the site. Whenever you copy the site to a new folder or publish it to the World Wide Web, that file will be included.

> A file included in a site doesn't have to be published. To cause it to be
> skipped when the site is published on a Web server, right-click the file in
> Folders view or the Folder list and choose Don't Publish from the context
> menu that appears.

An imported file can be dragged to a different folder of the site from Folders view or the Folders List pane.

## Delete a Site

A Web site managed with FrontPage can be deleted in two ways, a distinction that's extremely important to note before you attempt to remove a site.

The first way to delete a site is to remove it completely: This wipes out the folder containing the site, all its subfolders, and all the pages, graphics, and other files that comprised the site.

The second way is to only delete the files and folders that FrontPage uses to manage the site, leaving everything else intact.

As you work on a Web site with FrontPage, the software creates some folders and files used in the maintenance of the site (for example, FrontPage keeps track of when each of the site's files was last published from your computer to the World Wide Web).

Deleting the FrontPage information of the site deletes only the files and folders that FrontPage uses behind the scenes to manage the site. Everything else—pages, graphics, and other files—is not removed.

A site with none of its FrontPage material can still be viewed normally with a Web browser, but you won't be able to open it for editing in FrontPage. You can open individual pages in the site for editing, but you can't apply a theme to a site, add shared borders to several pages, or apply any other feature that involves an entire site.

To delete some or all of the files in a site, follow these steps:

1. If the site isn't already open, choose **File, Open Site**. The Open dialog box appears. Use it to select the site's main folder, and click **Open**.

2. If the folder list isn't displayed, open it: Click **View, Folder List**.

3. Right-click the name of the site—the top line in the folder list—and, in the context menu that opens, select the **Delete** command (as shown in Figure 5.3).

**FIGURE 5.3**

*Viewing a Web site's contents.*

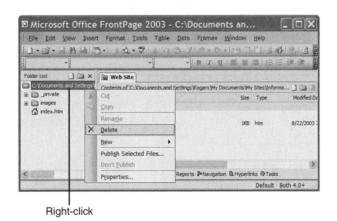

Right-click

A dialog box opens that enables you to delete FrontPage information or delete the entire Web site.

Both of these actions are permanent, so you should handle them with care.

4. To delete the site or its FrontPage information, choose an option and click **OK**.

5. To close the dialog box without deleting anything, click **Cancel**.

A site that is entirely deleted can't be brought back.

If you remove the FrontPage information from a site, it can be re-created later: Choose File, Open, and then use the Open dialog box to find and select the main folder of the site. FrontPage asks whether you want to convert this folder into a Web site—click Yes. FrontPage then creates the information it needs to manage the site.

---

**Hidden Files and Folders**

If you open a Web site's folder outside of FrontPage, you'll see that it contains folders and files that aren't shown in Folders view or the Folders List pane—most notably, a whole bunch of folders named _vti_cnf that appear to contain copies of the files that comprise your site.

These are not copies: Anything in a _vti_cnf folder is being used by FrontPage as part of its site management capabilities. Although their names make them appear to be Web pages, graphics, and the like, the files contain information about the files in your site—such as the last time a particular file was modified. The files in the _vti_pvt folder also are used for site management.

These files should not be deleted (although FrontPage is capable of recreating them if it becomes necessary).

When you delete the FrontPage information associated with a site, these folders and files are what's being removed.

---

# Use Word Documents on the Web

FrontPage is tightly coordinated with the other programs in the Microsoft Office productivity suite. As a result, you can easily incorporate data produced with one program into another.

For example, you can make documents created with Microsoft Word a part of your Web site. You can do so in two ways.

The easy way is to import a Word document in your site and leave it in that format. Visitors to your site who can view Word documents will be able to view the file by loading it with Word.

When you leave a document in Word format, you can't edit it with FrontPage. Instead, when you try to open it normally—by double-clicking the file in Folders view or the Folder list—it opens in Microsoft Word.

Web users will find it much more convenient to view your information if it is converted from Word document format into one or more Web pages.

To convert the contents of a Word document to a Web page:

1. Import the document using **File**, **Import**, as you would any file.

2. If you aren't in Folders view, click the **Folders** button below the editing window.

3. Right-click the document in Folders view, then select **Open With**, **FrontPage (Open as HTML)** from the context menu that appears (see Figure 5.4).

**FIGURE 5.4**

*Editing a Word document in FrontPage.*

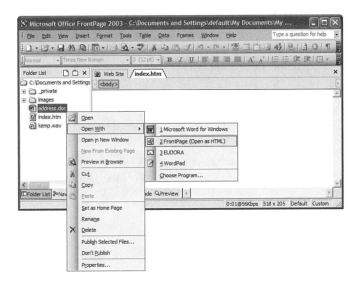

The first time you do this with a document, FrontPage might not have a converter available to display the file correctly. A dialog box appears asking whether you want to install one. Because you are converting the document into a Web page, click No.

When you use FrontPage to edit a Word document, a new Web page is created that contains the contents of the document.

This document might contain a lot of formatting—as much as possible, the font, alignment, and style choices employed in Microsoft Word will be carried over to FrontPage.

After the page has been converted, it can be saved normally: Click the Save button on the Standard toolbar or choose File, Save.

# Summary

In this hour, you learned how to turn the individual Web pages you have created into a cohesive, organized Web site.

Because FrontPage offers built-in support for opening folders, importing files, and moving files and folders around, you don't have to leave the program to handle these tasks.

In the coming hours, you will see more reasons why it's convenient to use FrontPage as a site-management tool. You can use it to keep hyperlinks current, publish the site on the World Wide Web easily, find and correct errors, and track visitors.

# Q&A

**Q** **I copied several files into the folder that contains my site. Why aren't they displayed in the Folder list?**

**A** If you added the files while the site was open in FrontPage, you need to make the software look over the site again to see what files it contains. Select the location of the site in the Folder List pane (the first item atop the list) and choose View, Refresh, or press the F5 key.

This should cause the missing files to appear in your site, even though they have never been imported. If this doesn't work, close the site and open it again.

# HOUR 6

# Develop a Site Quickly with Templates

As you begin to create your own Web sites with FrontPage 2003, the program might seem pretty imposing. Knowing where to start and what to do can be a daunting task when you've never used the software.

FrontPage makes the task more manageable through the use of *templates*, built-in sites that the software knows how to create by itself.

Templates enable you to develop a complete site in a few minutes and then spend your efforts customizing that site rather than creating one from scratch.

Templates are a huge timesaver when they are suitable for a project. In this hour, you will learn

- What templates are available
- How to choose a template for a new Web site
- How to edit pages created from a template
- How to work with hidden comments placed on template pages
- How to reuse the same content on different pages of a site with shared borders

# Select a Web Site Template

FrontPage comes with several dozen Web site and page templates that make it easier to get off to a fast start.

Each template is a framework that you can customize by adding and removing text and making other changes. The software includes templates for some of the most common ways that publishers use the World Wide Web.

The built-in site templates include a personal site, a corporate site, a customer feedback page, and a table of contents page.

All FrontPage sites and Web pages start from templates. The following templates can be used to start a site:

- **One Page Web Site**—A site with a single blank page and nothing else
- **Personal Web Site**—A site with pages where you can describe yourself, share digital photos, and write about your interests and favorite Web sites
- **Customer Support Web Site**—A site that enables a company to offer customer support through product description pages, a discussion forum, feedback form, site search form, and a frequently asked questions page
- **Project Web Site**—A site devoted to a collaborative project, with pages for member information, project status, a schedule, group discussions, and an archive
- **SharePoint Team Site**—A site for team collaboration that includes a calendar, a task list, a file library, and a contact list

There's also an Empty Web Site template that creates a site that contains no files. It differs from the One-Page Web Site template only by lacking an `index.htm` page.

# Create a New Web Site

In the first four hours of the book, you worked on Web pages without placing them into their own Web sites.

It's easier to begin a Web project by creating a new site before any pages have been created. Because all sites start from a template, you must choose one to start a project:

1. Choose **File, New**.

   The New pane opens in FrontPage along the right edge of the editing window.

2. Click the **More Web Site Templates** hyperlink.

   The Web Site Templates dialog box opens, listing the templates you can use to create a new site. It also lists wizards, which you'll be learning about in Hour 8, "Let FrontPage Create a Site for You."

3. Select the template to use for your site—click its icon.

   Next, you should create a new folder where the site will be saved on your computer.

4. Click the **Browse** button.

   The New Web Site Location dialog box opens (see Figure 6.1).

Create New Folder

**FIGURE 6.1**

*The New Web Site Location dialog box is used to tell FrontPage where to save your site.*

5. Use this dialog box to find and open the folder where you are saving your Web sites.

6. Each site should be given its own subfolder: To create one, click the **Create New Folder** button, which is shown in Figure 6.1.

   The New Folder dialog box opens.

7. Type a name for the folder in the **Name** field, and then click the OK button.

   The dialog box closes, returning you to the New Web Site Location dialog box again.

8. Click the **Open** button.

   The folder you have selected is displayed in the text field Specify the Location of the New Web Site.

9. Click **OK**.

FrontPage creates the site, filling the folder with Web pages, graphics, and subfolders.

6

# Customize Your New Web Site

After a new Web site has been created from a template, you can begin making changes to customize the site.

FrontPage displays a newly created site in Folders view so you can see all of the files that it contains, as shown in Figure 6.2.

**FIGURE 6.2**

*Viewing the contents of a newly created Web site.*

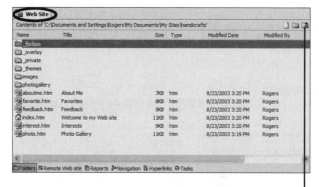

Up One Level button

All of the Web pages in the site are in its main folder. There are also several different subfolders used by FrontPage and a few that you'll want to use, such as images (for graphics), and _private (for files that shouldn't be shown to visitors).

When you use Folders view to open subfolders and explore the site, you might wonder how to get back to where you started. Click the Up One Level button, which is pointed out in Figure 6.2 because it isn't easy to spot.

A Web site's _private subfolder, which initially is empty, can be used as a place for files that should be hidden from visitors to your site. If you create a Web site where visitors can provide you with their mailing addresses, this folder could be used as a place to keep this information from prying eyes.

Before using the _private folder, you should always make sure that the file you expect to be hidden is actually hidden.

A Web server equipped with SharePoint Services 2.0, a feature that enhances the capabilities of FrontPage, will not let visitors see files in this folder unless you explicitly make the folder public.

> Web servers that do not have server extensions will not exclude visitors from files in _private.

Unless you used the Empty Web Site template, the main folder of your site will contain a special file named index.htm. This is the site's home page—the one that visitors will see when they request the main Web address of your site.

For example, when someone visits www.frontpage24.com to see a Web site created for readers of this book, they're seeing index.htm, the site's home page. (The full address for this page is www.frontpage24.com/index.htm.)

Several templates include folders that serve a particular purpose unique to that template. For example, the Personal Web Site template includes a photogallery folder used for pages that display digital photos.

To begin working on your new Web site, open one of the pages for editing: Double-click the page's name in Folders view.

The page opens in the editing window, where you can work on it as you would any other page, making changes and saving it with the Save button on the Standard toolbar.

To return to Folders view, click the Web Site tab atop the editing window, which is circled in Figure 6.2.

## Add and Remove Comments

On each of the sites created from a template, FrontPage offers guidance on several pages in the form of *comments*, text displayed in purple text that is preceded with the word "Comment," as shown in Figure 6.3.

Comments are displayed when a page is being edited in FrontPage but are hidden when it is shown in a Web browser. To see this for yourself, click the Preview button below the editing window. None of the comment text appears on the page.

**FIGURE 6.3**

*Viewing a page's hidden comments.*

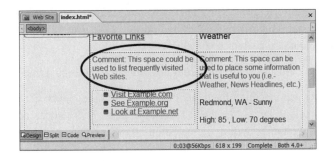

To edit a comment, double-click it. A Comment dialog box opens with the comment in a text area. After making changes, click OK to save them.

A new comment can be added to a Web page:

1. With the page open for editing, click the spot where the comment should be inserted.

2. Choose **Insert**, **Comment** to open a Comment dialog box.

3. Enter the text of the comment and click **OK**. The comment appears on the page in purple text.

You can delete comments at any time, even if they were part of a site or page template. Click the comment you want to delete and press the Delete key.

A little-known fact about comments in FrontPage is that they aren't completely hidden.

Although comments are not displayed by a Web browser, they are still present on the page and can be viewed by anyone who looks at the HTML formatting used to create the page.

Anyone can view this formatting easily—choose View, Source on Internet Explorer or View, Page Source on Mozilla and Netscape Navigator—so keep this in mind when writing comments.

## Making Changes to a Shared Border

Some Web site templates make use of *shared borders*, special page regions that can be shared by all of the pages of a site. Borders, which are comparable to headers and footers in Microsoft Word, can be defined for the top, bottom, left, and right edges of each page.

When a border is set up for a page, it appears outside the main contents of that page—a bottom border will appear below everything else, a top border appears above everything, and so on.

When you create a site using the Customer Support template, most of its pages use top, left, and bottom borders. The circled portion of Figure 6.4 shows the bottom border for this template on a support site's home page.

The boundaries of a shared border are indicated by dashed lines, as shown in Figure 6.4.

A border can be edited from any page on which it appears: Click within a border area to begin working on it—the dashed line disappears and you can edit the contents. Changes made to the border will be reflected on all other pages that share it.

FIGURE 6.4

*Editing a shared
border.*

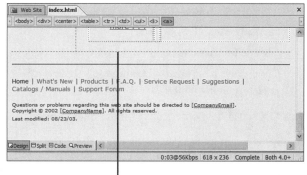

Shared Border

A Web site only may have one defined border for each of the four directions: top, bottom, left, and right.

When a border exists, it does not have to be displayed on every page of the site. Some pages can display it and others hide it.

To add and remove borders:

1. Choose **Format**, **Shared Borders**. The Shared Borders dialog box opens, as shown in Figure 6.5.

FIGURE 6.5

*Adding and removing
shared borders.*

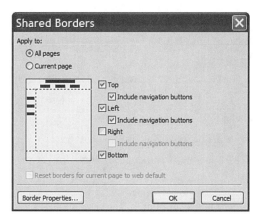

6

2. To add a border on a particular direction, check the Top, Bottom, Left, or Right boxes.

   For any border but the bottom, the Include Navigation Buttons check box becomes enabled. Check the box to fill the border with a *link bar*, a group of graphical or text links to pages of the site. Link bars are introduced in Hour 12, "Use Web Components to Jazz Up a Site."

3. To remove a border, uncheck any of the direction boxes.

4. Use the **Apply To** section to determine which pages will be affected:

   - Choose the **All Pages** option to set these borders for all pages of the site
   - Choose the **Current Page** option to set the borders only for the page that's presently being edited

5. Click **OK** to set the borders and exit the Shared Borders dialog.

Any Web page affected by the border change will be updated and saved automatically.

When a border is added to a site for the first time, it will be created with a comment that shows where the border is located. This comment should be replaced with the contents of the border.

Removing a border hides it from one or more pages but doesn't delete its contents—if the border is added again later, the contents will still be there.

# Explore the Personal Web Site Template

Sooner or later, most Web publishers create their own home page, a place to make a name for themselves on the World Wide Web. It's easy to create an autobiographical site for your professional or personal interests by using the Personal Web Site template.

This template consists of the following elements:

- index.htm, the site's home page, which provides a place to welcome visitors and introduce yourself
- photo.htm, a page for sharing digital photos or other graphics
- interest.htm, a good place to describe your interests and provide hyperlinks to relevant Web sites
- favorite.htm, a list of hyperlinks to your favorite Web sites
- aboutme.htm, a page where you can provide a longer version of your biography
- feedback.htm, a place where visitors to your site can leave you a message

Each of these pages contains a link bar, a row of graphical buttons that can be clicked to visit the rest of the site.

To see how link bars work on your new site, click the Preview in Browser button on the Standard toolbar. The site opens in your primary Web browser.

Figure 6.6 shows what a new site looks like after it has been created with the Personal Web Site template. The circled section of the page is its link bar.

FIGURE 6.6

*Visiting a new personal Web site.*

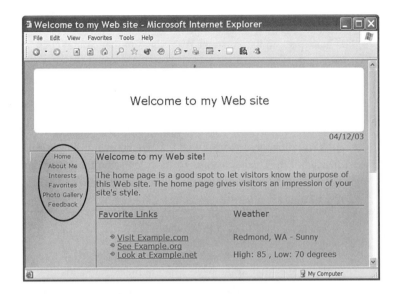

FIGURE 6.6

*Visiting a new personal Web site.*

After looking at this example, you might be a bit underwhelmed by the Personal Web Site template's extremely bland design. You'll learn how to replace it with something much more appealing in the next hour, "Make Your Site Look Great with Themes."

On the Web pages of your new site, you can change most text, headings, and hyperlinks by editing them normally. You've already learned how to work with these page elements in the first four hours of the book.

Templates also put some things on Web pages that can't be edited in the way you might expect: link bars, page banners that show the title of a page, and timestamps that display the calendar date.

These are *Web components*—special page elements supported by FrontPage that add functionality to a site.

You'll learn about components throughout this book as you work with the different aspects of Web design—especially as you read Hour 12.

To give you some familiarity with how components are used, the timestamp component is covered in this hour.

6

## Add a Timestamp to a Web Page

The main page in the Personal Web Site template, `index.htm`, contains a timestamp component at the bottom of the page, immediately following the text "This page last updated," as in "This page last updated 08/23/03."

The timestamp component displays the date that the Web page was last edited. It changes automatically each time anything on the page is altered.

Using this component, you can let visitors know how current the information on a page is. Instead of the time-consuming task of entering the date manually when you edit the page, you can put a timestamp component on it.

To add a timestamp to a Web page, follow these steps:

1. If the page isn't open in the editing window, double-click its filename in Folders view.
2. Click the spot on the page where a timestamp should be displayed.
3. Choose the menu command **Insert, Date and Time**. The Date and Time dialog box opens, as shown in Figure 6.7.

**FIGURE 6.7**

*Editing a timestamp component.*

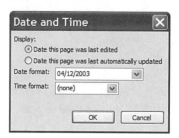

4. Pick one of the Display options to determine what causes the timestamp to change:
   - If it should change whenever you manually make a change to the page, choose **Date This Page Was Last Edited**.
   - If it also should change when FrontPage updates the page for some reason, choose **Date This Page Was Last Automatically Updated**.
5. In the **Date Format** drop-down menu, choose the way the date should appear.
6. If a time also should be displayed, in the Time format drop-down menu, change the value from (none) to something else.
7. Click **OK**.

The timestamp appears on the page, looking like you typed it in yourself.

After a timestamp has been added, to make a change, double-click it in the editing window. The Date and Time dialog box reopens. All of the other Web components are edited in the same manner.

> If you make a change to a timestamp component and it is not immediately reflected in the Web page, click the Refresh button on the Standard toolbar. This button works like the one on a Web browser—it causes a Web page to be completely redrawn.

## Save Changes to a Site

If you have created a personal Web site from the template, you should be able to work on most of it simply by editing text, headings, and hyperlinks.

To save a page after working on it, click the Save button on the Standard toolbar.

To delete a page or any other file, removing it permanently from the site, follow these steps:

1. Return to Folders view: Click the **Web Site** tab atop the editing window.
2. Right-click the filename in Folders view.
3. Choose Delete from the context menu.
4. A Confirm Delete dialog box asks if the file really should be deleted. Click **Yes** to confirm the deletion or No if you've changed your mind.

Some features offered in the Personal Web Site template are discussed in future hours:

- The Photo Gallery Web component on photo.htm is described in Hour 10, "Make a Site Look Great with Graphics."
- Link bars and page banners are described in Hour 12.

When you're ready to take a look at your handiwork, click the Preview in Browser button on the Standard toolbar. Your site opens in a Web browser, and you can experience it in the same manner as the people who will visit it—click the hyperlinks or link bar buttons to see each page.

**6**

# Summary

Figuring out where to get started is one of the biggest hurdles when you're authoring a Web site for the first time.

If one of the templates in FrontPage 2003 is applicable to a project you are undertaking, you're in luck—templates are an extremely helpful way to reduce the amount of time necessary to develop a site. You can spend your time customizing pages and making small adjustments instead of starting from scratch.

In the next two hours, you'll learn about themes and wizards, two more features that make it easier to create your own sites.

# Q&A

**Q How can you change the appearance of a Web template?**

**A** The colors and graphics in the Personal Web Site template and other templates are controlled by its theme. As you will discover in the next hour, themes are a way to establish a consistent and professional visual appearance for a Web site.

You can easily change the theme of a built-in template within FrontPage. You can change everything about the way the Web looks, including its background color, background image, component graphics, text color, and hyperlink color.

**Q Earlier, you said that the home page of a Web site is `index.htm`. The company that hosts my Web site said that this page is called `default.htm`. Which one should I use?**

**A** The name of a Web site's home page is established by the Web server used to present the site on the Internet. So, the short answer to your question is `default.htm`. Rename that page: go to Folders view, right-click the page, and then choose Rename from the context menu.

Some of the possible names for a site's home page are `default.htm`, `default.html`, `home.htm`, `home.html`, `index.htm`, and `index.html`. Many Web site hosting services are configured to look for several of these, so as long as you're using one of the ones they recognize, the site will load normally in a Web browser.

In most cases, FrontPage's choice of `index.htm` should work correctly. If you have problems, contact the hosting service and ask for the filename to give your site's home page.

# Hour 7

# Make Your Site Look Great with Themes

Even though the World Wide Web is barely a decade old, people who use the Web have come to expect certain things from the sites that they frequent.

One expectation is that all of the pages of a site will look alike, at least to some degree. The visual similarity serves as a landmark, letting visitors know they haven't left one site and gone to another.

Creating a consistent look for your Web site in FrontPage 2003 is made easier through the use of *themes*, a set of coordinated color choices and graphics that can be applied to a site's pages. More than 50 themes are available, each with its own distinct style.

In this hour, you will learn

- How to choose a theme for a Web site
- How to preview each of the built-in themes
- How to change the font, colors, and graphics of a theme
- How to create a custom theme

# Give a Site Personality

A good Web site has its own personality, reflected in both the content of its pages and the way the pages are presented. The latter part of that equation is determined by the choices you make as you design a site:

- The color of text and hyperlinks
- The color or graphic used as a page background
- The fonts used on text and hyperlinks
- The graphics and link bars it contains

These things can vary from page to page or can be consistent throughout an entire site. Repeating the same elements makes a site more cohesive and professional in appearance.

There's also a usability benefit: Visitors become accustomed to the placement of content and links on the site.

In the last hour, you used templates to quickly create a site and personalize it with your own content. This can be taken a step further with themes, which instantly define the colors, fonts, text, and graphics employed on a site.

You can apply a theme to any Web site you are working on: FrontPage 2003 comes with several dozen, and more themes are available on the Web, created by professional Web designers and other FrontPage users.

# Select a Theme

FrontPage themes are given short names that help describe their personalities. Expedition looks like a wildlife safari company's brochure. Topo features graphics inspired by maps. Evergreen takes on the dark colors of a forest. Blank, although not actually blank, is relatively plain.

Themes don't replace the need to offer your own graphics on a site, but they can provide a helping hand, especially where menu buttons, text fonts, and colors are concerned.

To get an idea of what they can do, take a look at two versions of the same Web page in Figure 7.1. The one on the left does not use a theme, while the one on the right uses the Pixel theme. That's the only difference between the two pages.

**FIGURE 7.1**

*Comparing unthemed and themed Web pages.*

Applying the Pixel theme to the page, the page content received several instant benefits. The link bar was transformed from text hyperlinks to graphical buttons that change whenever a mouse passes over them. The "About Me" headline and text below it adopted flashier new fonts. The list at the bottom of the page has graphical bullets. Also, the page background is now a textured graphic, although it's tough to see in the figure.

The switch to a theme in this example did not change the site's logo graphic—themes affect only the graphics used as a page background, list bullets, the page banner, and link bars. Everything else, including the graphics chosen for particular pages, is unaffected.

In Hour 6, "Develop a Site Quickly with Templates," you created a site using a template. Although you might not have realized it at the time, you were using a theme—all built-in templates, have a default theme that is applied to all pages in the site.

To apply a theme to a site or page you are working on, open the site (or page) for editing and choose Format, Theme. The Theme pane opens to the right of the editing window, as shown in Figure 7.2. The pane contains the names of each theme that you can choose below a small thumbnail preview that shows its colors and graphics (although some of these details are tough to see). Use the scrollbar to view the available themes.

To get a better look at a theme, hover your mouse over the theme's image until an arrow appears to the right of it; then click the arrow and choose Customize. The Customize dialog box opens.

This dialog box is used to view a theme and make changes to it. Because you're not altering the theme at this point, click Cancel to close the dialog box.

Each theme is available in several variations:

- Choose between vivid and subdued colors with the Vivid Colors check box.
- Choose between animated graphics and nonanimated graphics with the Active Graphics check box.

7

- Choose whether to use a background graphic with the Background Picture check box. If this is not checked, the graphic will be replaced by a solid-color background that's compatible with the other colors used by the theme.

FIGURE 7.2

*Selecting a theme.*

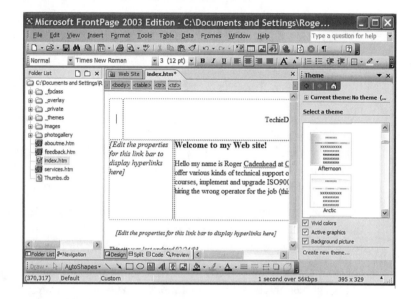

A theme can be applied to the current page being edited or to an entire site:

- For a page, double-click the theme's thumbnail image. The theme is applied to the page, changing its appearance in the editing window.
- For a site, hover your mouse over the thumbnail image until an arrow appears to the right of it. Click the arrow and choose Apply as Default Theme, as shown in Figure 7.3. The theme is applied to all pages in the site, aside from the pages that have been assigned their own theme directly.

You might need to save the page you are working on after its theme has been changed. In the tabs along the top edge of the editing window, pages with an asterisk next to their names have not been saved since changes were made to them.

After you've used a theme, click the Preview in Browser button on the Standard toolbar to open Internet Explorer and see how it looks.

FIGURE 7.3

*Choosing a site's theme.*

Take care when using the theme feature on a site—it replaces the existing design, removing your choice of background, link color, text color, and other elements.

> Themes are applied using Cascading Style Sheets (CSS), a standard for how graphics and text are presented on a Web page. Style sheets enable the visual elements of a page—its text, colors, fonts, and formatting—to be defined separately from the information the page contains.
>
> You'll learn more about them in Hour 22, "Format Your Site with Cascading Style Sheets."

## Using Animated Graphics in a Theme

Choosing to use active graphics in a theme adds some animation effects—the most noticeable is how graphical buttons on a link bar change when a mouse hovers over them. To see this, open a page with a theme that uses active graphics and preview it with a browser.

FrontPage creates these animation effects through the use of one of the scripting languages that it supports—either JavaScript or VBScript. All of that technical wizardry is handled behind the scenes by FrontPage, so you don't have to be a computer programmer to make use of this on your sites.

Because active graphics require scripting, three groups of people will never see the animated effects: Those who have turned off scripting in their Web browser, users of ancient versions of Internet Explorer and Netscape Navigator (versions 1 and 2, mainly), and users of text-only browsers. They'll see a nonanimated graphic or a text caption instead.

7

Wondering why some people would turn off scripting? Usually, it's to get away from obnoxious Web advertisers that pop up a bunch of different windows on your computer and don't let you close your browser. This browser feature requires JavaScript, so turning off all scripting gets rid of the annoyance (along with a lot of much cooler stuff, such as these animated menus).

## Testing a Theme in Different Browsers

You should always test your site in various browsers before publishing it. This is especially important when using FrontPage themes.

Themes will work successfully in current versions of Internet Explorer, Mozilla, Netscape Navigator, and other browsers. You might have problems in older browser versions.

For this reason, if you use themes, you should test the pages using the drop-down menu of the Preview in Browser button on the Standard toolbar.

This menu enables the site to be viewed with every browser installed on your computer at several different screen resolutions. It's an effective way to make sure that their users can successfully view a site.

If you decide that the animated effects in a theme will cause too many problems for your site's desired audience, you can turn them off:

1. Choose **Format**, **Theme** to open the Theme pane again.
2. Uncheck the **Active Graphics** box.
3. Apply the theme again to the current page or the entire site.

When fixing a problem with a theme or making some other change, the easiest route is often to simply choose another theme.

 One of the inconsistencies with animated graphics affects the display of background graphics and list bullets in Netscape Navigator 4. Users of that version of the browser will not see any of these graphics.

# Change to a New Theme

After you have put a theme to use on your own site, it's easy to experiment with alternatives. If you apply a theme to your site and don't like it, simply choose a different theme.

There's also a way to remove a theme from a site or page:

1. Open the site (or page) for editing.

2. Choose **Format, Theme**. The Theme pane opens.

3. Use the scrollbar to find the theme named No Theme, which can be applied to the current page or an entire site:

    - For a page, double-click the theme's thumbnail image. The page's theme is removed.

    - For a site, hover your mouse over the thumbnail image, and then click the arrow and choose Apply as Default Theme. All themes are removed from the pages of the site.

Removing a theme from a site does not delete any graphic that you have added, such as digital photos, a company logo, or the like. It only removes the graphics and formatting that were introduced to the site by the theme.

# Create a Custom Theme

As you have seen, themes are a quick way to enhance the appearance of a Web site. Whether your site contains 5 or 500 pages, a theme can be applied to it in minutes.

If none of the built-in themes suits the design you're trying to create, you can develop a custom theme.

Creating a new theme from scratch is a project for hard-core FrontPage experts. For the novice user, creating a custom theme is much easier to accomplish by modifying the things you don't like about an existing theme and saving it under a new name.

To create a new theme based on an existing design, follow these steps:

1. Choose **Format, Theme**. The Theme pane opens to the right of the editing window.

2. Select the theme variations you want to employ:

    - Choose vivid or subdued colors with the Vivid Colors check box.

    - Choose animated or nonanimated graphics with the Active Graphics check box.

    - Choose a background graphic or background color with the Background Picture check box.

**7**

3. Scroll to the theme you want to modify and hover your mouse over the theme's image until an arrow appears alongside it. Click the arrow and choose **Customize**. The Customize Theme dialog box opens, as shown in Figure 7.4.

FIGURE 7.4

*Customizing a theme.*

The Customize Theme dialog box is used to change the colors, fonts, and graphics employed on a theme.

Each of the customizable aspects of a theme is covered in the sections that follow. After a theme has been customized, click Save As to give the theme a name.

FrontPage saves all of the themes you customize in a folder of its own choosing. The newly saved theme then is listed with all of the other FrontPage themes you can use.

The location of that folder is dependent on your version of Windows. On Windows XP, customized FrontPage themes are stored in an `Application Data\Microsoft\Themes` folder inside a user folder of `Documents and Settings`.

## Select a Color Scheme

The Colors button is used to pick the colors that make up the theme's color scheme. You designate two color schemes that contain five colors each: vivid colors and normal colors.

These colors can be selected by borrowing a color scheme from another theme or selecting one predominant color and letting FrontPage choose four others to go along with it.

To select the colors for a new theme, follow these steps:

1. In the Customize Theme dialog box, click the **Colors** button. The dialog box changes to show the options available for selecting theme colors (see Figure 7.5).

**FIGURE 7.5**

*Selecting theme colors.*

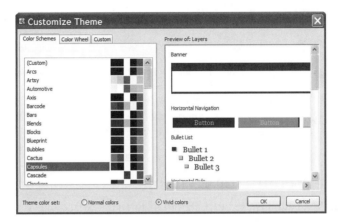

2. In the Theme Color Set Option, select either **Vivid Colors** or **Normal Colors** to customize that color scheme.

3. Choose one of the color-selection techniques:

   • To pick a five color scheme, scroll through the list of schemes, viewing the colors used by each alongside their names.

   The color in the middle is the page's background color. The other colors are used in a variety of different ways by a theme, as shown in the Preview Of window shown in Figure 7.5. Click a scheme's name to choose its color scheme.

   • To pick using the color wheel, click the **Color Wheel** tab to bring it to the front. The dialog box displays a color wheel—a circle containing hundreds of individual colors.

   Click a spot on the wheel to choose the main color in the scheme. The other four colors are chosen automatically on the basis of this choice—for example, picking a red area of the wheel creates a color scheme with several reddish hues.

   The Brightness slider changes all of the colors on the wheel. Drag it to the left to make the colors darker and more gloomy, or right to make them brighter and more vibrant.

7

4. To choose colors for the other color scheme, switch the **Theme Color Set** option from Vivid Colors to Normal Colors (or vice versa), and repeat step 3.

5. To save your newly chosen color schemes, click **OK**. The main Customize Theme dialog box appears again.

Every change that you make while selecting colors is reflected in the Preview Of pane.

There's also an advanced feature for experienced Web designers: With the Custom tab of the Customize Theme dialog box, colors can be manually assigned to specific Web elements such as the page background, active hyperlinks, and body text. This is more time consuming, but it provides total control over the colors employed in the theme.

## Select Fonts for a Theme

The Text button is used to assign fonts to body text and the six different heading sizes that are used on Web pages. You can use any of the fonts that are installed on your computer.

Before you dive into fonts, a few of the basics are worth reiterating here.

Fonts are a very system-specific element of Web page design. If you use a font on your site that isn't present on a visitor's system, that user won't see the font. Instead, a standard font such as Arial, Helvetica, Times New Roman, or Verdana will be used in its place.

If you're developing a Web site for a captive audience—such as a corporate or school intranet that won't be seen by anyone on the outside—you can use any font that you know will be present on all of the computers that have access to the site. If your Web site is available to anyone with a Web browser, you should make use of the most common fonts.

The best fonts to choose are Arial, Comic Sans, Courier New, Georgia, Impact, Times New Roman, Trebuchet, and Verdana—all of these are installed with Internet Explorer on computers running Windows and the Mac OS, so they're viewable by more than 95% of the people using the Web.

All of these fonts are suitable for use on headlines and other text 12 points or larger in size. For smaller text (such as paragraphs in the body of an article), Georgia, Verdana, and Trebuchet are the most readable fonts at small sizes.

1. In the Customize Theme dialog box, click the **Text** button. The dialog box changes to show the options available for selecting theme fonts, as shown in Figure 7.6.

**FIGURE 7.6**

*Selecting new fonts for a theme.*

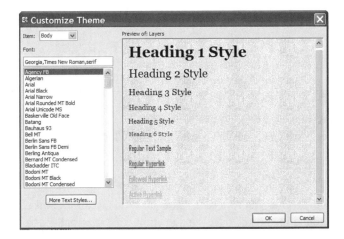

2. To select a font for body text and hyperlinks, choose **Body** from the Item list box and choose a font from the list of fonts.

   The name of the font appears in the Font text field, and the Preview Of pane changes, displaying your chosen font as "Regular Text Sample" and the two hyperlink samples.

3. To select a font for one of the six heading sizes, choose the heading from the Item list box and then select the desired font. The Font text field and the Preview Of pane are updated in response to your new choice.

If you're concerned that a font won't be present on a site visitor's computer, you can specify a list of fonts for the browser to choose from: the desired font followed by one or more alternative fonts and a generic font style: cursive, fantasy, monospace, sans-serif, or serif.

Web browsers will look for each font in the list and use the first one that's present on the system running the browser.

If none of the fonts are present and a generic font ends the list, the Web browser uses a font that fits that style. For example, Times Roman for serif, Arial for sans-serif, and Courier for monospaced.

7

4. If you'd like to specify alternate fonts and a font style, add them to the **Font** text field, separating each one with a comma.

   For example, Figure 7.6 shows that Georgia is the desired font for body text and hyperlinks. If it is unavailable, Times New Roman will be substituted. No Times New Roman either? The Web browser will use its preferred serif font when displaying the text.

5. To save your work, click **OK** to return to the main Customize Theme dialog box.

## Select Graphics Used By a Theme

The Graphics button is used to modify the graphics that appear on the pages of the theme.

This feature can be used to substitute graphics of your own creation, such as a company logo or photograph, for the theme's current graphics.

If you're not ready to customize graphics, you might want to take a look at it simply to learn more about how a theme makes use of them.

Every theme has graphics files associated with 10 different page elements, including the background image, the page banner, and both horizontal and vertical navigation bars. Some of these elements have several different graphics files associated with them—animated buttons have files for each image that appears on the button.

Changing graphics requires a strong working knowledge of how the different page elements function.

To see the graphics associated with a theme, follow these steps:

1. In the Customize Theme dialog box, click the **Graphics** button. The dialog box changes to show the options available for choosing a theme's graphics. An example of each graphic is shown in the Preview Of pane in Figure 7.7.

2. Use the Preview Of pane's horizontal and vertical scrollbars to see all of the graphics.

3. To find out more about the graphics for a particular page element, choose it from the **Item** drop-down box.

   The tabbed dialog box below the Item list displays the graphic (or graphics) employed by the element.

4. Click the **Font** tab to bring it to the front and see the font used by an element (see Figure 7.8). If the element does not use fonts, the list boxes on this dialog will be disabled.

**FIGURE 7.7**

*Selecting graphics for a theme.*

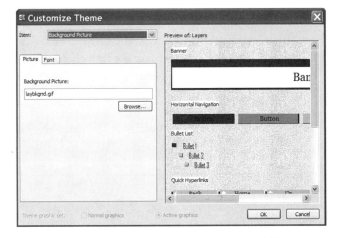

**FIGURE 7.8**

*Selecting the fonts used with graphics.*

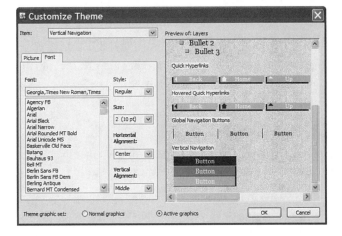

5. The Picture and Font tabs can be used to change the graphics:

- To choose a different graphic for the selected element on the Picture tab, click the picture's **Browse** button. The Open File dialog box appears. Use this to find and select the graphic to associate with the element.

- To choose a different font, click the **Font** tab to bring it to the front. Then use each of the list boxes on the tab to select the font, font style, and alignment to choose a different graphic file for the element.

Any changes that you make are reflected in the Preview Of pane.

6. Click **OK** to save any changes you made and return to the Customize Theme dialog box. To exit without making any changes to the graphics, click **Cancel**.

7

## Save the New Theme

After you have made changes to an existing theme, you can save the theme with its existing name or a pick a new one. If you save the theme under its existing name, it replaces the original version. Otherwise, a new theme is created with the specified name.

> While you're experimenting with creating your themes, you should always give them a new name rather than overwriting any of FrontPage's built-in themes. You might want to use them later.

To save your new theme, in the Customize Theme dialog box, click the Save As button to save the file under a new name. The Save Theme dialog box opens. Enter a name in the Enter New Theme Title field and click OK.

To save the new theme under the current name, click the Save button. This overwrites the FrontPage theme that you started from with your new, customized theme.

Your new theme and all of its graphics files are saved. From this point on, you'll see your theme as one of the selections whenever you go to choose a theme.

# Delete a Theme

To permanently delete your new theme (or any other theme that is available in FrontPage), follow these steps:

1. Choose **Format**, **Theme** to open the Theme pane.
2. Place your mouse over the thumbnail image of the theme. An arrow appears next to the theme.
3. Click the arrow and select **Delete** from the drop-down menu. A dialog box asks you to confirm the deletion of the theme.
4. Click **Yes** to delete it or **No** to leave the theme alone.

# Summary

Themes define several different aspects of a Web site, including its text and link colors, background graphic, navigation, and color scheme.

They also make it possible for everyone to benefit from Web design features that are used by experts, such as JavaScript-animated menu buttons.

In this hour, you learned how to use FrontPage 2003's built-in themes to instantly establish the visual personality of a site. FrontPage has themes suited to a variety of purposes, such as corporate sites, personal home pages, and online stores.

If the software's built-in themes do not fit a project, you can modify an existing theme and save it under a new name, making it available for any of your Web projects.

# Q&A

**Q I'm creating a new theme. I chose a background color as part of a color scheme, but it always shows up as white when I'm using the theme. What's causing this?**

**A** The background color of a theme is affected by whether you've opted to use vivid colors when you apply it to a Web. If you have not chosen vivid colors, FrontPage 2003 uses a white background with a more muted version of your color scheme.

To put your missing background color to use, reapply the theme with the Vivid Colors option selected.

**Q All of the FrontPage themes display a page banner graphic atop each page, which templates use to display a title. Should I be using these banners on my own sites?**

**A** You can, but in my opinion, it's tough to make a page look exciting with one of those giant, plain, solid-color banners on top of it.

One of the knocks against FrontPage has been the "cookie-cutter" nature of sites created with the software. You can get away from this perception by creating your own graphics, especially for the top of each page.

As you'll learn in Hour 10, "Make a Site Look Great with Graphics," you can create your own graphics and add text to them using FrontPage. These will almost always look better than a page banner because you can choose your own font and a visually interesting background.

7

# HOUR **8**

# Let FrontPage Create a Site for You

One of the things you learn quickly about FrontPage 2003 is how much work it can do for you. As you saw in the past two hours with templates and themes, FrontPage can create an entire Web site in minutes, complete with an appealing design and graphics.

FrontPage automates even more complex tasks through the use of wizards.

*Wizards* are programs that ask a series of questions about a project you'd like to undertake. Your answers control how the program does its work.

In this hour, you will learn

- How to create a site with the help of a wizard
- How to answer a wizard's questions
- How to change your answers
- How to create a Web site from existing pages using the Import Web Wizard

## Open a Site-Creation Wizard

Many software programs make use of *wizards*, dialog boxes that attempt to make a hard task easier by breaking it down into a series of questions.

FrontPage and other programs in the Office suite are set up on a computer through an installation wizard, so the format should be familiar to you.

In FrontPage, wizards can be thought of as templates with brains. They can be used to create sites and Web pages that are too complicated to be handled with a template.

By breaking down a task into a series of simpler steps, wizards make it possible to create complex Web sites—such as a 20-page professional corporate site or a customer support site—by answering a few simple questions.

Two kinds of wizards exist in FrontPage: Web site wizards, which create entire sites, and single-page wizards.

Wizards can be selected when you're creating a new site or adding a new page to an existing site.

To summon a site wizard, follow these steps:

1. Click **File, New**. The New pane opens (see Figure 8.1).

**FIGURE 8.1**

*Creating a new page or Web site.*

2. Click the **More Web Site Templates** hyperlink.

   The Web Site Templates dialog box opens with the General tab on top. You can use several wizards to create an entire site:

- The Database Interface Wizard creates a site that can connect to a Microsoft Access database, displaying records on Web pages and saving information collected on the site to the database. More information on this wizard is offered in Hour 19, "Connect a Database to Your Site."
- The Discussion Web Site Wizard creates a message board where visitors to your site can communicate with each other (as described during Hour 18, "Turn Your Site into a Community").
- The Corporate Presence Wizard creates a professional site for a business.
- The Import Web Site Wizard copies an existing Web site to your computer, even if it wasn't created with FrontPage.

3. To start a wizard, choose it and click the OK button. The wizard's main dialog box appears.

4. To use the wizard, answer each question that it asks and then click **Next** to see the next question.

   When you reach the last question, a Finish button is displayed.

5. When you're ready to put to work the options you've chosen in the wizard, click **Finish**.

Specific information on FrontPage wizards is offered in the remainder of the hour.

# Import an Existing Site into FrontPage

If you have created Web sites with other software before using FrontPage, you'll be interested in the Import Web Site Wizard, which can be used to bring an existing site and all of its files into FrontPage for editing.

With this wizard, you can take advantage of FrontPage's features on a site that wasn't originally created with the software.

The wizard can import a site from a folder on your computer, a folder on a network, or a Web site on the Internet.

To import a site, follow these steps:

1. Click **File, New** to open the New pane.
2. Click the **More Web Site Templates** hyperlink. The Web Site Templates dialog box opens, listing all of the site wizards you can select.

3. Choose the **Import Web Site Wizard** icon. In the Specify the Location of the New Web Site list box, FrontPage picks a name for a new folder where the site's files will be stored.

4. To choose a different folder, click the **Browse** button. The New Web Site Location dialog box appears, as shown in Figure 8.2. Use this dialog box to find and open the folder where you store the Web sites that you work on with FrontPage.

Create New Folder

**FIGURE 8.2**

*Choosing a location for an imported Web site.*

5. Each FrontPage site must be given its own folder. To create one for this imported site, click the **Create New Folder** button identified in Figure 8.2. The New Folder dialog box appears.

6. Give the folder a name in the Name field and click **OK**.

7. In the New Web Site Location dialog box, click the **Open** button. The folder is listed in the Specify the Location of the New Web Site list box in the Import Web Wizard.

8. Click **OK**. The Import Web Wizard opens.

## Choose an Import Method

The first question asked by the Import Web Site Wizard is how to retrieve the site, as shown in Figure 8.3.

A site can be imported in five ways, depending on where it is located and what kind of access you have to that location:

• FrontPage Server Extensions or SharePoint Services, an effective technique that requires a Web server equipped with one of these features

- FTP (File Transfer Protocol), the most common way that files are exchanged over the Internet

- HTTP (HyperText Transfer Protocol), a way to retrieve Web pages and other files that can be viewed on the Web

- File System, which retrieves files stored on your computer or a folder you have access to on a local area network

- WebDAV, a Web content authoring and versioning system that is less common than the alternatives

**FIGURE 8.3**

*Importing a Web site into FrontPage.*

The best way to import a site is to use FrontPage Server Extensions or SharePoint Services because this can retrieve all of the pages and other files included in a Web site—even if they aren't presented directly to visitors.

When you use FrontPage to create a Web site, it works with lots of files behind the scenes during the preparation of a page. For example, if your site uses a theme, there will be more than two dozen graphics and other files inside a folder called _themes and its subfolders. These files are never presented directly to people who visit your site. Instead, they're used by FrontPage to create the hover buttons, graphics, and formatting of your pages.

Using server extensions or SharePoint Services, the wizard also can import *subsites*— Web sites that are contained within folders of another site. (For example, a Web site in the C:\My Sites\sports\baseball\Cubs folder would be a subsite of a site in the C:\My Sites\sports\baseball folder.)

If the site to import is on a Web server extension or SharePoint, you can use them to import the Web site and all of its subsites:

1. Choose **FrontPage Server Extensions** or **SharePoint Services**.

2. Enter the Web address of the site's home page in the **Web Site Location** text field.

3. To include subsites, select the **Include Subsites** check box.

If the site that you want to import is on your computer (or in a folder on another computer in your network), you can copy it from that folder:

1. Choose the **File System** option and click the **Browse** button.

   The New Publish Location dialog box appears. Use this to find and select the Web site's primary folder (the one where its home page is stored).

2. Select the folder and click **Open**. The folder is displayed in the Web Site Location text field.

3. To import subsites at the same time (if there are any), select the **Include Subsites** check box.

The Import Web Site wizard isn't the easiest way to turn a folder on your computer or network into a FrontPage Web site. As an alternative, choose File, Open Site, select the folder, and then click Open. FrontPage asks if the folder should be converted so that it can be managed by the software. Click Yes.

If the site is on a Web server that you can access using File Transfer Protocol (FTP), a common standard for exchanging files with an Internet server, you can use your FTP account to import the site. Here's how:

1. Choose **FTP**.

2. In the Web Site Location text field, enter the address of the FTP server. Because it's using FTP, the address should be preceded with ftp:// instead of http://.

3. In the Root Directory field, type the location and name of the folder that contains the site's home page.

4. If the server requires Passive FTP, click the **Use Passive FTP** check box.

If you can't make use of extensions or SharePoint, FTP is probably the best choice of the remaining options.

If the site is on a Web server that isn't equipped with extensions or SharePoint (or if you don't know), you can save the files by retrieving them from the Web using HTTP.

The HTTP option isn't as effective as extensions, SharePoint, or FTP—it grabs only pages that are publicly linked from the home page. It also omits files that are used to create those pages, such as FrontPage themes and other files that were used to create the site.

However, as a last resort, HTTP can be used to import the site:

1. Choose **HTTP**.

2. Enter the Web address of the site's home page in the Web Site Location text field.

   FrontPage is finicky about the address: Instead of using a main address such as `www.example.com`, it's better to be more specific and refer to the name of the home page also (in other words, something like `www.example.com/index.html`).

3. After choosing one of the import methods, click Next to continue. The wizard is updated to reflect your choice.

4. If you are importing the site from a password-protected location, a Name and Password Required dialog box opens. Use the Name and Password fields to provide your login information, and then click **OK**.

> As a timesaver, whenever you log into a server, FrontPage saves your username and password so you don't have to enter them again later. This will come in handy when you publish your site.

After choosing an import method, click Next.

## Choose Where to Save the Site

The next question the wizard may ask is where to save the site. Because you've already chosen a folder, it appears in the Local Copy Location text field, which is disabled so that you can't change it.

However, there is a way to make a change if you've changed your mind and want to select a different folder:

1. Deselect the **Add to Current Web Site** check box. The Location Copy Location field and Browse button become enabled.

2. Click the **Browse** button. The New Page Location dialog box appears. Use this to select (or create) a new folder where the site's files should be saved.

3. Select the folder and click **Open**. The dialog box closes, returning you to the wizard.

4. Select the **Add to Current Web Site** box. Click **Next** to proceed to the next question.

## Choose How Much to Import

If you are importing a site using HTTP, you'll be asked an extra question at this point. Everyone else can skip to the next section.

For HTTP imports, the wizard asks how much you want to retrieve from the site, as shown in Figure 8.4.

**FIGURE 8.4**

*Choosing the elements of a Web site to import.*

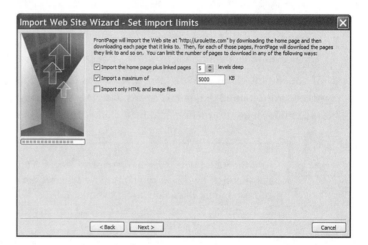

The download can be limited by the following three ways:

- Reducing the number of links that the wizard visits to find new files to import
- Limiting the site to a maximum disk size
- Limiting the retrieval to Web pages and image files only

The Import Web Site Wizard uses a concept called *levels* to determine how many links to follow when importing a site. Each level represents a link—the wizard finds and clicks links just like it was a person visiting the site with a browser.

For example, if the wizard visits a link on the home page to a What's New? page, it has traveled two levels into the site. If it continues further, using a link on the What's New? page to visit a Contact Me page, it has traveled three levels.

If this concept is still boggling your mind, a good choice for Web sites that are less than 100 pages in size is 5 levels.

Limiting the disk size and the type of files downloaded might cause FrontPage to retrieve only a portion of the site.

To choose how much of the site to import, follow these steps:

1. To set the number of levels, select the **Import the Home Page Plus Linked Pages** check box.

2. Use the arrows next to the **Levels Deep** list box to set the number of levels to import.

3. To set a maximum size, select the **Import a Maximum Of** check box. The KB text field next to the box becomes enabled with a default value of 5000K (5MB).

4. If you want to set a different value, type it in the KB field.

5. To limit file retrieval to Web pages and graphics only, select the **Import Only HTML and Image Files** check box.

If none of these check boxes is selected, the wizard retrieves everything in the site that it can find by visiting links and analyzing the content of Web pages.

After choosing how much of a site to import, click Next.

## Import the Site's Files

When the wizard is ready to begin copying the imported site's files, a Finish button appears. Click it.

The Import Web Wizard opens FrontPage's Remote Web Site view, which you'll see each time you publish a site to a Web server. It's shown in Figure 8.5.

**FIGURE 8.5**

*Beginning to import a Web site to your computer.*

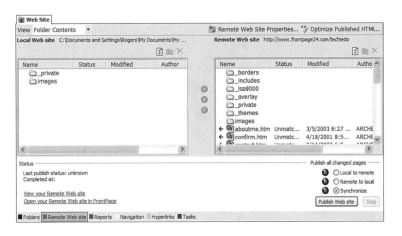

This view displays two folders side by side.

On the left, the Local Web Site folder displays the contents of the folder where the site will be imported. Because this is a new folder that you've just created, it contains only a few empty folders used by FrontPage: _private and images.

On the right, the Remote Web site folder displays the folder from which the site is being copied. Each file that will be imported has an arrow next to its name—the leftward direction of the arrow indicates that it will be copied to the folder on your computer.

To import the site, follow these steps:

1. In the Publish All Changed Pages section, make sure that the **Remote to Local** option is selected.
2. Click the **Publish Web Site** button. The wizard imports the site.

After the site has been imported (or it has failed for some reason), the Status section of the view is updated with the good or bad news—look for the Last Publish Status label to display "Successful" or an error message.

FrontPage copies the pages of the site, all of its graphics, and other files that are part of the same site (unless you're importing only pages and graphics). The folder structure of the site is re-created as well.

FrontPage also copies any other pages that are part of the same site. If there is a main home page and 20 other pages, each of these is retrieved along with all its graphics and other files.

If you are importing a site using the HTTP option, the wizard won't copy programs that run behind the scenes on a site, such as an email script, a hit counter, and the like. The only way to retrieve those programs is to use a better option, such as FrontPage Server Extensions or FTP.

As with other importing features of FrontPage, the Import Web Wizard makes it easy to incorporate existing site content into your work.

For obvious reasons, you only should make use of imported content that you have the legal right to publish on the World Wide Web.

## Work on the Imported Site

After you import a site, you can begin working on it like any other FrontPage site that you create.

FrontPage keeps the formatting of existing Web pages intact when they are imported into a site. As you start making changes and using FrontPage features such as link bars and themes, you may be changing or wiping out some of the existing features of the site.

An imported site should be tested thoroughly to make sure that it functions as intended.

# Create a Corporate Web Site

Another useful wizard for quick site development is the Corporate Presence Wizard, which can be used to establish a company's official site.

If you're developing a site for your own company or for a client that isn't on the Web yet, this wizard guides you through the process of developing a professional site. You'll be able to choose products or services that should be spotlighted, solicit feedback from customers, incorporate the corporate logo into each page, and perform other business-related tasks.

To make the most effective use of the wizard, you should know each of the following things about the site before you start:

- The products or services that will be promoted on the site
- Whether visitors should be able to contact the company using the site
- Whether the site needs its own search engine
- The company's mission statement, if one should be displayed on the site
- Other kinds of information, such as catalog requests, that will be collected
- All contact information about the company, along with the email address to use for the company and for Web-related inquiries

If you don't know some of these things, you can add them later, after the wizard has created the site. As a general rule, though, you'll be much closer to completing the site if you gather all the necessary information before using the wizard.

To call on this wizard, follow these steps:

1. Choose **File, New**. The New pane opens alongside the editing window.
2. Click the **More Web Site Templates** hyperlink. The Web Site Templates dialog box appears.
3. Select the **Corporate Presence Wizard** icon.

4. Click the **Browse** button. The New Web Site Location dialog box opens. Use it to open the folder where you keep Web sites.

5. Click the **New Folder** button.

6. Use the New Folder dialog box to name the folder and click **OK**, and then click **Open**.

7. In the Web Site Templates dialog box, click **OK**.

The Corporate Presence wizard opens with some introductory text. Click Next to begin.

## Choose Pages for the Site

The wizard's first question offers a checklist of pages that can be part of the site (see Figure 8.6).

**FIGURE 8.6**

*Choosing the pages to include.*

The wizard offers to create a home page (which is mandatory) and five optional pages:

- A "What's New" page

- A list of the products or services described on the site, each of which will receive its own page

- A feedback form to receive email from current and prospective customers

- A search form that can be used to search the site for key words and phrases

- A table of contents listing every page on the site

Check the box of each page that should be included. The wizard asks different questions based on the pages that have been chosen.

If you're answering questions and you change your mind about a previous answer, use the Back button to return to the question and revise it.

One of the dialog boxes asks exactly how many products and services you will be describing on the site. A page will be created for each of these, along with a main page connecting all of them with hyperlinks.

If you're not sure whether to include a feature in your corporate site, err on the side of excess. You can usually take things off a site more easily than you can add them later.

For each product, you can determine whether to display an image or pricing information (see Figure 8.7).

**FIGURE 8.7**

*Setting up a product page.*

Each service can be described along with the relevant capabilities and account information. You'll also be able to associate information request forms for each product and service so that prospective customers can use the site to ask for more details about the company's offerings.

After you answer all of the Corporate Presence Wizard's questions, it creates the site.

The wizard creates each of the main pages that you requested—pages for products, services, and other features, and the start of a navigational structure for the site.

Another thing the wizard does is add comments to each page offering tips on what you should add to that part of the site.

These comments show up in the editing window in a lighter color than the body text of the page, preceded with the word "Comment." Comments are not displayed when the page is loaded by a Web browser, so you can leave them on the page while you're working on the site.

> To add your own comment to a page, click a spot on the page where the comment should be added, and then choose Insert, Comment.
>
> A dialog box opens, and the comment you enter into it is added to the page at the current cursor location.

The Corporate Presence Wizard has numerous features that make it easier to establish a company's site. Here's one example: The wizard asks for some common information that should be available about any company: its mailing address, phone number, fax number, email address for customer inquiries, and the like. These things can be automatically placed on different pages, and when something changes, FrontPage updates every page where it appears.

## Summary

During the last several hours of this book, you learned how to take advantage of three time-saving features of FrontPage: templates, themes, and wizards.

Templates are default sites and pages intended for use in your own projects. The template gets you part of the way on a task you're working on, and you finish it by customizing the template.

Themes are built-in graphic styles that you can apply to either a Web page or an entire site. They define the background, colors, image buttons, and fonts that are used, and you can quickly establish a consistent look and feel for a site using themes.

Wizards are interactive programs that create templates based on your answers to a series of questions. You can create more complex sites with wizards than is possible with templates, including a corporate site, a discussion site, and an interactive form page.

By using these three features, you're able to solve one of the problems any Web designer faces: how to go from an empty file folder to an entire site, complete with pages, images, hyperlinks, and a navigational structure.

These features save a lot of development time on your own Web projects.

# Q&A

8

**Q** **One of the wizards, the Discussion Web Wizard, isn't introduced during this hour. Where can I learn how to use it?**

**A** That wizard is used to create a discussion board, a site in which visitors can read messages written by others and post their own in response. To use this wizard, you must be hosting the site on a Web server equipped with FrontPage Server Extensions. You'll find out how to work with this wizard in Hour 18.

**Q** **The WebDAV option of the Import Web Wizard is not covered in this hour. What is it?**

**A** WebDAV, which stands for Web-Based Distributed Authoring and Versioning, is a method for updating a Web site that's being worked on by a team of people. Using WebDAV, a folder on a Web server is treated as if it were located on your own computer.

If your Web site hosting service offers WebDAV, which is not as common as the other options covered in this hour, the service should have provided the information needed to make use of it in FrontPage.

# PART III

# Improving Your Site's Appeal

## Hour

9   Collect Information from Your Visitors

10   Make a Site Look Great with Graphics

11   Offer Animation, Video, and Games

12   Use Web Components to Jazz Up a Site

# Hour 9

# Collect Information from Your Visitors

As a Web publisher, you can collect information from the visitors to your pages, present it on your site, and use it in other ways to create a more engaging experience.

When you collect information on your site, you'll be using a Web page element called a *form*. Forms are made up of text boxes, lists, and other means of gathering information from visitors.

During this hour, you will learn

- How to use the feedback template and Form Page Wizard to create forms
- How to add questions to a form
- How to customize a form
- How to save the information collected on a form to a text file or a Web page
- How to receive form responses in email

## Collect Feedback from Your Visitors

One of the easiest forms to create is a *feedback page*—a place in your site where visitors can send you a private comment. This offers a convenient service to your visitors and has a second benefit—it makes it possible to omit your email address from your site.

Why is this useful? When you begin Web publishing, any email address you put on a page will quickly be discovered by *spammers*—junk email marketers who fill up inboxes with unsolicited commercial solicitations.

To find addresses to add to their mailing lists, spammers routinely use software to scour pages on the World Wide Web. It's inevitable that your site will be found quickly by these programs—often in as little time as one to two weeks.

By putting a feedback page rather than your address on your site, you'll reduce the amount of spam you receive.

> Some visitors to your Web site may prefer to contact you with their pre-
> ferred email program, so you might want to provide both a feedback page
> and your email address.

To add a feedback page to your site, follow these steps:

1. Open the site (if it isn't already) and choose **File,  New.**

   The New pane opens alongside the editing window.

2. Click the **More Page Templates** hyperlink.

   The Page Templates dialog box opens, displaying the pages that you can create using either templates or wizards.

3. Choose the **Feedback Form** icon and click **OK.**

   A feedback page is created,  using the same colors, text, and background as the rest of your site. It opens in the editing window, as shown in Figure 9.1. A dotted line indicates the borders of the form. Every part of the form must be located within this boundary.

   At the top of the page, a purple-tinted paragraph describes the form and offers some guidance for how it is used. This text is a *comment*, explanatory text that shows up only in the FrontPage editing window, not when the page is viewed with a Web browser. (To verify this, click the Preview button below the editing win-dow.)

4. To remove the comment, click it once and press the **Delete** key.

**FIGURE 9.1**

*Editing a feedback page.*

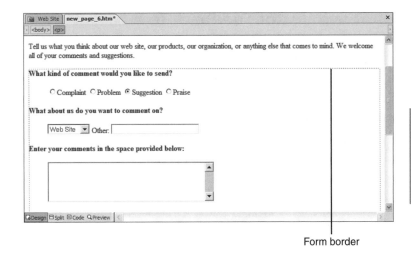

Form border

5. If you want to change the wording of a question, edit it as you would any other text in FrontPage: Click your cursor on the line and use your keyboard to add or remove things.

6. The positioning and formatting of the different elements of the form also can be changed like any other part of a Web page.

> Making changes to form elements is described in detail during Hour 20, "Use Your Site to Gather Information." When modifying a form, take care not to move anything outside its borders.

7. To delete any part of the form, drag your mouse over it and press the **Delete** key.

When a feedback page is created, FrontPage sets it up to save the answers to the file `feedback.txt` in the _private folder of your Web site.

For this to work, you must publish your site on a Web server that's equipped with FrontPage Server Extensions or SharePoint Services, enhancements that make it easier for people using FrontPage to add special features (like this) to their sites.

You'll learn about FrontPage server enhancements and how to save the `feedback.txt` file in Hour 13, "Publish Your Site."

At this point, you may want to change how visitor feedback is saved. It can be saved to a file in several different formats or sent to you in an email.

## Save Visitor Feedback to a File

The answers collected on a form can be stored in a file on your Web server in three different formats:

- **Text**—This can be viewed in a text editor or loaded in some database and spreadsheet programs such as Microsoft Access and Microsoft Excel.
- **HTML**—This can be read with a Web browser.
- **XML**—This is a popular format for data that's widely integrated into FrontPage 2003 and the rest of the Office suite.

  XML is a universal data format designed to make information reusable in other programs, such as those in the Office suite. Because it is a new feature, it won't work unless the server hosting your site is equipped with the SharePoint Services 2.0 enhancement.

To save feedback to a file, follow these steps:

1. Right-click anywhere within the form's borders—the dotted line identified earlier in Figure 9.1.

2. Choose **Form Properties** from the context menu. The Form Properties dialog box appears, as shown in Figure 9.2.

**FIGURE 9.2**

*Choosing how to save visitor feedback.*

3. Visitor feedback will be saved as text. To choose a different format, click the **Options** button. The Saving Results dialog box appears.

4. Use the **File Format** drop-down box to select a format for the feedback:

   - To make it easy to read with Microsoft Excel and other database programs, choose **Text Database Using Comma as a Separator**. This creates a text file with the filename extension `.csv`.

   - To read it with a Web browser, a good choice is either **HTML** or **Formatted Text Within HTML**. This creates an `.htm` file that uses the same formatting as the Web pages you create with FrontPage.

   - To save it as XML, choose **XML**. This creates an `.xml` file.

5. Click **OK**.

6. To choose the folder where the file should be stored, click the **Browse** button. The Current Web Site dialog opens. Use this to select one of the folders on your site.

7. Click **OK** to close the Form Properties dialog box.

The form will be set up to store responses in the designated file. If the file doesn't exist when someone uses the feedback form, it will be created.

## Receive Visitor Feedback in Email

Feedback also can be sent to you using email, rather than saved in a file on your site.

When it arrives, it looks like this:

```
MessageType:       Suggestion
Subject:           Web Site
Username:          Sam Snett
UserEmail:         snett@samspublishing.com
ContactRequested:  ContactRequested
Date:              22 Aug 2003
Time:              21:19:30

Comments:

Is this thing on?
```

In the email, the different answers on the feedback form are displayed on separate lines. In this example, Sam Snett with the email address `snett@samspublishing.com` has sent a suggestion with the subject "Web Site." The mail is displayed at the bottom. Sam asks, "Is this thing on?"

Feedback mail comes from an automated reply-to address established by your Web host—my server sends form data from `webmaster@frontpage24.com`. You can change this to the address of the person who is contacting you, as described in the next section.

9

To send feedback answers to an email address, follow these steps:

1. Right-click anywhere within the form and choose **Form  Properties** from the context menu that appears. The Form Properties dialog box opens.

2. Type an email address in the **E-mail Address** text field.

   This should be either your email address or the address of someone who is answering mail for your site.

3. Delete any text that's in the **Filename** box. Feedback will be mailed using the format of the Sam Snett example. To choose another format, click the **Options** button. The Saving Results dialog box appears.

4. Click the **Email Results** tab to bring it to the front.

5. Choose a format in the **Email Format** drop-down box. The same options are available as for files.

   Feedback email is given the subject line "Data posted to form 1," followed by the Web address of the feedback page.

6. To set a different subject line and make it easier to find these emails, type it in the **Subject Line** text field.

7. To make use of the email address of the person who filled out the form, type the text **UserEmail** in the **Reply-To Line** text field and select the **Form Field Name** check box right next to it (see Figure 9.3).

**FIGURE 9.3**

*Setting the reply-to address for visitor feedback.*

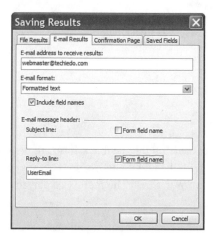

8. Click **OK** to close the Saving Results dialog box, and then click **OK** to close the Form Properties dialog box.

There appears to be a bug in how FrontPage handles form results that have been customized to be delivered by email.

When saving the results of a form as email, FrontPage may display a dialog box indicating that the form cannot send results by email and asking whether the email address should be removed.

If you know that your Web server offers server extensions or SharePoint, click No to retain the email address and ignore the warning. After you publish the feedback page, it should work correctly.

# Call on the Form Page Wizard

A feedback page is only one use among many for forms. You can take surveys, take orders, request mailing addresses, and gather lots of other information from the visitors to your site.

Creating one of these other forms can be done with the assistance of one of FrontPage's built-in helpers: the Form Page Wizard.

Like other wizards in FrontPage, this wizard asks a series of questions to determine what you want to add to your site:

- What questions do you want to ask?
- What kind of answers are acceptable?
- How should the questions and answers be formatted on the Web page?
- What should happen to the answers afterward?

As with all wizards, the Form Page Wizard asks a series of questions, each on its own page of the dialog box. After answering each question, you click either Next (if there are more questions) or Finish (if done).

When all of this has been determined, the wizard creates a new page with the form on it. You can either use this page or transfer it to another page using Copy and Paste.

See the next section, "Set Up Questions on a Form," for details on what types of questions you can create.

The first step in using the Form Page Wizard is to add a new page to an existing site:

1. With the site open for editing, choose **File, New**. The New pane opens to the right of the editing window.

2. Click the **More Page Templates** hyperlink. The Page Templates dialog box appears, listing templates and wizards that you can use to create a page.

3. Choose the **Form Page Wizard** icon and click **OK**.

4. Click **Next** to begin, answering each question according to the guidance offered in each of the subsequent sections. Click **Finish** after you answer the last question.

When the wizard runs out of questions to ask, it creates something based on your choices. The Form Page Wizard creates a form for the kind of information you want to collect from visitors to your site.

## Set Up Questions on a Form

Before you begin using the Form Page Wizard, you should learn a bit about what it needs to know when setting up a form.

The wizard requires two things for each question on the form: the wording of the question, which is called a *prompt*, and the type of information you are collecting in the answer, which is called an *input type*.

For example, "Please enter your mailing address" is a prompt that could be used if you're collecting contact information. "What is your birthday?" is a prompt that seeks a date.

### Ask a Single Question

Several of the wizard's input types are used for a single question:

- **Date**—A calendar date
- **Time**—A time
- **Number**—A numeric value
- **Range**—A number from 1 to 5 that's used to rate something from poor (1) to excellent (5)
- **String**—A single line of text
- **Paragraph**—One or more lines of text
- **Boolean**—A response limited to one of two options, such as yes or no, true or false, and on or off

For each input type, the prompt tells a visitor what kind of information to provide.

Two input types enable answers to be selected from a multiple-choice list:

- **One of Several Options**—A single item chosen from list
- **Any of Several Options**—Zero or more items chosen from a list

Each choice in a list must be a single line of text.

If a list allows only a single answer, the list can be presented in three different ways on a Web page—as a drop-down menu, radio buttons, or a list. All of these are shown on a Web page in Figure 9.4.

9

Drop-down menu

**FIGURE 9.4**
*Three ways a list can be presented on a form.*

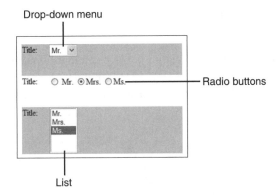

Radio buttons

List

As shown in Figure 9.4, a drop-down menu shows only one possible answer at a time. If you click the arrow next to the answer, a menu of other answers appears. Radio buttons and lists show several possible answers.

If a list allows multiple answers, each possible answer is shown next to a check box (see Figure 9.5).

**FIGURE 9.5**
*Accepting multiple answers to a question.*

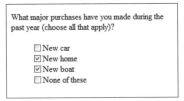

Both types of lists must have a named variable to store answers in, as explained in the section "Save Answers to Each Question," later in this hour.

## Ask a Group of Related Questions

The remaining input types ask several related questions at the same time:

- **Contact information**—Name, title, address, phone number, and other personal identification

- **Account information**—Username and password

- **Product information**—Product name, product version, and serial number

- **Ordering information**—Products to order, billing information, and shipping address

- **Personal information**—Name, age, physical characteristics, and related information

The Form Page Wizard automatically provides a prompt for each question in the group. Any prompt that you provide will be used to introduce the entire group. For example, if you're asking for personal information, the prompt could be "Please tell us more about yourself." Figure 9.6 shows a portion of a form created with this group.

**FIGURE 9.6**

*Using a prompt to identify a group of questions.*

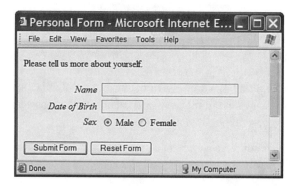

These input types make it easy to add some of the most common questions to a form. You can customize these questions by removing any questions that you don't want to ask.

After the wizard has created the form, the text of a prompt can be edited like any other text on the page.

## Save the Answers to Each Question

For each question you add to a form, you must define a place where the answer will be saved. Forms keep track of answers by saving each one in a *variable*, a special storage place for information in a computer program.

When you add a question to a form, the wizard may ask you to name its variable. A variable's name should describe its purpose. You can use any combination of letters, numbers, and the underscore character (_) when you're naming variables. For instance, if you ask for a visitor's birth date, a good name for its variable would be `birthday` or `date_of_birth`.

For some input types, the variable names will be provided by the wizard.

## Using the Form Page Wizard

When you begin using the Form Page Wizard, you will see a dialog box that contains no questions yet, as shown in Figure 9.7.

**FIGURE 9.7**

*Starting a new form.*

To add a question to the form, follow these steps:

1. Click the **Add** button.
2. To see what kind of information you can collect, choose an item in the list box **Select the Type of Input to Collect for This Question**.

    The Description pane helps explain what this input type can be used to collect. Also, you'll see an example prompt in the text field Edit the Prompt for This Question.

3. To add a question, fill out the dialog box and click the **Next** button.

    Next, you're asked for several things, including a variable name or a name for a group of variables.

4. Type a name for the variable (or variables) in the appropriate field.

Each input type can be customized in different ways, so the wizard asks different things.

5. Answer each question on the dialog box, and then click **Next**.

   After each question has been added, they are displayed by the Form Page Wizard, as shown in Figure 9.8. Questions are displayed in the same order in which they are listed by the wizard.

**FIGURE 9.8**

*Creating a new form.*

6. To change the order of questions, select one and click either **Move Up** or **Move Down**.

7. If you want to make changes to a question, select it and click **Modify**.

8. When you're done adding questions to the form, click **Next** and the wizard asks how the questions should be presented on a Web page:

   • To put each question on its own line, choose the **As Normal Paragraphs** option.

   • To display questions as a list, choose either **As a Bulleted List** or **As a Numbered List**.

9. Click **Next** to continue.

   The last step in creating a form is to decide how the answers will be saved:

   • To store answers as a Web page that you can read with a Web browser, choose **Save Results to a Web Page**.

- If you want to store answers in a text file that can be loaded with Microsoft Excel or Microsoft Access, choose **Save Results to a Text File**.

10. Click **Finish**.

To save a form's answers to a Web page or text file, you must be publishing your site on a server that is enabled with server extensions or SharePoint Services.

9

The file that contains form results can be loaded within FrontPage by opening the site directly from the Web server (a technique described during Hour 13, "Publish Your Site"). If you want to delete all existing results, delete the file on the server. A new file is created automatically when new results are submitted using the form.

# Summary

By using the feedback template and the Form Page Wizard, you can easily add interactive features to your site.

As you explored these capabilities and created your own form in this hour, some ideas on how to use this Web page capability probably sprang to mind.

Forms can be employed to offer user surveys, visitor feedback, polls, questionnaires, tests, and many other interactive features.

You'll learn more about how to create forms in Hour 20, "Use Your Site to Gather Information."

# Q&A

**Q** **Using the Form Page Wizard, I created a form and chose not to lay it out using tables. Some parts of the form extend beyond the right edge of the browser instead of wrapping around to the next line. Why is this happening?**

**A** The Form Page Wizard offers the choice to create forms without using tables because some of your visitors might not be using a Web browser that can display them.

At present, however, less than 1–2% of your audience is likely to be in this group (often considerably less).

To line up forms without using tables, the Form Page Wizard formats the page using a technique that causes text to appear exactly as shown, ignoring the normal rules of Web page formatting such as wrapping text around the right margin. This technique is useful when you want to use spaces to line up text.

The disadvantage to this approach is that the text is shown exactly as it appears, even if it scrolls off the right edge of the browser window. To avoid this problem, create forms that use tables.

**Q  Is there any way I can include my email address on my Web site without it being discovered by spammers?**

**A** The most effective technique is to create a graphic that displays the email address without using a `mailto:` link on the graphic or making the address the graphic's caption.

Spammers can find an email address anywhere in the text of a Web page, even in the HTML formatting used to present the page.

By presenting the address graphically, you enable visitors to write it down and type it into their email programs, but they aren't able to click a link to send mail to you. It's less convenient for them, but it's significantly more convenient where your own inbox is concerned.

If you are familiar with FrontPage's Word Art feature, which can be used to create graphics from text, you might think that it would be a good way to create a spam-proof email address graphic.

Unfortunately, this won't work: Word Art includes your email address as text in the HTML formatting of the page, where it can easily be discovered by spammers.

# Hour **10**

# Make a Site Look Great with Graphics

Because the visual appearance of your Web site is such a big contributor to its overall success, you'll be working a lot with graphics as you create pages for the World Wide Web.

Fortunately, FrontPage 2003 makes this easier by including sophisticated graphic-editing features. Tasks that used to require specialized graphics software such as Adobe Photoshop or PaintShop Pro can now be handled entirely within FrontPage.

In this hour, you will learn

- How to resize a graphic
- How to adjust its contrast and brightness
- How to crop a graphic
- How to share digital photos on a Web site

## Edit an Existing Graphic

Most of FrontPage's graphic-manipulation features can be found on the Picture toolbar, which shows up whenever you select a graphic in the editing window. (Another way to make it appear is to click View, Toolbars, Pictures.)

On the Pictures toolbar, hover your mouse over each of the buttons to find out its purpose. These buttons are organized into several different groupings. One group contains four buttons with pairs of right triangles on them. These buttons are used to rotate or flip the graphic. You can rotate a graphic to the left and right, and flip it horizontally and vertically.

Another group of four buttons contains icons that look like either a half moon or the sun. These control the contrast and brightness of the graphic, two things that any television owner should be familiar with (unless you have a much better TV than mine).

The black-and-white button turns a color graphic into a monochrome one, and the bevel button makes a photograph or other graphic look like a 3D button by giving it shadowed edges.

Because these buttons cause instantaneous changes to a graphic, you might get the impression that they just change the way it's displayed.

However, these buttons make permanent changes to a graphic. You can undo these changes before the page or your site has been saved, and then use the toolbar's Restore button to return the graphic to its last saved version.

You also can use this toolbar to change the size of a graphic permanently. If you have resized a graphic's display area and you want to make this the actual size of the graphic, click the Resize button.

# Reshape a Graphic

As you're working with drawings, photographs, and other graphics in FrontPage, you might decide that the shape of a graphic doesn't fit with the layout of a page or the composition of the graphic could be improved.

You can reshape a graphic in two ways: by changing its dimensions or by cropping it.

## Resize a Graphic

Resizing a graphic is necessary often in FrontPage because clip art and digital photos usually are in a much bigger size than you can use on a Web page.

This is by design because a graphic can often be reduced in size without reducing its quality. The opposite is not true: Enlarging a photo or another photo-quality graphic causes it to look blurry and jagged.

Before you can alter the size of a graphic, it must be placed on a Web page. To edit a graphic on a Web page, open the page and follow these steps:

1. Click a graphic. Selection handles appear at all four corners and the edges of the graphic, indicating that it can be edited using the commands of the Pictures toolbar. These handles are circled in Figure 10.1.

**FIGURE 10.1**

*Selecting a graphic for editing.*

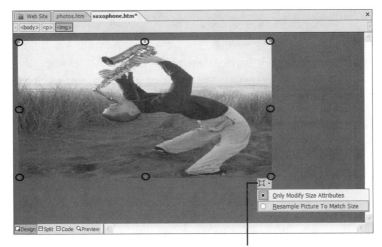

Picture Actions button

**10**

The graphic can be reshaped by dragging one of these handles to a new location. A handle is dragged toward the center of the graphic to make it smaller, or is dragged away from the center to make it bigger.

2. If you don't see the Pictures toolbar, choose **View, Toolbars, Pictures**.

> Having trouble finding the Pictures toolbar? Look for a vertical toolbar at the right edge of the editing window—FrontPage likes to open it there.

3. Reshape the graphic:

- If you want to resize the graphic while keeping the width and height in the same proportions, grab one of the corner selection handles and move it.

- If you want to change the width of the graphic, drag the handle in the middle of the left or right edge.

- If you want to change the height, drag the handle in the middle of the top or bottom edge.

  When you finish moving a selection handle, a Picture Actions button appears below or beside the graphic, as shown in Figure 10.1.

4. Click **Picture Actions**. When its drop-down menu opens, choose **Resample Picture to Match Size**.

   The graphic is altered so that looks exactly like what you see in the editing window. If you have reshaped the graphic to be smaller than before, it will appear more sharp and in focus after it is resampled.

5. If you don't like how it turned out, choose **Edit, Undo Edit Picture**.

6. Otherwise, click the **Save** button on the Standard toolbar.

The Save Embedded Files dialog box opens. Use it to save (and, if desired, rename) the graphic.

> You may be wondering what the other command on the Picture Actions menu accomplishes. When you select Only Modify Size Attributes, the graphic is displayed as the altered shape without altering the original graphic. This generally causes the graphic to appear at lower quality than it would if you resampled it.

## Crop a Graphic

*Cropping* is a photographic term that means to keep a portion of a graphic and discard the rest. Think of it like using a pair of scissors to cut out the portion of the image that you need and then throwing away the parts you cut off.

To crop a graphic on a Web page, follow these steps:

1. Select the graphic in the editing window. Selection handles appear at the corners and sides of the graphic.

2. If necessary, make the Pictures toolbar visible: Choose **View, Toolbars, Pictures**.

3. Click the **Crop** button. A thin cropping border appears atop the graphic, as shown in Figure 10.2.

FIGURE 10.2
*When the graphic is cropped, everything within the border is saved; the rest is discarded.*

Cropping border

4. Drag the handles on the cropping border until it displays the portion of the graphic you want to keep.

5. Click the **Crop** button again. The graphic is cropped and redisplayed.

6. If you change your mind, choose **Edit, Undo Edit Picture**.

7. If you like how it turned out, save the page: Click the **Save** button on the Standard toolbar.

   The Save Embedded Files dialog box opens, which gives you a chance to rename and save the newly cropped graphic.

Cropping a graphic alters it permanently, so you should always keep a copy of the original graphic for backup.

# Add Text to a Graphic

Another thing you can do to a graphic without leaving FrontPage is put text on top of it. This works only with graphics in GIF format, so if you attempt to add text to something in JPEG or PNG format, FrontPage will convert the file first.

Text can be added to a graphic in a manner similar to adding it to a Web page. You type the text and use FrontPage's formatting features to set the font, size, color, and other details.

10

Several text items can be placed on a graphic, each with its own hyperlink. This makes it easy to create a special kind of Web navigation called an *imagemap*, a graphic that contains links to several different places on the Web.

To add text to a graphic, follow these steps:

1. Click the graphic. Selection handles appear around its corners and edges.

2. Click the **Text** button on the Pictures toolbar (the button with a letter A on it).

   If you try to add text to a graphic that isn't in GIF format, FrontPage asks whether it should be converted—you can't add text to graphics in any other format. To continue, click **Yes**.

> If the graphic is a photograph or a complex image with lots of small areas with many different colors, the converted GIF graphic may be too large to use on your site. In general, GIF works best with simple images that contain lots of solid color, small graphics, and other images that don't contain much fine detail.

A rectangle with selection handles appears atop a small portion of the graphic.

3. Add text by clicking anywhere inside the rectangle and typing. The letters that you type appear on the graphic, as shown in Figure 10.3.

**FIGURE 10.3**

*Adding text to a graphic.*

This rectangular area shows where the text will be displayed. (The rectangle itself won't be shown—it's just a guide.)

4. The selection handles can be used to move the rectangle to a different position on the graphic or to change its width and height. Drag the selection handles to a new location. The text moves so that it remains centered within the rectangle and changes size based on the rectangle's dimensions.

5. To move the rectangle without changing its shape, click anywhere within its boundaries and drag it to a new location.

6. Use the buttons of the Formatting toolbar to adjust the font, size, and style of the text—the same way you format any text on a Web page.

   As you modify the text, the selection rectangle may move, changing its position atop the graphic.

7. To add a hyperlink to the text, double-click the rectangle. The Insert Hyperlink dialog box opens. In the **Address** text field, enter the Web address to which you're linking.

8. When you like the finished product, click the **Save** button on the Standard toolbar to save your work.

Although it appears that the text has been added to the graphic, it's actually displayed as an overlay on top of it, using a FrontPage Web component.

You can edit the text at any time: Click it once to select it, and use its selection handles or type within its boundaries.

# Make Part of a Graphic Transparent

Figure 10.4 shows a Web page that contains two GIF graphics on top of a gray page background. On one of them, the gray background of the page shows through part of the graphic, a feature called *transparency*.

**FIGURE 10.4**

*Viewing nontransparent and transparent graphics.*

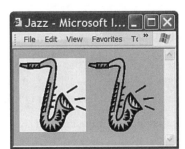

A transparent graphic has one color that has been chosen as the invisible color. Any part of the graphic that contains this exact color will not be displayed, exposing the background that would otherwise be hidden behind the graphic.

FrontPage can be used to set the transparent color of a graphic if that graphic is in GIF format.

To add transparency to a graphic on a Web page, follow these steps:

1. Click the graphic to select it. Selection handles appear on its edges.

2. Click the **Set Transparent Color** button on the Pictures toolbar.

As with text, if the graphic is not in GIF format, FrontPage opens a dialog box letting you know that it will be converted to that format.

If you think the graphic is suitable for conversion into that format, click **OK** to continue. The cursor changes from an arrow to an eraser-tipped pencil with a small arrow at one end.

3. Place the eraser end of the cursor over the color that should become transparent, and then click.

This color immediately vanishes as if it were deleted from the graphic, and is replaced with the page's background color or graphic.

Making a color transparent doesn't actually change the graphic's colors. If you remove transparency later, you'll see that the original color has been retained.

4. To remove transparency, click **Set Transparent Color** again and click the eraser on the transparent color.

Setting a transparent color changes the graphic, so when you save the page, a Save Embedded Files dialog box appears. Use this to save the modified graphic.

When you set a graphic's transparent color, it remains that way until you edit it again.

# Share Your Digital Photos in a Photo Gallery

Of all the features in FrontPage, the one I've been having the most fun with as I write this book is the Photo Gallery, a tool for sharing digital photos on a Web site.

The Photo Gallery is a Web component that takes the hassle out of publishing photos on the World Wide Web. Instead of importing individual graphics and creating pages to display each one, you add photos to the component, write captions, and edit the photos. Then you're done.

The entire gallery of photos is displayed on a single Web page. An example is shown in Figure 10.5.

**FIGURE 10.5**

*Displaying photos in a Photo Gallery.*

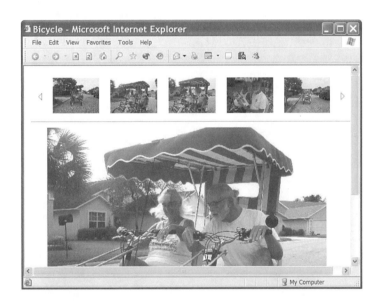

10

Before creating the photo gallery, save all of the photos or graphics you'll be using to a folder on your computer. There are other ways to do this—you also can retrieve photos directly from a camera or a scanner—but this is the easiest method. It also avoids a common problem of digital cameras: They eat a lot of batteries, and keeping them on while you work on a gallery can be costly.

The folder where photos are stored doesn't have to be part of your site; if you're saving photos in the My Pictures folder, they can be imported from there with no problems.

To create a photo gallery, follow these steps:

1. Choose **Insert, Picture, New Photo Gallery**. The Photo Gallery Properties dialog box opens (see Figure 10.6). It is used to select photos for the gallery, set their size, and decide how they will be displayed.

FIGURE **10.6**

*Creating a gallery of digital photos.*

2. Click the **Add** button. Then choose **Pictures from Files** on the drop-down menu that appears.

   This opens the File Open dialog box, which can be used to find the folder that contains your photos.

3. Click the photo to add it to the gallery, and then repeat step 2 for each photo you want to display.

> There's no limit to the number of photos that a gallery can contain. However, you'll get best results by featuring 12 or fewer in a single gallery.

Photos are displayed in the order they are listed in the Photo Gallery Properties dialog box.

4. To change the order, select a photo: Click its filename, and then click either **Move Up** or **Move Down**.

5. Each photo can have some text associated with it: a short caption and a longer description. To provide these for a photo, select the photo and fill out the **Caption** and **Description** text fields.

6. When you're working with digital photos, they usually are much larger in size than you can display on a Web page. To see how big a photo will be (and make changes, if needed), select the photo and click the **Edit** button.

   The Edit Picture dialog box opens, as shown in Figure 10.7.

**FIGURE 10.7**

*Editing a photo in the gallery.*

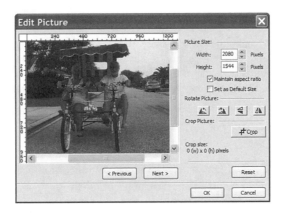

7. To set a new size, change the value of the **Width** field by either typing a new width or using the up or down arrows. When you've set the width, press the **Tab** key.

   The Height field is adjusted automatically so that the width and height remain proportionate to each other.

> You also can crop or rotate the picture, which works the same here as it does when graphics are edited using the Pictures toolbar.

8. Before you exit this dialog box, you might want to take advantage of a real time-saver by resizing every other photo to the same width and height you've just chosen. To apply the same width and height settings to all photos in the gallery, select the **Set as Default Size** check box.

9. If you want to edit the next photo in the gallery, click **Next**.

10. When you're done, click **OK** to go back to the Photo Gallery Properties dialog box. The last thing to do is to select a layout for the gallery.

11. Click the **Layout** tab to bring it to the front.

    Four layouts are offered in the Choose a Layout list. Select a layout to see how it will look in the Preview pane.

12. Choose a layout and click **OK**.

The Photo Gallery is displayed on the page. To add or remove photos from it and make other changes, double-click any of its photos in the editing window. The Photo Gallery Properties dialog box reopens.

 To make the Photo Gallery work, FrontPage uses JavaScript, a programming language that's supported by all of the popular Web browsers. If a visitor to your site has turned off JavaScript or is using a browser that doesn't support it, the gallery may not work correctly for that person.

## Summary

Now that you've edited graphics and worked with the Photo Gallery, you have seen what FrontPage's graphics-related features can accomplish.

Although the software's resizing, editing, and conversion features aren't on par with professional tools such as Adobe Photoshop, they handle some of the most common tasks extremely well.

When you combine these features with Web-specific features such as support for transparent GIF graphics and the Photo Gallery, it has never been easier to create an eye-catching site without ever leaving FrontPage.

## Q&A

**Q  I created a Photo Gallery and I want to adjust the contrast on a few of the pictures. How can I do this?**

**A**  The Photo Gallery supports only a few editing features: rotating graphics, resizing the photo, and cropping it.

To use the other graphics-editing tools on the Pictures toolbar, create a new Web page; choose Insert, Picture, From File; and add the photos. When you save the page after editing the graphics as desired, you'll have a chance to save the modified graphics. Save them in the same folder where they were stored originally, giving them the same filename.

Afterward, the Photo Gallery uses your new versions of those photos.

**Q** **I've been working with a graphic for a while and the edges are starting to look jagged. What can I do about this?**

**A** Any graphic that you edit within FrontPage changes each time you save or resample it. If you've altered the size several times, you'll lose some clarity each time as FrontPage tries to antialias the graphic.

*Antialiasing* is a graphic design term for adjusting the edges of a graphic so that it blends more smoothly with the background. FrontPage can't always antialias smoothly if graphics are repeatedly resized. If possible, revert to the original version of the graphic and redo your edits to get better clarity.

**Q** **Page backgrounds are mentioned during this hour. How do I set up a background?**

**A** A Web page can have a solid color or a graphic as a background: Choose Format, Background. The Page Properties dialog box opens with the Formatting tab on top.

Here's how to set up a background graphic that will be displayed underneath the rest of the Web page: Select the Background Picture check box, click the Browse button, then use the File Open dialog to find and select a graphic. Click OK; the Page Properties dialog closes and the background is displayed on the page.

To set up a background color: Choose Format, Background, then on the Page Properties dialog, choose a color in the Background list menu.

Tables and table cells also can have background colors or graphics: Right-click one and choose either Table Properties or Cell Properties.

**10**

# HOUR 11

# Offer Animation, Video, and Games

When you're viewing pages on the World Wide Web, few things grab your attention better than animated graphics. It can be difficult for static text and still pictures to compete with the moving graphics on banner ads and other trickery, such as spinning logos and dancing hamsters.

FrontPage 2003 makes it easy to add special effects like these to your own sites.

In this hour, you will learn

- How to create animated transitions that appear when a new page is loaded
- How to create buttons that change in appearance when a mouse passes over them
- How to place animated graphics, video, and game programs on Web pages
- How to create animated text

## Add a Scrolling Marquee

The simplest way to animate text on a Web page is to turn it into a *marquee*, a line of text that moves to the left or right like quotes on a stock ticker.

Marquees can be set up to scroll off the edge of the screen and come back on the other edge or slide to one edge and stop moving.

> Marquees work in Internet Explorer and current versions of Mozilla and Netscape Navigator. Some other browsers, most notably Opera, do not support the feature.

To add a marquee to a Web page, follow these steps:

1. Click a spot on the page where the marquee should be placed.
2. Choose **Insert, Web Component**. The Insert Web Component dialog box appears.
3. In the **Component Type** list box, make sure that **Dynamic Effects** is selected.
4. In the **Choose an Effect** list box, select **Marquee** and click **Finish**. The Marquee Properties dialog box appears, as shown in Figure 11.1.

**FIGURE 11.1**

*Creating a scrolling marquee.*

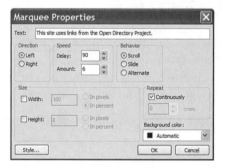

5. Type the text that should be displayed in the **Text** field.
6. Pick the direction text should move: Choose either Left or Right from the **Direction** section.
7. In the **Behavior** section, choose how the marquee should be displayed after it hits the far side of the page: Scroll or Slide.
8. If the marquee should move across the page repeatedly, make sure the **Continuously** check box is selected.
9. Click **OK**.

The marquee is added to the page. To see it moving, click the Preview button below the editing window or preview the page in a Web browser.

You may be prevented from adding marquees to a Web page—the Marquee item in the Insert Web Component dialog box will be disabled, making it impossible to use one.

This is determined by FrontPage's browser compatibility feature, which prevents you from using features of the software that are not supported with specific Web browsers or Web servers.

To see your current compatibility setting and make changes, follow these steps:

1. Choose **Tools**, **Browser Compatibility** to open the Browser Compatibility dialog box.
2. Click the **Change** button. The Page Options dialog box opens.
3. The use of marquees is determined by the setting of the Browsers list box. Your site's target Web browser can be Internet Explorer, Netscape Navigator, or both.

If marquee use is disabled, the only way to enable it is to choose the Internet Explorer Only item and click OK.

However, if you want Navigator and Mozilla users to have the full experience of your Web site, you shouldn't exclude them with the Browsers setting. Configuring your site to target Internet Explorer turns on several features of FrontPage that would be disabled otherwise.

This subject is discussed in detail in Hour 14, "Attract the Widest Possible Audience."

**11**

# Use Animation and Other Special Effects to a Page

Adding an animated GIF file to a page is no different than adding any other graphic.

Animated GIF graphics are the primary form of animation on the Web. Almost all non-static banner ads are in this format, as are many of the moving images that you see on personal pages, such as spinning envelopes and other small graphics.

The animation sequence embedded in the GIF graphic isn't displayed after it is added to a page. To see it in action, switch to Preview mode, or preview the page in a Web browser.

These GIF files are created by software that combines several GIF pictures into a single file. This file also contains information that determines the order in which to display these pictures, how much time to pause between each picture, and how often to cycle through all the pictures.

The final product is treated like a graphic within FrontPage and has the same filename extension: `.gif`. You can import this graphic, add it to pages, and resize its display area.

One thing that you can't do within FrontPage is edit your animated GIF. You can't add beveling, adjust its contrast, or use any of the other image-editing features that you learned about in Hour 10, "Make a Site Look Great with Graphics." This is because any changes to the GIF will remove its animation and reduce it to a single picture. FrontPage prevents this from happening by graying out everything on the Picture toolbar that would damage the animated GIF.

> FrontPage's Clip Art Library includes animated GIF graphics. To search them in the library, choose Insert, Picture, Clip Art to open the Clip Art pane; open the Results Should Be drop-down menu; check the Movies box; and then check the Animated GIF box. Subsequent searches will be limited to these graphics.
>
> When you're done and you want future searches to look through the entire library, check the All Media Types in the Results Should Be drop-down menu.

## Create Page Transition Effects

One of the special effects you can add to a page in FrontPage is a *page transition*, which changes what a Web browser displays when a visitor loads the page or leaves the page to load something else.

Figure 11.2 shows a Web page in midtransition.

**FIGURE 11.2**

*Transitioning between two Web pages with the Circle effect.*

In Figure 11.2, two Web pages are visible: a page from URouLette and a page depicting a beach. This is called a *circle transition* because the new page is shown in a growing circle until it fills the browser window.

Page transitions are supported only by Internet Explorer, so users of other Web browsers will not see them—instead, the page will be displayed normally.

To trigger a transition, an event must take place. You can associate transitions with four different events:

- When the page first loads
- When the page is exited
- When the site first loads
- When the site is exited

You can use 25 page transitions, each with a name that describes the special effect (such as Wipe, Blend, Circle, and Checkerboard).

Some transitions are associated with a direction, such as Wipe Right, which wipes the new page onscreen from left to right.

There also is a Random transition that loads a different transition each time the event occurs.

When you select a transition, you can select its duration, measured in seconds. This determines how long it will take to display the effect. You can choose longer transitions, such as a 10-second or 20-second effect, but keep in mind that this slows down people who are using your site. Anything longer than 5 seconds is likely to aggravate some of your visitors.

To add or remove transitions from a page, follow these steps:

1. Open the page and choose **Format, Page Transition**. The Page Transitions dialog box opens (see Figure 11.3).
2. In the **Event** list box, choose the event that will trigger the transition.
3. In the **Transition Effect** list box, choose the transition to display (or choose No Effect to remove an existing transition from the page).
4. Choose a display duration for the transition by typing a value from 1 to 30 in the **Duration** text field.
5. If you want to add transitions to one of the other events, repeat steps 2–4.
6. When you're done adding transitions to the page, click **OK**.

11

FIGURE 11.3

*Choosing a Web page transition.*

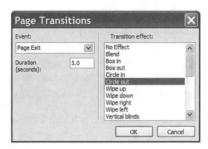

Preview the Web page with Internet Explorer to see the transition in action.

An easy way to see all of the transitions is to apply a Random page transition effect to the loading and exiting of a test page, preview the page in a browser, and then reload it repeatedly by clicking the Refresh button.

# Animate Page Elements with Dynamic HTML

FrontPage offers another group of special effects that you can apply to specific elements of a page instead of the entire page. They make use of Dynamic HTML, a group of Web publishing techniques that cause Web pages to change in appearance after they are loaded by a browser.

These effects can be associated with text, hyperlinks, and graphics. You can cause animations to be triggered by such events as loading a page, clicking a link, or hovering a mouse over the element.

Dynamic HTML effects work in Internet Explorer and current versions of Netscape Navigator and Mozilla.

## Apply a DHTML Effect to Text

Many Dynamic HTML effects can be applied to text. You can cause it to move into its correct place onscreen in a variety of different ways.

Here are the effects to choose from for text:

- **Elastic**—The text moves onscreen until it is slightly beyond its destination and then bounces back to the correct place.
- **Drop in By Word**—The text drops into place one word at a time.
- **Fly in**—Words fly in from several different directions.

- **Hop and Wave**—Words move into place one at a time in a leisurely circular motion.
- **Spiral**—Words spin onscreen, ending up in the right place.
- **Wipe**—Words are drawn in from the left or top edge of the page in a wiping motion.

Dynamic HTML effects are set to occur when an event takes place. One of these events is the loading of the page that contains the text. For hyperlinks and pictures, you also can trigger an effect based on mouse actions. You can animate a text hyperlink when it's clicked or double-clicked, and cause a picture to react when the mouse hovers above it.

To add a Dynamic HTML effect, follow these steps:

1. Open a page for editing.
2. Select the page element that should be animated:
   - For text and hyperlinks, drag your mouse over the area you want to select. The selected area then is highlighted.
   - For graphics, click the graphic. Selection boxes then appear at the corners and sides of the graphic.
3. Choose **View, Toolbars, DHTML Effects**. The DHTML Effects toolbar is displayed over the editing window (see Figure 11.4).

   You can use the list boxes on this toolbar to pick a special effect that will be applied to the selected item.

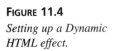

**FIGURE 11.4**

*Setting up a Dynamic HTML effect.*

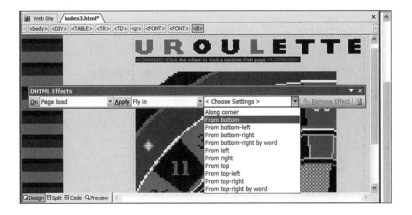

4. In the **On** list box, choose the event that triggers the animation:

  - For any element, choose **Page Load** to cause the effect to begin when the page is first loaded by a Web browser.
  - For pictures or hyperlinks, choose **Mouse Over** or **Click** to trigger the event when the mouse is used on the element in the specified manner.

5. In the **Apply** list box, choose one of the seven Dynamic HTML Effects. The Effect list box (immediately to the right) contains options to fine-tune how the effect works.

6. In this list box, choose one of the options.

The Remove Effect button becomes active, which is the only indication that the effect has been added to that page element.

View the page with Internet Explorer to see how the effect looks. Some of them are a bit hokey—a little bit of spiraling or waving text goes a long way—but they can call a little attention to something if used judiciously.

To remove a dynamic HTML effect from an element, follow these steps:

1. Select the element the same way you did when you added the effect.
2. Choose **View, Toolbars, DHTML Effects**.
3. In the DHTML Effects toolbar, click **Remove Effect**.

## Create a Mouseover Graphic

One of the most popular Dynamic HTML effects is the *mouseover graphic*, an image that changes when a visitor moves a mouse on top of it.

The mouseover effect is supported by most of the popular browsers, including Internet Explorer, Netscape Navigator, Mozilla, and Opera.

FrontPage themes make use of mouseover effects on their link bars. If you're using a theme with graphical link bars, the buttons on the bar change as a mouse passes over them.

Before you can create this effect on your own using Dynamic HTML, you need two graphics: the original graphic and a swap graphic that will appear when a mouse is over it. The swap graphic can be a modified copy of the original or a different graphic entirely.

The swap graphic should be the same size as the original. If it isn't, FrontPage resizes the graphic's display area so that it fits the space available to it.

To use two graphics in a mouseover animation, follow these steps:

1. If the graphics aren't a part of the site yet, import them into the site: Choose **File, Import** and use the Import dialog box to find and add them.

2. Open the page that contains the original graphic for editing.

3. Click the graphic and then choose **View, Toolbars, DHTML Effects**.

4. In the On list box, select **Mouse Over**.

5. In the Apply list box, select **Swap Picture** (see Figure 11.5).

**FIGURE 11.5**

*Adding a mouseover effect to a graphic.*

**11**

6. In the Effect list box, select **Choose Picture**. The Picture dialog box opens.

7. Use the dialog box to find and click the swap graphic—the graphic that should be displayed when a mouse is over the original graphic.

The Remove Effect button on the DHTML Effects toolbar becomes enabled, indicating that the mouseover graphic is in place.

Preview the page in FrontPage or Internet Explorer to see the effect.

# Copy Formatting from One Place to Another

Using Dynamic HTML can be a tedious process when you're applying the same effect to several different elements of a page, such as a row of graphics.

FrontPage has a feature that makes it much easier to copy a page element's formatting to another part of the page: the Format Painter.

The Format Painter stores the fonts, colors, special effects, and other formatting associated with a page element. Users of Microsoft Word may recognize this feature because it's offered in that software also.

Here's how to use it:

1. Select the item that has the formatting you want to duplicate.

2. Double-click the **Format Painter** button on the standard toolbar.

   The button is highlighted to show that it has saved some special formatting for use elsewhere.

3. Select each element that should receive the stored formatting information. Each element is reformatted immediately as it is selected.

4. When you're done, double-click the **Format Painter** button again.

# Add Video to a Page

Working with video in FrontPage is similar to working with graphics. You insert the video on a page, and you can make changes to its presentation by double-clicking the video in the editing window.

Although FrontPage handles Windows Media and Real Video format best, the software can be used to add any of the popular video formats to your sites, including QuickTime and MPEG files.

To add a video to a Web page, follow these steps:

1. Open the page for editing and click the place where the video should be displayed.

2. Choose **Insert, Picture, Video**. The Video dialog box opens.

3. Using this dialog box, find and double-click the video file.

   The video is added to the page. If it's in a format recognized by FrontPage, the first frame of the video is displayed in the editing window as a placeholder. Otherwise, a small video icon appears.

> When a video is placed on a page, FrontPage sets it up to play once and then stop.

4. To set up the video to loop one or more times, double-click it in the editing window.

   The Picture Properties dialog box appears with the Video tab up front.

5. Set up looping:

- If the video should continuously loop, select the **Forever** check box. (The looping may annoy some of your visitors, however.)
- If it should loop a fixed number of times, use the **Loop** list box to enter the number.

6. Click **OK**.

Videos are edited with the same Picture Properties dialog box, which has other options to change the display size, add a border, and the like.

When you save the page that contains the video, a Save Embedded Files dialog box opens if the file needs to be imported to your Web site.

If the video does not display in preview mode, you should be able to view it by saving and previewing the page.

# Add Flash and Java Content

In addition to graphics, video, and audio, the World Wide Web can be used to offer interactive games and other software.

11

You add animation, games, and other interactive programs to your Web pages in several ways. The most popular ways are to use Flash and Shockwave, two offerings from Macromedia that are used on graphical programs and multimedia presentations.

Both Flash and Shockwave require special player software to run within a Web browser. These players are preinstalled with Internet Explorer and can be downloaded and installed to work with other browsers. Macromedia estimates that 497 million Web users can run these programs.

Flash and Shockwave make use of vector graphics, a way to present pictures by drawing shapes, lines, and text. Because of this, it's extremely easy to change the size of a program on a Web page without altering its image quality.

If you have created (or been given) a Macromedia program to present on a Web site, you can add it to a Web page by following these steps:

1. Import the program's file (which usually has the .dcr or .swf file extension) into your Web site as you would a graphic or any other file.

2. Open the page that will contain the program, and click your mouse at the spot where the program should be displayed.

3. Choose **Insert, Picture, Flash** (even if the file is a Shockwave program).

   FrontPage adds a placeholder to the page that's as wide and as tall as the program will be when it runs.

4. To see how it will look, save the page and click the **Preview** button below the editing window.

   Interactive programs run within their own window. If the area devoted to this program is too small for your taste, you can change it easily—and, unlike a graphic, it can be enlarged without reducing quality.

5. Click the **Design** button to return to the editing window.

6. If you want to change its size, double-click the program's placeholder.

   The Flash Properties dialog box appears, as shown in Figure 11.6.

**FIGURE 11.6**

*Changing how a Flash or Shockwave program is presented.*

7. In the **Size** section, you can change the size of the window in which the program runs: Select the **Specify Size** check box and use the **Width** and **Height** list boxes to set its dimensions.

   FrontPage keeps the width and height in the same proportions, so any change to one measurement causes the other to change automatically.

8. If you don't want to keep the same width-height proportions, deselect the **Keep Aspect Ratio** check box and then choose values for **Width** and **Height**.

9. Like a GIF file, the program can have a transparent background: Select the **Transparent** check box.

10. After making any other desired changes, click **OK**.

FrontPage displays a placeholder for the program in the editing window. You should be able to view it by clicking the Preview button or viewing the page with a Web browser—although FrontPage 2003 appears to have some trouble showing these programs in preview mode.

Another way to present software on a Web page is to use Java, the widely used programming language from Sun Microsystems. If a browser is equipped to run Java, special programs called applets are run by a Java interpreter. This interpreter was once a standard part of Web browsers, but today it's an optional feature of Internet Explorer, so many Web users won't be able to run Java applets until they download and install the Java plug-in, an interpreter offered for free by Sun.

Unlike Shockwave and Flash programs, Java applets aren't always made available as a single file. Although many are packaged into a Java archive file (which has the file extension .jar), others are composed of one or more .class files, graphics files, and other files required by the program.

FrontPage 2003 does not offer a way to identify a Java applet's JAR file, so there's no way to use this procedure with an applet packaged in that manner. If you have to work with a JAR file, you can use FrontPage's code view to add the HTML markup tags required to present an applet. For more information on working with markup tags, see Hour 21, "Create and Edit Pages Using HTML."

11

To add a Java applet to a page, follow these steps:

1. Collect all of the files required by the applet, and then import them to your site.

   The easiest way to do this is to keep all of the files in the same folder as the Web page that will contain the applet.

2. Open the Web page where the applet will be displayed, and then click a spot to choose a position for it on that page.

3. Choose **Insert, Web Component**. The Insert Web Component dialog box opens.

4. In the **Component Type** list box, choose **Advanced Controls**.

5. In the Choose a Control list box, choose **Java Applet** and click **Finish**. The Java Applet Properties dialog box opens (see Figure 11.7).

**FIGURE 11.7**

*Adding a Java program to a Web page.*

6. Type the name of the applet's main class file in the **Applet Source** field.

7. Identify the folder in your site where that file is located:
   - If it's in the same folder as the Web page, leave the Applet Base URL text field empty.
   - If it's in a subfolder, type the name of that folder in the Applet Base URL.

8. Because some of your visitors won't be using a Web browser equipped with Java, you should offer some guidance letting them know that the program requires it: Type an explanation in the field **Message for Browsers Without Java Support**.

9. If the applet makes use of one or more parameters, click the **Add** button.

   The Set Attribute Value dialog box opens.

10. Type the parameter's name in the **Name** field and select the **Specify Value** check box.

    The Data text field becomes enabled.

11. Type the parameter's value in that field, and then click **OK**.

12. Repeat steps 9–11 for any additional parameters.

13. Unlike other programs, applets do not have a default size. Type values in the **Width** and **Height** fields to determine the size of the program's window. (Usually, an applet's developer indicates the size at which to display the program.)

14. After making any other customizations required by your applet, click **OK**.

    A gray box with a small J icon is displayed in the editing window. To make any changes to the Java applet, double-click this window.

For the program to work, the Web page, the Java applet's main class file, and any other files required by the applet must be published to the Web server hosting the site.

Also, a Web browser must be equipped with a Java interpreter to display applets. This has become more of an issue in recent years because Microsoft has stopped including a Java interpreter with Internet Explorer.

When presenting a Java applet on a Web page, you should let visitors know that they can download a Java interpreter for their browser from the Web site www.java.com.

> If you're still a bit foggy on what these programs can do, a few good examples will help make things clearer. Macromedia offers a Showcase site that highlights some new and noteworthy uses of Flash and Shockwave. To see it, visit www.macromedia.com/showcase. Also, Java game programmer Karl Hörnell offers a portfolio of his work—including applets that you can add to your own sites—at www.javaonthebrain.com.

# Summary

This hour's workshop showed you many of the animation and multimedia effects that are possible in FrontPage.

FrontPage makes it easy to apply some impressive animation effects to your sites: mouseover graphics, page-to-page transition effects, and Dynamic HTML tricks such as elastic text and zooming pictures.

If you have video files or interactive programs such as a Macromedia Flash presentation or a Java game applet, you can add them to a page in a manner comparable to working with graphics.

# Q&A

**Q  FrontPage won't let me use View, Tools, Dynamic HTML Effects or any other features like it—the Dynamic Effects toolbar is all grayed out and inactive. What's causing this?**

**A**  You should use FrontPage's browser compatibility feature to see whether your site's targeted Web browsers support Dynamic HTML. As described in Hour 14, "Attract the Widest Possible Audience," FrontPage enables developers to target a site to a specific audience by specifying some features they can't use. Versions 3 and earlier of Netscape Navigator and Microsoft Internet Explorer do not support effects created with Dynamic HTML, so these options may be disabled if you are including those versions in your target audience.

To check this and similar options, click Tools, Browser Compatibility to open the Browser Compatibility dialog box; then click the Change button. If the selected browsers do not support Dynamic HTML, FrontPage prevents you from using its special effects in your site.

# HOUR 12

# Use Web Components to Jazz Up a Site

Looking at the World Wide Web today, it's hard to believe that it began as an all-text medium. Before graphics were added to the Web, the only significant difference between the Web and a book was the presence of hyperlinks.

Today the World Wide Web is composed of a dazzling assortment of media: text, pictures, sound files, movies, Java programs, Flash animations, streaming audio, PDF files, vector graphics, and other files delivered in conjunction with Web pages.

In this hour, you will learn

- How to use Web components—special kinds of content that enhance a Web site
- How to add components that present information from Web sites such as Expedia and MSNBC
- How to add link bars and page banners
- How to create a dynamic Web template that can be used to reliably develop pages that share most of the same content

# Add Components to a Web Site

New ways to present information and engage an audience are introduced constantly on the World Wide Web.

FrontPage 2003 includes more than 40 components that you can incorporate into your Web sites. Some of them, such as the Web search component and discussion forums, are described in upcoming hours of the book. Others, such as comments and timestamps, have already been covered.

The other components include the following:

- Dynamic effects such as marquees and rotating banner ads
- Excel spreadsheets
- Hit counters
- Photo galleries, which create their own thumbnail images
- Page banners
- Pages and pictures that are displayed only at specified times
- Link bars
- Links to maps on Expedia.com
- MSN search boxes and stock quotes
- MSNBC headlines and weather reports
- Java applets and ActiveX controls
- Browser plug-ins

In this hour, you'll see how to add several of these components to a Web page, a process that usually takes less than five minutes.

Here's a basic rundown of how to add a Web component to a page:

1. Open the page for editing.
2. Click your cursor at the spot the Web component should be placed.
3. Choose **Insert, Web Component**. The Insert Web Component dialog box appears, as shown in Figure 12.1.
4. Choose the type of component to add in the **Component Type** list box. Components are displayed in the list box to the right.
5. Select one of the components in that list box.

6. If the **Next** button is enabled, click it.

   You'll be able to customize the Web component. Keep clicking **Next**, when possible, to make more choices.

7. If the **Finish** button is enabled, click it.

**FIGURE 12.1**

*Adding a component to a Web page.*

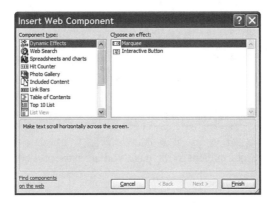

If the Web component does not require anything else to set up, it appears on the page in the editing window. Otherwise, a dialog box opens where you can configure the component.

# Put MSNBC Features on a Page

FrontPage offers six Web components that display news headlines and weather reports from MSNBC, the television network and online news service founded by Microsoft and NBC.

You can add headlines in five topic areas to any page of your Web: business, living and travel, news, sports, and technology. There also is an MSNBC weather component that can be set up to present a city's current forecast and temperature.

Figure 12.2 shows what several of these components look like on a Web page.

These headlines are offered as pictures stored on MSNBC's Web server, so you can use them on any of your Web sites. The pictures are updated automatically by MSNBC to keep the information current.

If you select the MSNBC weather component, you must also choose a city to associate with the component. MSNBC offers weather information for 14,000 cities.

12

FIGURE 12.2
*Viewing MSNBC news and weather on a Web page.*

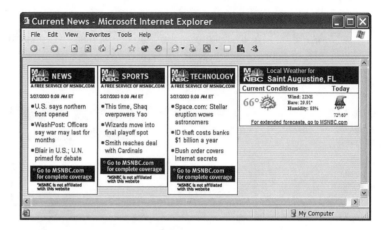

To add an MSNBC component to the page you are currently editing, follow these steps:

1. Connect to the Internet.

2. Choose Insert, Web Component. The **Insert Web Component** dialog box appears.

3. In the Component type list box, select **MSNBC Components**.

4. In the Choose an MSNBC Component list box, select the MSNBC component to add and click **Finish**.

   If you're adding headlines, the graphic appears on the page immediately, displaying the current headlines in the selected topic.

   If you're adding a weather forecast, the Weather Forecast from MSNBC Properties dialog box opens. You must use this to select a city, using either its name or its ZIP code. When you have selected a city, click **Next**; then click **Finish** to confirm your choice.

The picture is added to the page. You can move it around like any other picture.

 When you add a weather component, FrontPage displays Seattle's forecast and temperature in the editing window, regardless of the city you have selected. To see the correct information, preview the page in a Web browser: Click the Preview button on the standard toolbar.

To change the city associated with a weather forecast, double-click the component in the editing window.

# Link to Maps on Expedia

If your Web site needs a map to a specific location, such as a place of business or the site of a party, you can use two Web components offered by the Expedia travel site.

In less than five minutes, you can create an Expedia Web component that's either a graphical map or a hyperlink to a map on Expedia. In both cases, the map shows the location you have specified and the surrounding streets.

Figure 12.3 shows what a map and a hyperlink look like on a Web page.

**FIGURE 12.3**

*Viewing an Expedia map and hyperlink on a Web page.*

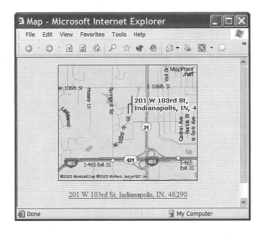

Here's how to add one of these to a Web page:

1. Connect to the Internet.
2. Choose **Insert, Web Component**. The Insert Web Component dialog box appears.
3. In the Component Type list box, select **Expedia Components**.
4. In the Choose an Expedia Component list box, select one of these choices:
   - To add a graphical map, choose **Static Map**.
   - To add a hyperlink to a map page on Expedia, choose **Link to a Map**.
5. Click **Finish**. An Expedia wizard opens and asks for the location that should be at the center of the map. Click **Next** after answering each question; click **Finish** when you reach the end.

   The wizard closes and then adds an Expedia Web component to the page.

To make changes to an Expedia component after it has been added to a Web page, double-click it. The Expedia wizard reopens so you can review and change the location.

**12**

# Add a Link Bar

It's easy to get lost when you're visiting a large site on the World Wide Web. One of the ways to make your site easier to use is to incorporate link bars.

*Link bars*, which were called navigation bars in versions of FrontPage earlier than 2002, are related hyperlinks that are represented as a group of graphical, animated buttons.

Every FrontPage theme uses link bars to provide navigational links to the different pages in the Web site.

Most commercial news and sports sites have link bars that lead to the main topics they cover. For example, the sports site ESPN.com has links to NFL, NBA, NHL, and MLB pages on a link bar that's part of every page. If you ever get lost as you're reading articles on the site, you can get back to a starting point by using the link bar.

When you are working with a link bar, you don't create any of the hyperlinks that it contains. Instead, these links are determined by the navigational structure you have created for the Web site in Navigation view.

Figure 12.4 shows a page in a Web site that uses a link bar. The bar, which runs vertically along the left edge of the page, includes links to seven pages: Home, About Me, Services, Contact Me, Search, Site Map, and Discussion. Link bars also can be arranged horizontally.

**FIGURE 12.4**

*Navigating a Web site using link bars.*

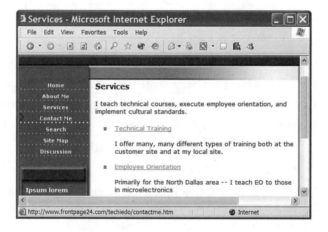

To add a link bar to a page, follow these steps:

1. Open the page for editing. If you're adding a link bar based on the site's navigational structure, the page must be present in Navigation view (which is covered in detail in the next section).

2. Choose **Insert, Navigation**. The Insert Web Components dialog box opens with the Link Bars item selected in the Component type list box.

3. In the Choose a Bar Type list box, select the type of bar to add:

   - To create a link bar based on the site's arrangement in Navigation view, choose **Bar Based on Navigation Structure**.

   - To create a link bar for pages that should be viewed in a specific order, choose **Bar with Back and Next Links**.

   - To create a link bar with any hyperlinks of your choosing, even if they aren't part of your site, pick **Bar of Custom Links**.

4. Click **Next**. The Insert Web Components dialog box lists styles that you can use for the bar's buttons. Styles are based on FrontPage themes.

5. Pick an item from the Choose a Bar Style list:

   - If you're using themes, to make the bar match the rest of your site, choose the **Use Page's Theme** option.

   - Otherwise, use the scrollbar to see the possible choices and make a selection.

6. Click **Next**.

7. The last choice is whether to display links horizontally or vertically. Click an icon in the **Choose an Orientation** list box and click **Finish**.

   If the link bar needs a name, the Create New Link Bar dialog box appears. Type a name in the **Name** field and click **OK**.

The Link Bar Properties dialog box opens. Use this to set up the links that will appear in the bar, as described in the next two sections.

**12**

## Add a Navigational Link Bar

The Link Bar Properties dialog box determines which links will appear on the bar.

A link bar based on the navigational structure of a Web site uses Navigation view, a method of organizing a site in FrontPage that's one of its more innovative features.

Every site has a Navigation view, even if it hasn't been set up yet. Sites created from one of the FrontPage site templates include one automatically.

To see a site's Navigation view, choose View, Navigation.

Figure 12.5 shows the Navigation view for a newly created site that uses the Personal Web site template.

Home page icon

FIGURE 12.5

*Examining a Web's
navigational structure.*

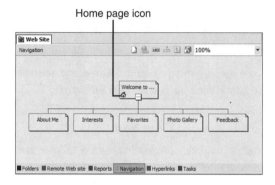

All six pages in the template are represented in the Navigation view: the home page, which has a home page icon, and five pages displayed below it.

Navigation view establishes a parent-child relationship among the pages of a Web site. In Figure 12.5, the home page is the parent of the other five pages: About Me, Interests, Favorites, Photo Gallery, and Feedback.

In this view, a parent can have as many children as desired, but a child has only one parent.

The view also provides the text that will be used on link bars for each hyperlink. To change this text for a page, follow these steps:

1. Right-click the page's icon and select **Rename** from the context menu that appears.
2. Type a new name and press **Enter**.

Link bar text should be reasonably short—anything more than 13–15 characters is probably too long to fit on a button. This text also is used on the page's banner, a Web component covered later this hour.

After you create a Web page, it can be added to Navigation view in several ways.

With the view open, here's one of the easiest methods to add an existing Web page to the view:

1. Right-click the Web page that will be its parent (you can change your mind easily later).
2. Choose **Add Existing Page** from the context menu that appears. The Insert Hyperlink dialog box opens.
3. Use this dialog box to find and select the page, and then click **OK**.

The page is added to Navigation view and linked to its parent. You can associate it with a different parent—or no parent—by dragging the page to a new location.

The easiest way to get a feel for this is to drag a page and drop it at several different places to see what relationship is established.

As you drag a page, a dotted outline indicates the relationship that would be established if you dropped the page at that spot. The outline changes depending on where you have dragged the page and which page it is closest to, as shown in Figure 12.6.

**FIGURE 12.6**

*Dragging a page around Navigation view.*

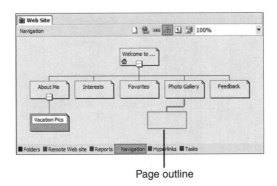

Page outline

In general, a page dropped above another page becomes its parent. A page dropped below a page becomes its child. A page that's dropped beside a page is its sibling and shares the same parent.

An exception applies: Pages dropped above a Web's home page are orphans—no lines connect them to other pages. You can use this to start new parent-child groups that are completely unrelated to other pages of the site.

If you're setting up a link bar based on the site's Navigation view, the Link Bar Properties dialog box displays a navigational graphic and several options that you can select, as shown in Figure 12.7.

The graphic includes a legend that describes how it is arranged. When you choose an option, the graphic changes to show you what will appear on the link bar.

A link bar can display six different groups of hyperlinks, depending on the option you choose on the Hyperlinks to Add to the Page panel:

- **Parent Level**—Links to the current page's parent and all of its siblings
- **Same Level**—Links to the current page's siblings
- **Back and Next**—Links to the siblings immediately to the left (back) and right (next) of the current page

**12**

- **Child Level**—Links to all pages that are children of the current page
- **Global Level**—Links to all pages that have no parents
- **Child Pages Under Home**—Links to all pages that have the Web's home page as a parent

**FIGURE 12.7**

*Working on a naviga-tion-based link bar.*

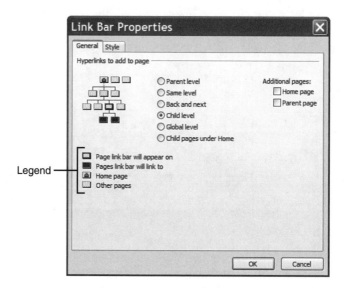

You also have the option of adding extra links to the Web site's home page and the cur-rent page's parent, if these aren't already in the group.

This is a lot of options to consider as you're working on a link bar for the first time. The most common (and useful) choice is Child Pages Under Home, with the Home page check box selected, which creates a link bar to all of the main pages of a site. The Web page shown in Figure 12.4 uses that kind of link bar.

After you have selected the hyperlinks that will appear on a bar, you can change its appearance and orientation: Click the Style tab to bring it to the front and make your choices.

When you're done setting up the link bar, click OK. The link bar is displayed on the Web page.

## Add a Back/Next or Custom Link Bar

FrontPage supports two other kinds of link bars:

- A link bar with Back and Next buttons that can be used on several pages of your site, helping visitors read them in a specific sequence (like pages in a book).

- A link bar with Back and Next bars that can be used on several pages of more than one Web site.

To add one of these bars to a Web page, follow these steps:

1. Open the page for editing and click the place where it should be inserted.

2. Choose **Insert, Navigation**. The Insert Web Components dialog box opens with link bars selected in the Component Type list box.

3. In the Choose a Bar Type list box, select either **Bar with Custom Links** or **Bar with Back and Next Links**, and then click **Next**.

4. The dialog box displays a list of styles that determine the link bar's appearance. Choose one and then click **Next**.

5. Choose vertical or horizontal orientation for the link bar.

6. Click **Finish**.

7. The Create New Link Bar dialog box appears, asking for a name to give the bar. Give it a name in the **Name** text field and click **OK**.

The Link Bar Properties dialog box appears, as shown in Figure 12.8.

**FIGURE 12.8**

*Working on a back/next link bar.*

**12**

These link bars are created by adding links to the pages that should be read in sequence. The order of pages is determined by the order, from top to bottom, of the Links list.

To set up the sequence of links, follow these steps:

1. To add a link to a page, click the **Add Link** button and choose the page using the Insert Hyperlink dialog box.

2. To move a link in the Links list, select it and click either **Move Up** or **Move Down**.

3. To delete a link, select it and click **Remove Link**. This doesn't remove the page— it just takes it out of the sequence.

4. If all of the pages in the Links list share a common parent, select the **Parent Page** check box to add a link to it on the bar.

5. Select the **Home Page** check box to add its link.

6. When you've finished setting up the sequence of links, click **OK**.

The back/next bar appears on the Web page. For it to work correctly, however, it needs to be on every one of the pages that was in the sequence of links.

To handle this quickly, first select the link bar and press Ctrl+C to copy it to the Clipboard. Then open each page, click the spot where the link bar should be placed, and press Ctrl+V to paste it there.

## Put a Banner on a Page

Page banners are specified with all of FrontPage's built-in themes, so you should already have experience working with them. The banners, which provide a way to display some kind of title on a Web page, can be text or a graphic; the graphical ones look like giant link bar buttons.

In all of the built-in themes, pages banners take up a lot of space on a Web page and don't provide much information, which makes it tough to incorporate them into an attractive design (I typically avoid using them for this reason.)

However, some of the themes created by FrontPage Web designers include smaller and more attractive page banners.

One of the best sources for FrontPage add-ons such as new themes and templates is FrontPageTools.Com, run by Paul Colligan, the co-author of *Special Edition Using Microsoft FrontPage 2003* (Que Publishing, 2003). To see what products Colligan has for sale, visit the Web site www.frontpagetools.com.

To add a banner to a page, follow these steps:

1. With the page open for editing, click the spot where the banner should appear and choose **Insert, Page Banner**.

2. The Page Banner Properties dialog box opens. The page's title (from Navigation view) appears in the Page Banner Text field. In the Properties section, choose **Picture** for a graphical banner or **Text** for text.

3. To change the banner text (and the title in Navigation view), edit the **Page Banner Text** field.

4. Click **OK**. The banner is displayed on the Web page.

The text of a page banner will be the same as its title in the Navigation view window. If the page isn't in the navigational structure of the Web yet, it must be added before a banner can be displayed.

To make changes to a banner, double-click it in the editing window. The Page Banner Properties dialog box opens again.

If you'd like to see other Web components that have been offered for FrontPage users, often at no cost, choose Insert, Web Component, and then click the Find components on the Web hyperlink. You will be taken to the Downloads for FrontPage section of Microsoft's Web site.

You also can visit the site directly at `www.microsoft.com/frontpage/downloads`.

# Create Dynamic Web Templates

Web components reduce the amount of work that's required to create several kinds of Web content for your site.

Another useful timesaver is a *dynamic Web template*, a new kind of page template in FrontPage that makes it easy to create different pages that contain many of the same things.

Dynamic Web templates are pages that have been divided into parts that can be edited and parts that must remain unchanged.

Using one of these templates, you can easily create a group of Web pages in which things such as the logo, link bar, and footer text stay the same, while the body of the page can change from page to page.

12

The template serves as a master copy, setting the basic layout, style, and formatting of each page that is created from it.

An example use of these templates is shown in Figure 12.9.

FIGURE **12.9**

*Editing a page that uses dynamic Web templates.*

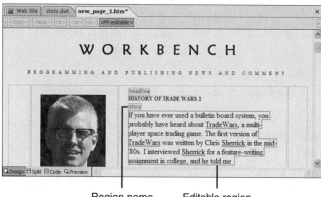

Region name        Editable region

A template is set up by loading an existing page and defining its *editable regions*, the parts of a page that will change. Anything that is not within these regions cannot be edited. Regions are denoted by boxes with orange borders. The name of the region is displayed in the upper-left corner of the box.

In Figure 12.9, an editable region named Story is being worked on. There's also an editable region named Headline that contains the text "History of Trade Wars 2."

Each editable region on the template is given a name. A page can have as many regions as desired.

To create a dynamic Web template, follow these steps:

1. Open a Web page that will be the basis for all of the other pages that use the template. It can be any page of your site.

2. Give it a new name: Choose **File**, **Save As** to open the Save As dialog box, and then switch the Save As Type list box to **Dynamic Web Templates (*.dwt)**.

   In the Filename field, the extension switches to .dwt.

3. Choose a descriptive name for the template, making sure to keep the file extension .dwt. Click **Save**.

   Changing the file extension converts the page into a dynamic Web template.

4. Select a region of the template that should be editable. The region will appear highlighted.

5. Right-click anywhere within the highlighted regions and choose **Manage Editable Regions** from the context menu that appears. The Editable Regions dialog box opens (Figure 12.10).

FIGURE **12.10**

*Adding an editable region to a dynamic Web template.*

6. Type a name for the region in the **Region Name** field, and click **Add**. Click **Close** to shut the Editable Regions dialog box.

7. Repeat steps 4–6 for each editable region that you want to define.

8. Save the file: Choose **File**, **Save** or click the Save button on the Standard toolbar.

Any page created from this template is only editable in the regions that have been defined.

When you have a dynamic Web template, a new page can be created from it:

1. Choose **File**, **New** to open the New Pane.

2. Click the **From Existing Page** hyperlink. The New From Existing Page dialog box opens.

3. Select the template and click **Create New**. (FrontPage may display a dialog box indicating that the page has been created.)

4. A page is created that has the dynamic Web template attached to it. Anything within the orange-boxed editable regions can be modified—the box expands or shrinks to fit the changes.

**12**

A dynamic Web template also can be associated with an existing page: Choose Format, Dynamic Web Template, Attach Dynamic Web Template; then choose the template file and click Open.

If you decide to stop using the template on a page, making it possible to edit everything on it, choose Format, Dynamic Web Template, Detach from Dynamic Web Template.

After a page has been attached to a dynamic Web template, any change to the template can be applied automatically to that page. Whenever you save the template file after making a change, FrontPage asks if the pages using the template should be updated.

## Summary

One of the biggest selling points for FrontPage is the capability to create interesting Web sites without a lot of work.

As you concentrate on the appearance of your Web site and the information it contains, FrontPage uses HTML, CSS, and other Web technology behind the scenes to put everything together and make it work.

FrontPage Web components embody the same principle, making it easy to incorporate unusual things into your Web site such as link bars, news and weather reports, page banners, and many other offerings you'll be learning about in coming hours.

Another timesaver is a dynamic Web template, a new feature of FrontPage 2003 that makes it possible to share content on related pages of your site, giving them a consistent and professional appearance.

## Q&A

**Q In FrontPage 2002, I was able to create a link bar with text links instead of graphical buttons. Is this still possible?**

**A** You can still use text instead of graphics, but the feature has moved. When selecting a style for the link bar, scroll all the way to the bottom of the Choose a Bar Style list. You'll find several choices where the links are text rather than graphical buttons. After selecting one, click Next to choose the orientation of the bar.

**Q** **Several of FrontPage's Web site templates use shared borders instead of dynamic Web templates. Which is better?**

**A** Dynamic Web templates are more useful because they protect the shared parts of a page from being changed. Shared borders enable content to be shared among several Web pages, but that content can be modified at any time without restriction. Also, a dynamic Web template can be defined in a single file, while borders require up to four files.

Microsoft's documentation for FrontPage 2003 states that shared borders are offered so that Web sites created with earlier versions of the software can be edited normally.

12

# PART IV

# Making Your New Site a Success

## Hour

13  Publish Your Site

14  Attract the Widest Possible Audience

15  Promote a New Site

16  Learn More About Your Site's Audience

# HOUR 13

# Publish Your Site

All the sites you have created so far were viewed locally on your own computer. After 12 hours of dress rehearsal, you might be wondering when this production is ever going to open to the public.

It's showtime.

In this hour, you will learn

- How to choose a Web hosting service for your site
- Whether you need a hosting service that offers extended support for FrontPage 2003
- How to publish a Web site from your computer to the Web
- How to publish a Web site in the reverse direction from a Web server to your computer
- How to synchronize copies of your Web site stored in two different locations

## Find a Server to Host Your Site

Before you can publish your site with FrontPage, you must have a place to publish it. Unless your company has its own Web servers, you must set up an account with a Web hosting service.

Thousands of companies offer Web hosting, competing for your business in several different ways:

- **Price**—Some hosts are free if they can put banner ads on each page of your Web, but they usually offer no assistance if anything goes wrong with their service. Others generally range in price from $9 to $49 per month.
- **Disk storage**—Hosts offer from 5MB to 200MB of storage space for all the pages and files in your site.
- **Bandwidth**—Hosts often put restrictions on how often pages and files in your site are requested, limiting it to a set amount such as 3GB per month. Going over this can result in an additional charge or a total shutdown of the site until the next billing period—it's important to find this out before you join.
- **Operating system**—Some hosts specialize in hosting on servers that use a specific operating system, such as Windows 2000, Windows XP, Linux, or Mac OS.
- **Features**—Hosts offer different features based on the technology they have implemented on their servers.

The features offered by a Web hosting service vary greatly. They can include Common Gateway Interface (CGI) scripting, Java servlets, PHP, and MySQL database access.

For FrontPage users, the most important features to look for in a Web host are support for SharePoint Services, FrontPage Server Extensions, and Active Server Pages.

FrontPage Server Extensions are programs that run on a Web server to extend the capabilities of a site. These extensions are designed to make it easy for FrontPage users to add sophisticated features to their sites.

Windows SharePoint Services 2.0 is a Web server–based tool for team collaboration and Web site administration. For FrontPage 2003, it has been enhanced to include the functionality of server extensions.

Active Server Pages are Web pages that include HTML formatting and programming code that creates Web content when the pages are loaded by a server.

Microsoft calls a Web server that offers FrontPage extensions or SharePoint Services an *extended server*.

Although several popular Web servers can be upgraded to function as an extended server, the one that's best suited to FrontPage hosting is the Microsoft Internet Information Server. That server software has the added advantage of supporting Active Server Pages.

When seeking a host for your FrontPage site, the best choice is one that offers SharePoint Services 2.0, which makes it possible for your site to include all of the features that require server extensions and some additional features offered only by a server running SharePoint.

> Multiple versions of FrontPage Server Extensions and SharePoint Services are implemented by hosting services on the Web. The best choice is a service that offers Windows SharePoint Services 2.0, followed by a host with either SharePoint Services 1.0 or FrontPage Server Extensions 2002.

By hosting your site on an extended server, you can make use of several Web components described in the preceding hour, "Use Web Components to Jazz Up a Site," and many other features introduced in future hours.

FrontPage components that require an extended server include the following:

- **Form handler**—Collects information from a form on a Web page and sends it using email
- **Hit counter**—Counts the number of times a page is loaded
- **Web Search**—Searches a site for specific text and returns a results page
- **Photo Gallery**—Displays a group of photos on a page, automatically creating small "thumbnail" versions of each image

An extended server also is required to see the Web usage reports that FrontPage offers, which are described during Hour 16, "Learn More About Your Site's Audience."

Another important feature offered by Web hosts is domain name service. One of the best ways to promote your site and make it look professional is to give it a short, memorable Web address.

Many hosting services will let you pick out a domain name for your site—an Internet address that begins with a descriptive word or phrase and ends with .com, .net, .org, or another designation.

If you can find a domain name that you like, or if you already own one, you can use it as the address of your site. The cost ranges from $10 to $45, although some companies offer free domain registration as a benefit to paid subscribers.

Microsoft offers a Web Presence Providers directory that you can use to find a hosting service that offers extended servers. To view the directory, follow these steps:

1. Connect to the Internet.
2. Open any site that you have never published.

**13**

3. Choose **File, Publish Site**. The Remote Web Site Properties dialog box is displayed.

4. Choose the **Click Here to Learn More** hyperlink.

The Web Presence Provider site opens in your browser. If it doesn't work, you also can go there directly by visiting the Web address `www.microsoft.com/frontpage/wppsearch`.

You can search the directory by region or by criteria, such as price and operating system. When you find one you like, you can go directly to that site to learn more and sign up for an account.

After you have set up an account with a hosting service, you are ready to publish a site.

# Publish Your Site for the First Time

FrontPage can publish sites to three different places:

- A folder on your computer or another computer on a local network
- A Web server on your computer
- A Web hosting service

Publishing a site to another folder on your computer is a way to copy it. Using a Web browser, you can view pages in the site, test hyperlinks, and try out features that do not require an extended server.

The only difference between publishing on your computer and publishing on the World Wide Web is how you specify the destination. In both cases, you're copying files from one location to another.

Before you can publish a site to a Web server on the Internet, you need a username and password that grant you permission to store files on that computer. You also might need the name of the folder where the site can be stored.

Using FrontPage 2003, the easiest and most reliable way to publish a site is to use an extended server. All you need to know are your username, your password, and the location of your site—a Web address that you can use to visit it with a Web browser.

If you're using a Web host that is not an extended server, you can publish the site using File Transfer Protocol (FTP). To use this, you must have a username, a password, the address of the host's FTP server, and the folder where your site should be stored.

The Web host you have chosen should have provided all of this information when you signed up. You'll need it before you can proceed.

When that information is at hand, here's how to publish your site:

1. Open the site and choose **File, Publish Site**.

   If you have never published the site, the Remote Web Site Properties dialog box opens, as shown in Figure 13.1.

**FIGURE 13.1**

*Publishing a Web site for the first time.*

2. In the Remote Web Server Type list box, choose the method that will be used to publish files to the server:

   • If you are publishing the site to an extended server, choose **FrontPage or SharePoint Services**.

   • Otherwise, choose **FTP**. An extra text field appears on the dialog box: FTP directory.

3. In the **Remote Web Site Location** field, type the Internet address where the site will be published.

   When using server extensions, this will be a Web address that begins with `http://` (such as `http://www.example.com`).

   When using FTP, this will be the address of an FTP server. The address will begin with `ftp://` instead.

4. FTP users have an extra step: If you know the folder where the site should be published on the FTP server, type it in the **FTP Directory** field.

13

5. Click **OK**.

6. If this is the first time the site has been published, you'll be asked whether a Web site should be created at that location. Click **Yes**.

   At this point, FrontPage opens the Remote Web site view, which displays your site's folder alongside a folder on your Web host. This view is shown in Figure 13.2.

**FIGURE 13.2**

*Preparing to publish a Web site.*

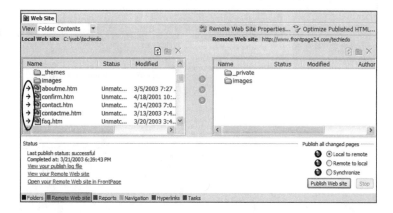

Before anything is published, FrontPage compares the two folders. If a page is the same in both places, it is not published.

You can look in the Local Web site folder (on the left) to see what files will be published—they have right arrows next to their names, as circled in Figure 13.2.

7. In the Publish All Changed Pages section, make sure that **Local to Remote** is chosen.

8. Connect to the Internet (if you haven't already) and click **Publish Web Site**.

9. If you have never published a site to this server, you're asked for your username and password. Type them in the **Username** and **Password** fields, and click **OK**.

FrontPage copies the files in your site to the Web server, displaying a status bar that tracks its progress.

As files are being published, FrontPage also reports any files that are found on the Web server but not in the folder on your computer. You're asked whether to delete these files as they turn up.

Unless you know that that it's okay to delete a file, you shouldn't let FrontPage delete it. Many Web hosting services put files in your folder that support some of their features. If the files are deleted, the features might no longer work correctly (or at all).

When everything has been published correctly, the Status section displays the message "Last publish status: successful." If something went wrong, you'll see an error message instead.

To see the site on the Web server, click the View Your Remote Web Site hyperlink. Your site's home page opens in your primary Web browser.

Publishing a site to a Web server can take 5 minutes or more, depending on the speed of your Internet connection and the number of files in your site.

After you have published a site for the first time, it is set up to use the same publishing location until you choose a different one.

## Solve Any Publishing Problems

When you're learning how to publish a site, several different problems can stymie the process.

If you're having trouble getting your work published, try the following suggestions:

- Double-check your username and password to make sure that they're correct.
- If you're publishing to a Web address using an extended server, load this address in your Web browser to see if it works. In most cases, if the address is correct, you will see a test page—Web hosting services usually create a site's main folder before you ever publish to it.
- If you're using FTP and are specifying an FTP directory, try taking it out and specifying only the FTP server's address. Some Web hosting services will find the right folder for your username automatically.

These examples cover the most common problems that might occur as you're publishing a site. In some instances, you might encounter problems because the hosting service doesn't offer FrontPage extensions or SharePoint, although this normally doesn't prevent pages and files from being copied to the Web server.

**13**

Most Web hosts provide rudimentary documentation on publishing sites using their hosts. At the very least, they can provide the HTTP or FTP address that you should use when publishing, along with your username and password.

## Prevent Something from Being Published

By design, FrontPage publishes all of the files that you create or import into a site—even if they are in the _private folder.

You can exclude a file from being published, keeping things you are still working on from showing up on the site.

Here's how:

1. With the site open for editing, choose **View, Folders**.

   FrontPage displays the Folders view of the site.

2. Right-click the page that should not be published.

   A context menu appears.

3. Choose **Don't Publish**. An X appears on the icon next to the file.

4. When the file is ready to be published, right-click it again. On the context menu, the Don't Publish command has a check mark next to it.

5. Choose **Don't Publish** again to deselect it and allow the file to be published.

## Keep a Web Site Synchronized

If you manage your site by keeping one copy on your computer and publishing it to a Web server, you probably don't need to do anything to keep both copies synchronized with each other. Publishing the site periodically ensures that both copies contain the same Web pages, graphics, and other files.

However, it's possible to use FrontPage to design Web sites that modify and create files on a Web server as they are used. For example, if you use the Form Page Wizard to collect information from your visitors, their responses are saved in a file in your site.

Several of the Web components you will learn about in upcoming hours also create files on the Web server that you'll want to save. In Hour 18, "Turn Your Site into a Community," you learn how to add a discussion board to your site where visitors can post their own messages. Each message is saved in a file on the site.

These files won't exist on the copy of your site stored on your computer.

When you're working on a site that creates or modifies files on the server, you should periodically use FrontPage's synchronization feature to copy these files to your computer:

1. Open the local copy of the site—the one stored on your computer.
2. Choose **File, Publish**.

   The Remote Web Site view is displayed, as shown in Figure 13.3. You might also be asked for the username and password used to publish the site.

**FIGURE 13.3**

*Synchronizing a Web site in two places.*

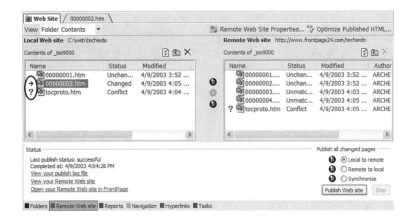

3. In the Publish All Changed Pages section, choose the **Synchronize** option.

   Before continuing, you should look at both folders in the Remote Web Site view to see which files will be copied—based on the arrow icons next to particular files, as circled in Figure 13.3.

   The following rules apply:

   - If a file has been changed on the server but not on your computer, the changed file is copied to your computer.
   - If a file has changed on your computer but not the server, it is copied to the server.
   - If a file has changed in both places, FrontPage displays a question mark next to it.

   Files with a left arrow are copied from your computer to the Web server. Files with a right arrow are copied in the opposite direction.

   Files with a question mark aren't copied at all because FrontPage can't figure out which one is the right one to store in both places.

**13**

4. For each file with a question mark, decide which copy is the right one. Then right-click it and choose **Synchronize Selected Files** from the context menu that appears.

5. Click **Publish Web Site**. FrontPage attempts to make the files on your Web server match the ones on your computer.

6. If any unresolved conflicts remain, caused by files with question marks, a dialog box asks how to deal with them. Click **Ignore and Continue** to skip each of these files, and then repeat steps 4–5.

After a site has been synchronized, you can make changes to the files copied to the folder on your computer and republish the site. When you're running a discussion board, this is how you can remove messages from the board, if necessary.

# Summary

In this hour, you learned how to publish a site to a folder on your system and a folder on a machine that could be anywhere else in the world. Thousands of Web hosting providers are available to use as the home for your sites.

Publishing a site in FrontPage is a task that's easy after you've done it successfully, quickly becoming as simple as saving files from one folder to another.

Getting to that point can be a challenge sometimes, depending on how FrontPage and your Web hosting service work in conjunction with each other.

# Q&A

**Q If a Web hosting provider doesn't offer an extended server with either FrontPage Server Extensions or SharePoint Services, should I use that provider?**

**A** The answer depends on whether your site is reliant on server-specific features and you can live without some FrontPage maintenance features.

To see whether a site is reliant on the extensions, publish it to the hosting provider and try all of its features. Some of them, such as forms, can be rewritten to use an alternative. Others, such as threaded discussions, require the extensions and can't be replaced easily.

When you are publishing a site, FrontPage 2003 works faster and more reliably with a host equipped with an extended server. My advice is to choose a host that offers them—you get this advantage along with a bunch of Web components and wizards that aren't available otherwise.

**Q** **My Web hosting service puts a bunch of files in the folder where I publish my site. Is there a way to make FrontPage stop asking me if I want to delete them?**

**A** One way to solve the problem is to make copies of those files in your site. Use the Import Web Wizard or FTP software to create a second copy of your Web on your system, including the files your hosting service put there for you.

After making the copy, open your original site and import your hosting service's files into it. When that's done, select the files in the Folder list or Folders view, right-click, and then choose Don't Publish from the shortcut menu that appears. From that point on, FrontPage will stop asking whether you want to delete the files when you publish the site.

**13**

# Hour **14**

# Attract the Widest Possible Audience

One of the most important things to remember about the World Wide Web is that it is a completely unpredictable medium. The way a page looks on your computer is often very different than how it looks when other people view it on theirs.

As a Web designer, you have very little control over how your work will be presented when it is shown to your visitors. Though you can take a look at your site in the most popular Web browsers, literally hundreds of different programs can be used to view Web pages.

Although the Web is built on official standards such as the Hypertext Markup Language (HTML) and Cascading Style Sheets (CSS), these are often implemented inconsistently by different products. The only standard that you can count on is chaos.

In this hour, you will learn

- How to use FrontPage 2003 to create a site that's targeted to specific Web browsers
- How to create a site that's targeted to a specific Web server
- How to make your Web site usable by a much larger group
- How to turn features of FrontPage on and off based on the technology used in their implementation

# Cope with a Diverse Audience

Trying to make a Web page work in all leading Web browsers is a challenge. The audience is split largely among five programs—Microsoft Internet Explorer, Mozilla, Netscape Navigator, Opera, and Safari—and dozens of others are in use.

Each Web browser has quirks in how it presents different World Wide Web features, bugs that haven't been fixed yet, and special support for things that haven't been adopted by the other browser developers. This makes it challenging to create a Web site that looks presentable in all of them.

FrontPage makes it easy to add many of these nonstandard features to your sites (especially if the feature works best in another Microsoft product, Internet Explorer). Fortunately, it also makes it easier to sort through the chaos and decide which features to use and which to avoid.

The World Wide Web Consortium has been entrusted with creating a standard version of HTML, the language used to create Web pages. You can visit the group's site at www.w3.org to learn about the current version of the standard and proposed improvements for the next version. The consortium also develops other standards that affect Web development.

> The World Wide Web Consortium offers a service that has been a real boon for Web designers: a validator that checks a Web page to make sure it's not using any nonstandard HTML. If you're familiar with HTML and want to check a page's validity so you can correct errors, visit the Web page http://validator.w3.org.

Since Netscape launched its first browser in 1994, the Consortium's standards have often been at odds with the companies that are most involved in following them: the browser developers. There has been fierce competition between different companies to introduce their own enhancements to HTML, Web page scripting, and Cascading Style Sheets.

Many of these new features are appreciated by Web users—displaying images on a page was once a nonstandard enhancement, for instance. However, it has been common practice to introduce new features in the browsers without waiting for them to become standards.

One of the simplest examples of this involves blinking text. For an early version of its browser, Netscape added a way to make text on a Web page blink on and off like a

"VACANCY" sign outside a motel. It's a simple, eye-catching effect that calls attention to a word, sentence, or more.

Making your text blink is easy in FrontPage:

1. Select the text in the editing window.
2. Choose **Format, Font**. The Font dialog box appears.
3. Select the **Blink** check box (if you can) and click **OK**.

Try this in one of your own sites. You're likely to find that the Blink check box has been disabled and can't be selected in the Font dialog box. You're being prevented from doing this by FrontPage's built-in browser compatibility feature, which prevents you from using features that can't be viewed by your target audience.

By default, FrontPage is set to create sites that work in both Navigator and Internet Explorer. Because Internet Explorer does not support blinking text, the feature is unavailable.

"To blink or not to blink?" is only one of the questions you must ask when you design a site. The software includes more than a dozen different features that are affected by differences among the popular Web browsers.

# Make Your Web Compatible with Multiple Browsers

One of the goals of FrontPage is to shield you from many of the complexities of Web design.

At this point, you might not be too familiar with technology such as HTML, Dynamic HTML, and JavaScript because FrontPage uses these things behind the scenes as you work on a site. You can focus on the effects and presentation that you want on your page, not the techniques used to make it happen.

The easiest way to keep from having to learn about these topics is to ask yourself four questions before you start a site:

- Which Web browsers will be used by my target audience?
- Which versions of those browsers will the audience use?
- Which Web server will my site be published on?
- Does that Web server have server extensions of SharePoint?

**14**

Although there isn't a definitive source for Web usage statistics, a look at several different surveys provides a pretty good picture of what people are using to browse the World Wide Web.

As of this writing, it appears that the Web audience is composed of the following users:

- Around 65% of all Web users are running Microsoft Internet Explorer.
- Around 15% use Netscape Navigator or one of the other Web browsers based on the same software (such as Mozilla).
- Around 10% use America Online's Web browser, which is presently Internet Explorer.
- Around 10% use browsers such as Opera, Safari, Lynx, or other Web-presentation programs.

Additionally, around 80% of Internet Explorer and Navigator users have upgraded to the current versions of the software (at this time, Internet Explorer 6, Navigator 7, and Mozilla 1.4).

Netscape Navigator is based on Mozilla, another popular Web browser that was created by hundreds of programmers collaborating in an "open source" project. When I refer to Navigator in the rest of this hour, I'm referring to all of the browsers based on Mozilla. The same can be assumed in FrontPage 2003, which refers to Navigator but not Mozilla. Anything that works in the current version of Navigator should also work in Mozilla.

These statistics are based on several reports of browser market share, most notably the report produced by Janco and Associates that's summarized on the Web at www.psrinc.com/browser.htm, and the usage statistics for my own sites, which receive around 12 million visits a year.

Although Internet Explorer has the largest share of the browsing audience, most Web sites are developed for recent versions of Internet Explorer and Navigator so that Web designers can take advantage of the newest features in these browsers.

You can also choose to design a site specifically for Internet Explorer, which enables you to use specific features that aren't available in any other browser. However, as many as one in three of your visitors could be using something else, so you'll be leaving out a considerable portion of your audience.

Another thing that you can determine when you're selecting a browser's target audience is whether you'll be relying on an extended server. Several of the features of a

FrontPage-designed site rely on these extensions, including some of the feedback form options, the search engine, and the site created with the Discussion Web Wizard.

Aside from these features, the Web server that you use to host a site doesn't have much effect on browser compatibility: Most of the Web content that you can create with FrontPage will work regardless of the server software that you are using.

## Choose Your Target Audience

After you've decided upon a target audience and Web server for your site, you can configure the information in FrontPage, which makes it easier to tailor your work to them.

To set your site's compatibility, follow these steps:

1. Choose Tools, Browser Compatibility. The Browser Compatibility dialog box opens.

2. Click the **Change** button. The Page Options dialog box appears with the Authoring tab in the front, as shown in Figure 14.1.

FIGURE **14.1**

*Choosing a Web site's target audience.*

The choices you make in the Authoring tab don't change existing features of a site. Instead, they prevent you from adding new features unless your target audience is capable of using them.

14

You don't have to know anything about these to select a target browser and Web server, as you'll see in the next step.

3. Choose a target Web browser (or browsers) from the **Browsers** list box. Check boxes for special features will be selected or deselected depending on your choice.

   Though you can select Internet Explorer only or Navigator only, the most sensible choice is **Both Internet Explorer and Navigator**. You'll be able to focus on features that work for at least 90% of your visitors.

4. In the **Browser Versions** list box, choose one of these values:

   - For a site that makes use of cutting-edge features available to 80% of the users of your target browser, select **5.0/6.0 Browsers and Later**.

   - For a site that uses most current features, omitting a few that are unavailable to 5–10% of your target users, select **4.0 Browsers and Later**.

   - For the most conservative choice, select **3.0 Browsers and Later**, which would apply to just about anyone using the Web.

5. Choose an option from the **FrontPage and SharePoint Technologies** list box:

   - If you are hosting your site with a server that offers server extensions of SharePoint Services, select **Complete**.

     You'll be able to make use of some of FrontPage's most innovative features, such as site search engines, discussion boards, and site maps.

   - If not, select **None** and then select the **Author-Time Web Components** and **Navigation** check boxes.

     The FrontPage and SharePoint Technologies list box changes to Custom. You'll be able to use FrontPage features that are created on your computer when a page is being drafted. Features that are handled by a server will be omitted.

6. Click **OK**. The Target Browser section of the Browser Compatibility dialog box displays your selected audience.

As you might expect, FrontPage works best when you're aiming directly for the most recent versions of Internet Explorer. Every one of these special features works in Microsoft's most current browser.

You can change browser compatibility settings as often as you want during the development of a site. However, you might end up with features on your site that aren't suited to your intended audience.

One way to keep this from happening is to occasionally check your entire site for incompatible features:

1. Choose **Tools, Browser Compatibility**. The Browser Compatibility dialog box opens.

2. In the Check Where section, choose **All Pages** to inspect all pages of your site.

3. Click the **Check** button. FrontPage 2003 looks over all pages of your site in search of features that are not supported by your target Web browsers or target server.

   Each possible problem is listed in the bottom half of the Browser Compatibility dialog box, as shown in Figure 14.2. The description of each issue is shown in the Problem Summary column, although you may need to drag a column-divider line to increase the width of the column to read the full description.

**FIGURE 14.2**

*Checking a Web site's compatibility.*

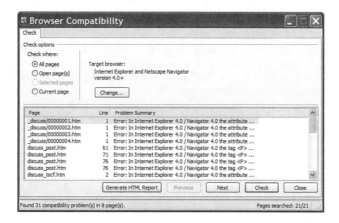

4. For a more readable list of problems, click the Generate HTML Report button. FrontPage creates a new Web page with a list of problems and their descriptions, and adds the page to your site.

5. Click **Close**.

If you created an HTML report of possible problems, it will be open for editing (although there isn't much reason to edit it). To read the report, click the Preview button at the bottom of the editing window.

## Restrict Specific Technology on a Web Site

The check boxes on the Authoring tab enable you to override the selections that were determined when you picked a browser audience.

14

If you use this, you might spend time on features that aren't really usable by your audience. For example, if you enable the Browse-Time Web components for a site, you can add things such as a photo gallery and hit counters. However, if you're hosting the site on a Linux server that doesn't offer FrontPage Server Extensions, the pages that you create won't work when the site is published.

You might find it handy to disable a technology simply because you don't want to use it anywhere. For example, some Web developers choose not to place any Java applets on their pages. Although these programs can be a compelling way to present interactive content on a Web page, Java can reduce the speed with which a page loads and is not available on some browsers—users can turn off the feature, and some versions of Internet Explorer do not support Java unless the user has chosen to install it.

Along the same lines, PNG graphics are not supported in version 3.0 of either popular browser. If you want to include the small number of users who are still using Netscape Navigator 3.0 in your target audience, FrontPage won't allow you to add PNG graphics to a page unless you change the selected audience in the Authoring tab.

In addition to PNG graphics, the following features can be turned on or off with the check boxes of the Authoring tab:

- **Active Server Pages**—Web pages that contain programs that are run by Microsoft Internet Information Server as they are loaded
- **ActiveX controls**—Programs that run as part of a Web page using a standard developed by Microsoft
- **Cascading Style Sheets (CSS)**—A language that specifies how the contents of a Web page should be presented
- **Frames**—A way to divide a single browser window into smaller sections, each holding its own Web page
- **Java applets**—Interactive programs, written with the Java programming language, that run as part of Web pages
- **JavaScript/JScript**—Netscape's Web scripting language, which preceded VBScript and is still the most commonly used and widely supported in browsers
- **VBScript**—A scripting language developed by Microsoft that enables some interaction between a user and a Web page

To turn off a specific special feature, follow these steps:

1. Choose **Tools, Browser Compatibility**. The Browser Compatibility dialog box opens.

2. Click the **Change** button. The Page Options dialog box appears with the Authoring tab in the front. The check boxes in the dialog box reflect your choice of target Web browser and server.

3. To turn off a feature, deselect its check box so that it no longer has a check mark in it.

   The value of either FrontPage and SharePoint technologies or Browser Versions changes to Custom, indicating that you are no longer using the default settings.

4. Click **OK**.

When a feature has been turned off, FrontPage disables any of its functionality that requires that particular technology, making it impossible for you to employ it on your site.

## Handle Differences Between Web Browsers

As you start to deal with the issue of browser compatibility, you're more likely to restrict yourself than to expand the possible features employed on of your sites. Like most Web designers, you probably want to reach both Internet Explorer and Navigator users as your primary audience.

Using FrontPage, you can take two routes to use browser-specific features on a site aimed at everyone:

- **The longer route**—Duplicate some of the pages in your site and create two navigational structures, one for Navigator users and one for Internet Explorer users. Visitors can click hyperlinks on one of the site's main pages to select the site that matches their browser, and each one can have different compatibility options.

- **The shorter route**—Put browser-specific features on separate pages and provide hyperlinks to those pages for people with the right browser.

For example, if you have a page that uses a Java applet, you could provide a link to it indicating that it requires a browser equipped with Java. This prevents visitors from wasting time loading a page that they can't use.

These two techniques expand the amount of work you have to do, especially if there are a lot of duplicated pages.

Given the present statistics on browser usage, anything that's limited to one of the popular browsers will be unusable by at least 20% of the site's audience. This might not be a problem in some cases—for example, if you're working on a site that will be published on a corporate intranet, you might know that the only browser used at the site is Internet Explorer.

**14**

# Preview a Page with Different Browsers

The easiest way to sort through the chaos of multiple browsers is to test a Web site thoroughly with several of them.

The most popular Web browsers are available from the following sites:

- Microsoft Internet Explorer: www.microsoft.com/ie
- Netscape Navigator: www.netscape.com/download
- Mozilla: www.mozilla.org
- Opera: www.opera.com
- Safari (for Mac OS X): www.apple.com/safari

It's easy to download and install browsers for testing, as long as you're not trying to set up multiple versions of the same browser. Doing that is a recipe for disaster—if you attempt to install an older version of Internet Explorer or Netscape Navigator on your system, you're likely to wipe out the settings or functionality of your existing browser.

You can install Navigator and Mozilla at the same time, but you can't run both simultaneously without running into a few problems because they require some of the same resources on a computer. Because the browsers are so similar, there's less reason to test a site with both of them.

If you have access to a second computer, hold off on upgrading its Web browser (or browsers). That way, you can use the PC to test how your site looks using that software.

Another way to test a wide range of browsers (and even operating systems) is to use emulator software such as Microsoft Virtual PC or VMware Workstation. These programs make it possible to install virtual computers that run in their own window and can have their own operating system and software.

For more information on these products, visit their Web sites:

- Microsoft Virtual PC: www.microsoft.com/windowsxp/virtualpc
- VMware Workstation: www.vmware.com

After you have installed a browser, you can add it to the list of browsers that can be used to preview a site in FrontPage:

1. With a page open for editing (or a page selected in the Folders list), click the arrow next to the Preview in Browser button and choose **Edit Browser List** from the drop-down menu that appears (see Figure 14.3).

Preview in Browser arrow

The Edit Browser List dialog box opens.

2. Click the **Add** button. The Add Browser dialog box appears. You can use this to select your Web browser and then give it a descriptive name.

3. Click the **Browse** button. Use the Add Browser dialog box to open the folder where the browser was installed and then select the program.

   The Command field of the Add Browser dialog box displays the location and name of the program.

4. Type the browser's name in the **Name** field.

5. Click **OK**. The browser is added to the Browsers list.

6. To include this browser when you use FrontPage's Preview in Multiple Browsers feature, select its check box.

7. Repeat steps 2–6 for each new browser you have installed.

8. When you're done, click **OK**.

After you have added browsers to FrontPage, they appear in the Preview in Browser drop-down menu and when you choose the menu's More Browsers command.

Use this menu to view a Web site with several different browsers at different screen resolutions—you can open a page at 640×480, 800×600, and 1024×768 to see what it looks like for visitors with their monitors at those resolutions. (As you probably expect, all three choices are available only if your resolution is set to 1024×768.)

14

# Summary

One of the biggest headaches for Web designers has been the differences and bugs in how the leading Web browsers implement the standards used to create sites—the Hypertext Markup Language (HTML) and Cascading Style Sheets (CSS).

Although it has gotten better in recent years as browser developers became better at implementing the official standards, FrontPage 2003 makes it even easier to do two things on your sites:

- Stick with the features that different browsers share with each other
- Avoid using features that your audience can't use anyway

By determining your site's audience before you develop the site, you can concentrate on the features offered in FrontPage rather than thinking about the technology that makes them possible.

# Q&A

**Q  What's the point of having an HTML standard if none of the browser developers follows it to the letter?**

**A**  The idealist's answer is that Microsoft and other developers can be persuaded to begin complying with the standard. If enough developers insist on following the HTML standard and Web users support sites that adhere to it, the browser developers will start following the standardization process instead of trying to stay ahead of it.

The pessimist's answer is that the browser makers use new features to gain a competitive edge over each other, so HTML's standard will always be disregarded in pursuit of market share.

Frustrated Web developers who want to stop spending so much time dealing with incompatibilities have been lobbying both companies to standardize. One such effort is the Web Standards Project, at www.webstandards.org.

These efforts have made an impact: Current versions of the five most popular Web browsers—Internet Explorer, Navigator, Mozilla, Opera, and Safari—are closer than ever to the full, official standards for HTML and CSS.

# Hour 15

# Promote a New Site

In some ways, the real work begins after you have published your Web site for the first time. To make all of your efforts worthwhile, you ought to promote your site so that it finds an audience.

In this hour, you'll learn some of the most useful and inexpensive methods to call your site to the attention of World Wide Web users.

During this hour, you will learn

- How to get your site listed in search engines, computer-compiled databases containing billions of Web pages
- How to get listed in Web directories, human-crafted directories of sites organized by category
- How to increase the number of hyperlinks to your site
- How to join a Web ring, a group of publishers with similar sites who promote each other
- How to find out which Web publishers are linking to your site

Although most of these techniques apply to any Web site publisher, the last topic covered is specific to FrontPage 2003: Using the new weblog package, a template that makes it easy to publish content on your site that attracts more visitors.

# Let Search Engines Know About a New Site

After your Web site has been published, it's only a matter of time before it will be found by *search engines*, Web sites that compile a searchable database of the contents of billions of Web pages.

The most popular search engine at this time is Google, which is available on the Web at www.google.com. If you are unfamiliar with the site, it's a fast and reliable search engine with a distinct method of ranking search results based on how popular the site is and how people refer to it on Web pages. It's remarkably effective—search for the name of any large company or public figure in Google, and the first result is extremely likely to be its official home page, if one exists.

Other popular search engines are Teoma, at http://www.teoma.com; Altavista, at http://www.altavista.com; and All the Web, at http://www.alltheweb.com.

Search engines find Web sites on their own using software that "crawls" (searches) the hyperlinks that are found on Web pages. Even if you haven't promoted your new site, if someone has published a link to it on the Web, search engines will eventually find that link, follow it to your site, and add it to their databases.

Instead of waiting for search engines to find you, a process that can take months, it's better to submit your site to them.

> Before you submit your site, take a few steps to ensure that it will be most likely to be accepted: Check to see that you can reach all of the pages of the site from the home page, give each Web page an effective and descriptive title, and choose your words well in the hyperlinks and link bars that connect each of the site's pages.

When submitting your site to a search engine, you provide the Web address of its home page (and other pages, if desired). The search engine visits the site at some point with WebCrawler software, looking at that page and others that are linked from that page. Submitting one page is often sufficient: If the home page contains links to all of the main sections of the site, those pages should be found by the crawler.

Visit the following Web addresses to add your site to the most popular search engines:

- Google: http://www.google.com/addurl.html
- Altavista: http://addurl.altavista.com
- All the Web: http://www.alltheweb.com/add_url.php

- Inktomi and Fast: `http://insite.lycos.com/searchservices`
- Teoma and Ask Jeeves: `http://www.teoma.com` (click the Submit Your Site hyperlink)

Some search engines will consider your site for inclusion at no charge. Google and All the Web fall into this category.

Others offer free site submissions but will give you additional consideration for a price. Altavista, Inktomi, and Fast have both free and for-pay offerings. The cost of the pay service varies, but it's around $20–$40 for the submission of a single Web address, and $10–$20 apiece for 10 or more—those costs must be paid yearly.

There's also some that consider sites only if you pay for submission, such as Teoma and Ask Jeeves.

Submitting a site to a search engine is no guarantee that it will be included. However, in my experience, all of the pay services add sites quickly, and Google is extremely likely to add any sites that are submitted within two to four months.

When your site is showing up in search engines, you're likely to see a considerable jump in the number of visits that it receives, especially if you offer something on your site that's hard-to-find, unique, or particularly interesting.

# Submit the Site to Web Directories

Search engines are compiled by computers, enabling users to look through billions of World Wide Web pages for specific occurrences of text.

Another popular resource for finding things on the Internet is a Web directory, a service compiled by editors instead of software.

The most popular of these is a directory offered by Yahoo!, at `http://dir.yahoo.com`. Although Yahoo! offers news, stock quotes, email, Web hosting, and dozens of other services today, it began as a Yellow Pages–style directory of Web sites, and that's still one of its most popular features.

The Yahoo! Directory is compiled by a staff of editors who will consider sites at no cost, as described on the site at `http://docs.yahoo.com/info/suggest`.

The general procedure is to find the directory page on Yahoo! on which your site belongs and then click the Suggest a Site link on that page.

Getting a new site added to Yahoo! in this manner is often futile: I've tried for several years to have a few sites included, to no avail. Other Webmasters have shared similar experiences on professional mailing lists.

Yahoo! also offers a paid Express service that will review your site for inclusion within seven days of submission. The cost is $299 for most Web sites, paid yearly, and is not a guarantee that the editors will add the site. As with search engines, though, paying site publishers are unlikely to be rejected.

To find out more about Express, visit the Yahoo! Directory at `http://dir.yahoo.com` and click the Suggest a Site link.

Another Web directory that's becoming increasingly popular is the Open Directory Project (also called Dmoz), a catalog of more than three million sites.

Dmoz is published at the address `http://www.dmoz.org` and is republished with permission by dozens of Web sites, including Google, at `http://directory.google.com`.

All submissions to the directory are free—visit the main site at `http://www.dmoz.org`, find the category most appropriate for your site, and then click the Add URL hyperlink on that page.

Dmoz is prepared by more than 55,000 volunteers, each of which has responsibility for particular pages of the directory.

Your chances of being listed largely depend on whether the editors of a category are working actively on the project at the time (and how well your site fits that particular subject).

In general, there's a much better chance of being listed on Dmoz than using the Yahoo! free submission service, but it can take patience. After submitting your site, if it hasn't shown up in the directory in two to three months, submit it again. At times, if submissions are piling up, editors will skim over them, selecting a few and deleting everything else.

If no one is editing the category you want to be listed in and you're particularly determined to be included, you can volunteer to join the project and take responsibility for it. However, you'll need to prove that you aren't playing favorites with your own work, reviewing and selecting sites submitted by other publishers.

To make it easier for a Dmoz volunteer to add your site, use FrontPage to give the home page a good title and description.

Titles are a standard part of Web page design and show up on the title bar of a Web browser displaying the page. Descriptions are less commonplace and make use of a special feature of Web design called parameters.

*Parameters* are hidden lines of text on a Web page that describe something useful about that page. They are placed on a page using *metatags*, descriptive information on a Web page that isn't displayed to the visitors of your site but may be used by Web browsers and other software.

An example is the `Content-Type` parameter, which tells a Web browser the character set and file type of a Web page. If you look at a Web page in Code view to see the HTML tags employed to create the page, you'll see that FrontPage gives every page one of these tags. The default content type is `text/html; charset=windows-1252`.

Parameters can be added to a page without using HTML.

Here's how to add a `description` parameter to your site's home page:

1. Open the home page for editing.

2. Choose **Format, Page Properties**. The Page Properties dialog box opens with the General tab in front (see Figure 15.1). This can be used to set up some advanced features that apply to the page.

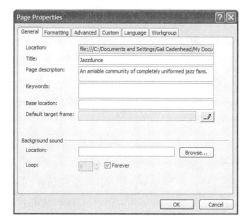

3. If you haven't already, give the page a title by filling out the **Title** field.

   The title should be short—generally 25 characters or less—and will presumably be your site's name or something similar.

4. Provide a succinct description of your site in the **Description** field.

   This also should be short but can be longer than a title—perhaps 50–60 characters, at most.

5. Click **OK**.

The description is not displayed on the Web page, but a Dmoz editor can make use of it when preparing your site for publication in the directory.

If your description is used, you'll begin to see it on Google and other Web sites that make use of data from the Dmoz directory.

# Exchange Links with Similar Sites

Search engines and Web directories are likely to be the major sources of new visitors to your Web site, but you shouldn't overlook another opportunity to build an audience: hyperlinks from sites similar to your own.

The best way to get people to link to your site is to offer an excellent, interesting, and up-to-date site.

However, as you're starting out, you could benefit greatly from some help from more established Web publishers.

Depending upon the kind of site you are offering, you might be able to encourage other publishers to link to your site in exchange for links to theirs.

This could be a formal process—contacting publishers to reach an agreement to exchange links—or an informal process by which you link to other sites in the hopes that they'll reciprocate at some point.

The latter is probably the best way to begin when your site is new and has not established an audience yet.

Many Web site publishers avidly keep track of the sites that have published hyperlinks to their work. If you are hosting your site on a Web server equipped with server extensions or SharePoint, you can look for these links in FrontPage using the Referring URLs report, one of the statistical reports created by the software that are covered fully in the next hour, "Learn More About Your Site's Audience."

Whenever a visitor reaches your site using a hyperlink, the Web server hosting the site keeps track of this information, which is called a referrer (or an HTTP referrer).

To see the Referring URLs report, you must open the copy of your site on the Web server and view its Reports view. Here's how:

1. Choose **File**, **Open Site**. The Open Site dialog box appears.

2. In the **Site Name** text field, enter the Web address of your site's home page (the same address that you use to view it in a Web browser) and click **Open**.

   The Web site opens in Folders view, listing the pages, graphics, and other files that it contains.

3. On the Views bar at the bottom edge of FrontPage's user interface, click the **Reports** button.

   The Reports view is displayed, showing you some statistics about the site and listing more than a dozen links to more detailed reports.

4. Click the **Usage Data** hyperlink.

   Reports detailing the visitors to your site are shown.

5. Click the **Top Referrer** hyperlink. The Referring URLs report is shown (see Figure 15.2).

**FIGURE 15.2**

*Tracking referrals to your Web site.*

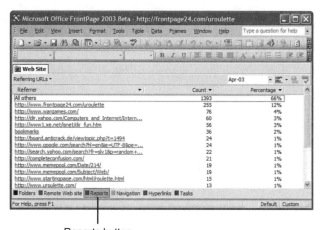

Reports button

The report shows the Web addresses of the top 20 pages that send the most visitors to your site, ranked in order, with the percentage of visits they generated.

Your own site is likely to be one of the top sites in the list because your pages link to each other, and each of these is considered a referral.

6. To load one of these pages in a Web browser, click its hyperlink.

7. When you're done looking at the report, choose **File**, **Close Site**.

By keeping up with the Referring URLs report, you can find links to sites that are related to your own.

To encourage other publishers to link to your site, create a link list on your home page or another page of your site. Populate the list with some of the sites that link to you and others of interest.

As the size of your site's audience grows, more of your visitors will find and use those links. When the publishers of the linked sites take note of the amount of visits they're receiving, some of them will begin linking to your site as well.

Each link to your site has an additional benefit: It increases your site's prominence in the Google search engine (and perhaps others). Google ranks search results based on how many people link to your site and the words that they use in the links. As your site becomes more established and is linked on dozens or hundreds of Web pages, you'll see considerably more visitors from people who use Google.

Google keeps track of these referring links. To see all of the pages that link to your site, visit Google at http://www.google.com and search for the keyword link: followed by the address of your home page or another page. Google will display all of the pages in its database that contain links to that part of your site.

# Join a Web Ring

As you might expect of a computer network, the World Wide Web is a great place to collaborate. People with similar sites on the Web often work together to publicize their work, and one of the most popular ways to do this is to form a Web ring.

A Web ring is a group of related Web sites that link to each other in an unusual way. Instead of offering a list of hyperlinks to all of the sites, each ring member may publish common things on their home page:

- A graphic or title for the Web ring
- A link to the Web ring's home page
- A link that can be used to join the ring

15

- A link that loads a random site in the ring
- A link to the previous and next sites in the ring

The last thing is what gives the ring its name. By clicking this "next site" link on each ring member's page, you should be able to see every site in the ring, eventually circling back to the page where you started.

Figure 15.3 shows a Web page that belongs to the FrontPage Resources Web ring. The links and graphics for the ring, which resemble a banner ad in some ways, are circled.

**FIGURE 15.3**

*Offering a Web ring on a site.*

The Web site that originated the Web ring concept is WebRing, which is published on the Web at http://webring.com.

WebRing currently has more than 60,000 rings that contain 1 million Web sites. Each ring is run by a volunteer who created it and defined the membership requirements (presumably, that person has one or more sites in the ring).

To participate in WebRing, you find an existing ring that's looking for sites like yours and apply to join it. WebRing publishes a directory of rings organized by category.

The Web page shown in Figure 15.3 is from FrontLook.Com, a site that offers themes, Web components, and other excellent resources for FrontPage users. The site is available at http://www.frontlook.com.

If you are approved for membership in the ring by the person who created it, you'll receive some special HTML code that must be added to your site's home page to participate.

Behind the scenes, FrontPages uses HTML, which stands for Hypertext Markup Language, to create your Web pages as you work on them.

Instead of creating Web ring links and graphics by hand, you should insert the ring's HTML code directly on a page.

If you're familiar with HTML, you can click the Code button on the Views bar and add Web ring HTML.

Everyone else can add the HTML easily using a Web component:

1. Open your home page in the editing window.

2. Click the spot on the page where the Web ring code should be displayed. Often they are placed at the bottom of the page or at a location dictated by the creator of the ring.

3. Choose **Insert**, **Web Component**. The Insert Web Component dialog box appears.

4. Scroll down the Component Type list and select **Advanced Controls**.

   The Choose a Control list displays several Web components that you can add to the page.

5. Choose **HTML** from this list and click **Finish**.

   The HTML Markup dialog box opens, as shown in Figure 15.4.

**FIGURE 15.4**

*Adding a Web ring's HTML code to a page.*

6. On the Web page or email that contains the Web ring's HTML code, select all of the code and press Ctrl+C to copy it to the Windows Clipboard.

7. Return to the HTML Markup dialog box, click once in the **HTML Markup to Insert** text field, and then press Ctrl+V to paste the HTML code from the Clipboard.

   HTML markup text added to a Web page in this manner will not be displayed as it is being edited. Instead, a small box with the text <?> is shown.

**15**

8. To view the Web ring HTML, click the **Preview** button on the Views bar (or click the Preview in Browser button on the Standard toolbar) .

This procedure can be used for any Web service that requires HTML code to be added to a page. To modify Web ring code, open the page for editing and double-click the <?> box. The HTML Markup dialog box reappears with the existing code, which can be changed or replaced.

Web rings appear most often on personal and hobbyist sites, an association you may want to keep in mind before adding one to a corporate or professional site.

As one of the more popular no-cost promotional services for Web publishers, Web rings can increase the visitors and links to your site, especially if the ring you have joined is popular. As an added benefit, participation in a Web ring can increase your site's ranking on Google, making it appear closer to the top in search queries conducted on that site.

# Add a Weblog to Your Site

Because the World Wide Web is such a dynamic medium, people who use it regularly expect that their favorite sites will be dynamic also. To develop an audience of repeat visitors, which is essential to the success of most sites, you need to continually offer new material, which can be very time- and labor-intensive.

In recent years, a new kind of Web content has become an extremely popular, largely because it makes it easy to add fresh material to a site: the Weblog.

Weblogs, which are also called blogs, are a form of online diary that's published in reverse chronological order, with the most recent entry displayed first.

The writing style varies widely among weblogs, but most feature similar traits:

- Entries are short, from 1 to 4 paragraphs.
- Hyperlinks to other Web sites occur often in those entries. The first weblogs were published with the purpose of sharing interesting discoveries on the World Wide Web, and that's still popular today.
- New entries are frequent—some are updated several times a day, while many average at least three to five entries a week.
- Promotion of other weblogs is common: Many of them feature a "blogroll," a list of weblogs being read by that author.
- The writing style tends to be informal, personal, and opinionated.

Weblogs are an addictive form of writing that can be as easy to do as writing an email. By some estimates, there are more than a quarter million weblogs being published today, usually by people who saw and liked an existing weblog and decided to start one of their own.

I've been publishing one, Workbench, to discuss technology, talk about subjects of interest as I work on books like this one, and promote my personal Web site. It's shown in Figure 15.5 and can be viewed at http://www.cadenhead.org/workbench.

**FIGURE 15.5**

*Presenting diary-style entries on a weblog.*

If you can offer a weblog as part of your site, or as an entire site unto itself, every entry that you add to the weblog gives visitors a reason to bookmark your site and keep checking it on an ongoing basis.

It's also a way to increase the number of links to your site because so many weblog authors publish links to the blogs that they read.

Since I began Workbench, which takes around one to two hours a week, the number of visits and links to my personal site has quadrupled.

 If the subject matter of your site lends itself to a weblog, you can use FrontPage 2003's new weblog package to add one to the site.

**15**

A new feature of this edition of FrontPage, *packages* are templates for sites that make heavy use of databases on the Web server hosting the site. Like the other packages, the weblog package requires a host that fully supports FrontPage 2003 and offers SharePoint Services, a collaboration and workgroup server from Microsoft that complements FrontPage.

A weblog created with this package includes a discussion feature, a search capability, and a list of favorite links.

To create one, follow these steps:

1. Choose **File**, **New** to open the New pane alongside the editing window.
2. In the New Web Site section, click the **Web Package Solutions** hyperlink.

   The Web Site Templates dialog box opens with the Packages tab up front, displaying the special package templates that can be used to create data-using sites.
3. Create the Web site as you would any other site, with one exception: The location of the site must be on the Web server instead of your computer.

After you create the weblog, you'll be able to update it using your Web browser instead of FrontPage.

FrontPage's weblog publishing feature is new and lacks some of the features offered by some of the other weblog authoring services and software.

Here's a few of the ones that are popular and reasonably easy to use:

- Blogger, at `http://www.blogger.com`
- LiveJournal, at `http://www.livejournal.com`
- Weblogger.Com, at `http://www.weblogger.com`
- Radio UserLand, at `http://radio.userland.com`

# Summary

If you've created an excellent Web site that's well designed, entertaining, and useful, it's a reasonably safe bet that it would find an audience even if you didn't spend any time promoting it.

However, most of the suggestions covered in the proceeding hour are quick to implement and cost nothing.

Getting listed in search engines such as Google, Web directories such as the Open Directory Project, and a Web ring is free. You also can exchange links with the publishers of sites like your own.

Other promotional efforts cost money—Yahoo! evaluates site submissions much more quickly for a fee than it would otherwise.

By calling your site to the attention of these services, and perhaps going even further by offering a weblog, you give your site an advantage in a very competitive medium.

# Q&A

**Q My Web site has started showing up in Google. This causes some of my visitors to miss my home page because they show up directly on a different page. How can I prevent this?**

**A** One way to prevent it is to add a `robots` parameter to pages that has the value `NOINDEX`. If this was on every page but the home page, Google would drop all of those pages from its database.

However, this solution will eliminate a large source of visits to your site because your pages won't be in Google anymore to be found during searches.

A better solution is to make sure your site can be navigated by users regardless of which page they start on. If every one of your pages contains a link to your home page and a link bar to the main sections of your site, you can give visitors from Google and other search engines an easy way to find their way around.

# HOUR 16

# Learn More About Your Site's Audience

As a Web site developer, the first question you're likely to have after publishing a site is whether anyone is visiting it.

Though it takes time for a Web site to build up an audience, you can often improve the site by observing how your initial visitors are using your site and how they go about finding it by using search engines such as Google, Web directories such as Yahoo!, and other means.

If you host your Web site on a server equipped with server extensions or SharePoint, you can use FrontPage's usage reports to find out a wealth of information about your audience.

During this hour, you will learn:

- How to view the number of times your site is visited each day
- How many times each page is requested
- What terms are used to find your site in popular search engines
- What pages on other sites contain links to your site
- Which Web browsers are used by your visitors

# Explore a Web Server's Logging Capability

The introduction to this hour contained all the *sensible* reasons to use FrontPage's site usage reports.

There's also another reason: Tracking the visits to your sites in obsessive detail is one of the most entertaining things about publishing on the World Wide Web.

As a Web publisher, you have the capability to continuously receive information on how popular your work is and what people are saying about it. It's like being a network TV executive with an unlimited budget to spend on overnight Nielsen rating reports and focus groups.

You can learn a lot about the people visiting your site and the ways they get there by checking out a few simple reports.

The data used by FrontPage to create usage reports is stored on the Web server that hosts your site. This data requires a server that is equipped with server extensions or SharePoint, enhancements that are available primarily on Windows servers that run Microsoft Internet Information Server; server extensions also are offered for the Apache Web server and other Web hosting software.

If you open a site stored on your computer or on a Web server that doesn't have FrontPage extensions, you won't see any evidence of usage data in FrontPage.

> If your Web hosting service doesn't offer server extensions, it might offer its own usage reports created with a program such as WebTrends, Webalizer, or Analog. The reports from those programs are a lot different than the ones described this hour, but they are produced using the same kind of usage data.

## See Usage Information for a Web Server

To produce reports like the ones available in FrontPage, a Web server must keep track of how it is used.

Servers accomplish this by producing data files called *logs*. Typically, a server can generate four kinds of log files:

- **access_log**—A list of requests for Web pages and other files that the server was asked to transmit
- **agent_log**—A list of Web browser identification tags that were sent along with each request

- **referer_log**—A list of Web addresses that contain hyperlinks requesting pages from the server
- **error_log**—A list of errors generated by the server as it is used

The log files kept by your Web hosting service might be different, but they all are capable of saving four kinds of information: page requests, Web browser use, referrals from other sites, and errors.

FrontPage uses Web server logs behind the scenes to prepare usage reports, so you don't have to work with them directly. However, they're worth a short look to see what you can learn from a Web server.

## Track Page Requests with Access Logs

Listing 16.1 contains 10 lines from an access_log file produced in the NCSA Common Log Format, the most commonplace way that log files are kept on the World Wide Web.

**LISTING 16.1** An Example of a Server's access_log

```
rb01.proxy.aol.com - - [01/Apr/2003:00:05:50 -0800] "GET /images/amazon.gif
➥HTTP/1.1" 200 1338
216.136.153.219 - - [01/Apr/2003:00:06:41 -0800] "GET / HTTP/1.1" 200 14081
216.136.153.219 - - [01/Apr/2003:00:06:41 -0800] "GET /images/amazonclock.gif
➥HTTP/1.1" 200 9867
216.136.153.219 - - [01/Apr/2003:00:06:41 -0800] "GET /images/retort.gif
➥HTTP/1.1" 200 11897
216.136.153.219 - - [01/Apr/2003:00:06:42 -0800] "GET /images/gray.gif
➥HTTP/1.1" 200 56
216.136.153.219 - - [01/Apr/2003:00:06:42 -0800] "GET /images/amazon.gif
➥HTTP/1.1" 200 1338
208.23.188.210 - - [01/Apr/2003:00:06:57 -0800] "GET / HTTP/1.1" 200 14081
208.23.188.210 - - [01/Apr/2003:00:06:58 -0800] "GET /images/amazonclock.gif
➥HTTP/1.1" 200 9867
208.23.188.210 - - [01/Apr/2003:00:07:00 -0800] "GET /images/retort.gif
➥HTTP/1.1" 200 11897
208.23.188.210 - - [01/Apr/2003:00:07:03 -0800] "GET /images/gray.gif
➥HTTP/1.1" 200 56
```

Each line in the access log contains the following information, in order from left to right:

- The Internet address that requested the file
- The date and time of the request
- The file that was requested
- The HTTP protocol used to make the request

- A status code
- The amount of data transferred, in bytes

Each request from the server is logged separately, whether it is looking for a page, graphics displayed on a page, or a request for a listing of files in a folder. If a Web page contains three graphics, four items show up in the log—one for the page and three for the graphics.

The Internet address requesting a file can be represented as a number (such as 208.23.188.210) or a machine name (such as rb01.proxy.aol.com). This address could represent any number of things, such as a home computer with a high-speed Internet connection, an Internet service provider machine used by different dialup users, or a server at a corporate office that takes employee requests for Web files.

The requested file is based on the location of the folder that contains a site's home page. In Listing 16.1, the request for /images/gray.gif is seeking a graphics file called gray.gif in the site's images subfolder.

## Track Browser Use with Agent Logs

Listing 16.2 contains 10 lines from an agent_log file in NCSA format.

**LISTING 16.2**    An Example of a Server's agent_log

```
Mozilla/4.0 (compatible; MSIE 4.01; Windows 98)
Mozilla/4.0 (compatible; MSIE 6.0; Windows 98; PeoplePC 1.0; HP)
MSProxy/2.0
Mozilla/4.61 (Macintosh; I; PPC)
Mozilla/4.61 (Macintosh; I; PPC)
Mozilla/4.0 (compatible; MSIE 5.01; Windows NT 5.0)
Mozilla/4.75   (X11; U; Linux 2.2.14-4.0 i686)
Mozilla/4.76 (Windows 98; U) Opera 5.02
None-of-your-business!
Mozilla/4.0 (compatible; MSIE 6.0; Windows NT 5.1)
```

Each line in the agent log contains only one item: the identification text sent by a program as it requested a file from the server. The program, which is usually a browser, is also known as a *user agent*.

Most lines in an agent log refer to browsers, and by far the most common is Microsoft Internet Explorer. Listing 16.2 contains several references to Microsoft Internet Explorer, which uses the acronym MSIE, along with a version number such as 4.01, 5.01, and 6.0.

There's also a line that contains the word "Opera," which indicates that the Opera browser was used.

Netscape Navigator and Mozilla generally show up as the text "Mozilla" followed by a slash, a version number, and additional information.

> As you can see in Listing 16.2, Internet Explorer also identifies itself as Mozilla. This is a throwback to the mid-1990s, when Navigator was the most popular Web browser and Internet Explorer was just being introduced. Microsoft was trying to achieve full compatibility with Navigator in page presentation, so it identified itself as "Mozilla" and "compatible."

**16**

One line that you might have been surprised by in Listing 16.2 is `None-of-your-business!`

The text used to identify a browser or Web-retrieval program is at the discretion of the visitor to your site. Some people consider agent logging to be an invasion of their privacy, so they change their user agent text to prevent their browser from being identified. `None-of-your-business!` is actually one of the tamer things I've seen in the server logs of my own sites over the years.

## Track Linking Sites with Referral Logs

Listing 16.3 contains 10 lines from a server's referer_log in NCSA format.

**LISTING 16.3**    An Example of a Server's referer_log

```
http://www.cadenhead.org/ -> /images/amazonclock.gif
http://www.cadenhead.org/ -> /images/retort.gif
http://www.cadenhead.org/ -> /images/amazonclock.gif
http://www.cadenhead.org/ -> /images/gray.gif
http://www.cadenhead.org/flash.shtml -> /images/lilretort.gif
http://google.yahoo.com/bin/query?p=screensaver&hc=0&hs=0 -> /flash.shtml
[unknown origin] -> /index.shtml
http://search.msn.com/results.asp?RS=CHECKED&FORM=WEBTV&v=1&cfg=WEBTV
➥&q=yellow+journalism -> /index.shtml
http://www.google.com/search?q=preshrunk+stalinist -> /tshirt.shtml
http://www.google.fr/search?q=zapruder+movie&hl=fr&meta= ->
➥/1998/07/073198.shtml
http://www.cadenhead.org/ -> /images/amazon.gif
```

Each line in a referral log contains two items, from left to right:

- The page containing the link to the file
- The file that was requested

The bulk of a referer_log file consists of referrals from your own site because the pages of your site contain links to each other and links to graphics displayed on each page. (The filename is sometimes spelled as referrer_log instead.)

Most Web usage reports can be configured to ignore these kinds of referrals, focusing on the ones that come from other Web sites.

The most useful information in a referral log is links to search engines, which often contain the text used in the search that led someone to your site.

In Listing 16.3, there are several of these from Google, a search engine that is rapidly becoming the most popular on the World Wide Web. The following searches brought people to the site: "screensaver," "yellow journalism," "Zapruder movie," and "preshrunk Stalinist."

 In regard to "preshrunk Stalinist," referral logs are often filled with so many bizarre, off-color, or vulgar search terms that Web publishers compile lists of the oddest ones on their sites. There's even a Web site devoted to these called Disturbing Search Requests, at http://searchrequests.weblogs.com. (Note: the content of the site, like your own referral log, is likely to contain things that you might consider to be objectionable.)

If your Web analysis software can recognize these links in a referral log, as FrontPage does, a report can be compiled of the most popular search terms used to find your site.

## Track Problems with Error Logs

Listing 16.4 contains five lines from the last of the log files kept routinely by a server, error_log, in NCSA format.

**LISTING 16.4**   An Example of a Server's error_log

```
[Sun Apr  1 01:01:52 2003] [error] [client 38.144.151.137] File does not
➥exist: /usr/local/etc/httpd/cadenhead.org/htdocs/1900/10/110700.shtml
[Sun Apr  1 06:02:24 2003] [info] [client 198.77.58.123] (32)Broken pipe:
➥client stopped connection before rwrite completed
[Sun Apr  1 06:02:24 2003] [info] [client 198.77.58.123] (32)Broken pipe:
➥client stopped connection before rwrite completed
[Sun Apr  1 07:52:30 2003] [info] [client 63.44.198.51] (32)Broken pipe:
➥client stopped connection before send body completed
[Sun Apr  1 17:56:53 2003] [error] [client 63.251.248.45] File does not
➥exist: /usr/local/etc/httpd/cadenhead.org/htdocs/1900/10/110700.shtml
```

Each item in this log file contains the following information, from left to right:

- The date and time it took place
- A status term indicating whether it was an error or some other kind of unusual event
- The Internet address that requested the file involved in the error
- A message describing the error

The most common errors in the log are "File does not exist" messages and interrupted connections between the Web server and the machine requesting a file.

FrontPage does not include error log analysis in its usage data reports. Consult your Web hosting service to see whether it offers its own reports—these usually include a summary of the error messages that appear most frequently in your logs.

# View the Usage Reports for Your Site

An example of FrontPage's Usage summary report for a Web site is shown in Figure 16.1.

**FIGURE 16.1**

*Viewing reports for a site.*

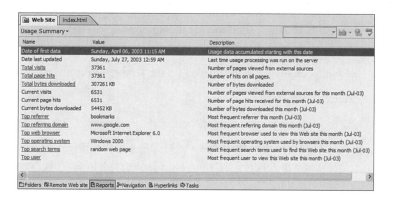

Before you can make use of FrontPage usage reports, you must publish your site on a server equipped with server extensions or SharePoint and wait until your host has processed the server logs.

To see the usage data for a site you have published, you must open it in an unusual way. Instead of opening the folder on your computer that contains a copy of the site, you must open it directly from the Web server.

FrontPage usage reports are organized into the following subjects:

- **Page hits and visits**—The number of times each page is requested
- **Operating systems**—The number of visits received from people on Windows, Macintosh, Linux, and other systems
- **Browsers**—The software used to request pages and navigate your site
- **Referring domains and URLs**—The Web pages that contain links used to visit your site
- **Search strings**—The text used in search engines to find your site
- **Users**—The signed-in users visiting your site (useful only if your site requires a username and password for each visitor)

The visit and page hit reports are two attempts to determine how popular your site is. A *hit* is a request to the Web server for a file contained in your site. If someone requests a page containing 13 graphics files, 14 hits are counted. The visit count disregards requests for image files contained on a page, ignoring requests for graphics files presented as part of a page.

The other reports use other data stored in server logs, tracking pages that refer to files in your site, browsers used to visit it, and operating systems that can be determined from the browser identification.

When your site has been opened on the server, you can view its usage reports.

Here's how:

1. Connect to the Internet.
2. Choose **File**, **Open Site**. The Open Site dialog box appears.
3. Enter the address of your site's home page in the **Site Name** field and click **Open**. (You may be asked for the username and password you use when publishing the site.)

FrontPage opens the site for editing directly on the Web server. While you're working in this way, you will have access to some FrontPage features that are not available when you're editing the copy of the site that is stored on your computer.

One of these server-only features is usage reports.

To find out about how your site is being used, follow these steps:

1. With the site open for editing, click the **Reports** button below the editing window. FrontPage switches to Reports view and displays the Site Summary, which contains more than a dozen reports about your site, as shown in Figure 16.2.

**FIGURE 16.2**

*Viewing reports for a site.*

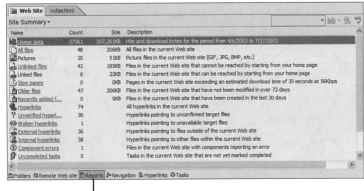

Reports button

**16**

2. Click the **Usage Data** hyperlink. The Usage Summary opens, displaying a collection of information and linked reports about how people are accessing your site.

   A few reports in the Usage Summary contain a single line of information, such as the number of visits during the current month. Others include a link to a more detailed report, such as Total Visits and Top Referrer Links.

3. To see a detailed report, click its hyperlink. Each report is displayed as a table of data. To see a pie chart, a bar graph, or another visual report, click the arrow next to the **Chart** button and choose a chart type from the pop-up menu that appears (see Figure 16.3).

**FIGURE 16.3**

*A graphical Web usage report.*

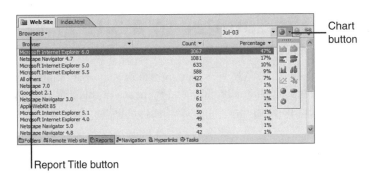

Chart button

Report Title button

4. After you are done viewing a report, click the button next to the report title to open a drop-down menu and select another report to view.

5. To view the main Usage Summary, choose **View**, **Reports**, **Usage**, **Usage Summary**.

One of the most important reports for many site developers is the Total Bytes Downloaded report—a "traffic report" that approximates how much demand your site puts on the server that hosts it.

Many Web hosting services put a cap on the amount of data users can request from a site in any month. A typical limit is 3GB (3 million bytes).

When you reach this limit, some hosting services shut off your site and stop responding to requests for your files until the next month.

Others charge an additional fee based on how much extra traffic you attract. Some publishers don't know about this policy until they see an unexpected charge of $100 or more on the credit card they use to pay for hosting.

Occasionally, these fees can be even more expensive—recently, the computer book author Glenn Fleischman offered one of his books for free as an e-book on his Web site. After thousands of people downloaded the book in a few days, he could have been responsible for up to $15,000 in extra traffic costs (fortunately, he was not billed for the usage).

 Unless you are publishing a large site with an audience numbering in hundreds of people each day, you are unlikely to reach a host's traffic limit. On a 1,000-page site that I publish, my files were requested 589,000 times in one month and still amounted to only 3.2GB of downloaded data.

## Add a Hit Counter to a Site

Hit counters are another way FrontPage supports tracking of your site's popularity.

A *hit counter* is a Web page element that displays the number of times the page has been viewed. It's an extremely rudimentary means of tracking site popularity; if someone loads your page 10 times in a row, the counter increases by 10.

Often counters are implemented by putting a graphic on your Web page using HTML, the formatting language of Web pages.

If your site is hosted on a server equipped with server extensions or SharePoint, you can add a hit counter easily using a Web component.

To add a hit counter to a Web page, follow these steps:

1. Open the page for editing and click a spot where the counter should be inserted.
2. Choose **Insert**, **Web Component**. The Insert Web Component dialog box opens.
3. In the Component type list box, select **Hit Counter**. A Choose a Counter Style list box is displayed, showing several styles for the counter (see Figure 16.4).

**16**

**FIGURE 16.4**

*Adding a hit counter to a page.*

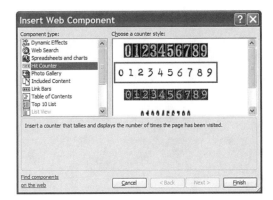

4. Select one of the styles and click the **Finish** button. The Hit Counter properties dialog box opens.
5. To control the number of digits displayed on the counter, select the **Fixed Number of Digits** check box and type a number from 1 to 10 in the adjacent text field.
6. Click **OK**.

That's it; the counter is displayed on the page with a dummy value. To see it in action, publish the page, open it with your Web browser, and click the browser's Refresh button a few times.

# Share Usage Reports with Your Visitors

If you'd like to share some of your site's usage information with your visitors, you can use a Top 10 List Web component (provided that your Web server supports server extensions or SharePoint).

Your site can display seven different top 10 lists with the top results for the current month: Visited Pages, Referring Domains, Referring URLs, Search Strings, Visiting Users, Operating Systems, and Browsers.

To add one to a page, follow these steps:

1. With the page open for editing, click the spot where it should be added and then choose **Insert**, **Web Component**. The Insert Web Component dialog box appears.

2. In the Component Type list box, select **Top 10 List**. In the adjacent list box, seven usage reports are listed: Visited Pages, Referring Domains, Referring URLs, Search Strings, Visiting Users, Operating Systems, and Browsers.

3. Choose the report you'd like to display on a page, and then click **Finish**.

   The Top 10 List Properties dialog box opens, as shown in Figure 16.5.

**FIGURE 16.5**

*Displaying usage reports on a Web page.*

4. Type a title for the list in the **Title Text** field.

5. To include a date also, select the check box **Include Date Usage Processing Was Last Run**. The list can be displayed as a table, a numbered list, a bulleted list, or text.

6. Select the desired appearance by clicking an icon in the **List Style** panel, and then click **OK**.

A placeholder for the top 10 list is added to the page. Publish it to your Web server to see it with real usage data.

## Summary

Because you are publishing your first sites with FrontPage, the software's Usage data report might not seem useful or particularly important.

By the time your sites show up in search engines and attract a following, you'll probably be consulting your usage reports on a regular basis.

Checking these reports enables you to learn which parts of your site are most popular, what people are saying about your site on other sites, and how your site is being found by people using Yahoo!, AltaVista, Google, and other search engines and directories.

# Q&A

**16**

**Q** **When I use the Top Referrers report, some of the pages that show up don't contain any links to my site, and the content of those pages makes me doubt they ever did. What causes this to happen?**

**A** The most likely cause is a Web browser that transmits inaccurate referral information to your Web server. A browser is supposed to log a referral only when someone uses a hyperlink to reach your site. If a user visits your site by typing its address in the browser's Address bar, no referral should be reported.

Some Web browsers transmit this information anyway, revealing the last page someone visited before they came to your site. As a result, you'll see some odd things in the Top Referrers report from time to time, such as the main page of popular sites like Yahoo!, CNN.com, and Hotmail.

A good rule of thumb is to ignore any referral that shows up fewer than five times in a month.

**Q** **My server's logs don't look anything like the ones listed in this hour. Why are they different?**

**A** Each Web server saves log files differently. The ones displayed in this hour use Common Log Format (CLF), the most popular format for logging Web server activities. The Apache Web server, currently the most popular on the Web, uses this format.

Microsoft Internet Information Server, which is frequently used by companies that offer FrontPage hosting, keeps logs in its own format. Most of the same information is contained in these logs—file requests, referrals, and user agents—although there's no error log kept by the server.

**Q** **Isn't referer_log misspelled?**

**A** It is. The creators of the Hypertext Transfer Protocol, the standard used by Web browsers and Web servers to exchange information with each other, spelled it as *referer* instead of *referrer* in the document that told programmers how to use the protocol. When HTTP quickly became part of hundreds of software programs used by millions of people, there was no way to remove the incorrect spelling, much to the bane of technical writers, copy editors, and grammarians everywhere.

# PART V

# Enhancing Your Site

## Hour

17   Add a Search Engine to Your Site

18   Turn Your Site into a Community

19   Connect a Database to Your Site

20   Use Your Site to Gather Information

# Hour **17**

# Add a Search Engine to Your Site

FrontPage 2003 has several different features that make your Web sites easier to use.

If your site has been organized in Navigation view and makes use of link bars, most visitors should be able to quickly find what they're looking for.

For the times when a user can't find something, it's helpful to offer a search engine that can look through all pages in a site for specific text. FrontPage offers a personal search engine that functions like Google and AltaVista, two popular Web sites that scour millions of Web pages for specific text, hyperlinks, and other content.

In this hour, you will learn

- How to add a search form component to your FrontPage site
- How to choose the parts of a site that will be searched
- How to keep the search form's index up-to-date

The search form component is a text search engine that requires a Web server equipped with FrontPage Server Extensions or SharePoint services.

# Make Your Web Site Searchable

FrontPage's search form component requires server extensions or SharePoint, so you'll need a Web-hosting service that supports them to use this feature.

The easiest way to add a search engine to your Web site is with the Search Page template, one of the standard templates that you can choose when adding a new Web page. This template adds a search page containing a search form component with Start Search and Reset buttons and text describing how searches are conducted.

Figure 17.1 shows how the search form looks on a Web page. As you'll see, the drab appearance of the form can be changed.

FIGURE **17.1**

*Searching a FrontPage Web site.*

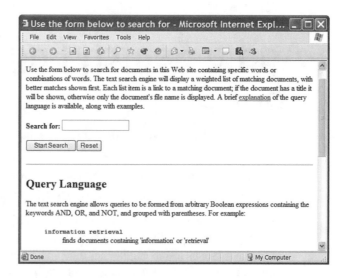

To add a search engine to a FrontPage Web site, follow these steps:

1. Choose **File, New**.

   The New pane opens to the right of the FrontPage editing window.

2. Click the **More Page Templates** hyperlink.

   The Page Templates dialog box is displayed, listing templates on which your new page can be based.

3. Choose the **Search Page** icon and click **OK**.

   A new page opens in the editing window that contains a search form component and text that explains how to use it.

The search page takes its colors and text appearance from the site's theme. However, it will look plain compared to the rest of your site—lacking page graphics, link bars, and other things that give it personality.

To better incorporate search functionality into your Web site, you can duplicate the contents of this page on one that better resembles the rest of your site.

Here's how:

1. With the search page open for editing, click anywhere on the page and press **Ctrl+A**.

   The entire page is selected for copying.

2. Press **Ctrl+C** to copy the page's contents to the Clipboard.

3. Choose **File, New**.

   The New pane opens alongside the editing window.

4. Click the **From Existing Page** hyperlink.

   The New from Existing Page dialog box opens, listing the pages and folders in your site (as shown in Figure 17.2).

**FIGURE 17.2**

*Creating a new page based on an existing page.*

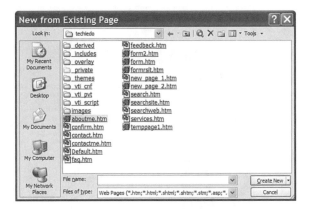

5. Click the page that you want the new search page to look like.

   A new page opens for editing that's a copy of the original.

6. Drag your mouse over the text that should be replaced with the contents of the search page.

7. Press **Ctrl+V** to paste the search page from the Clipboard.

If you change the text provided on the Search Page template, you should keep or rewrite the documentation that explains how to conduct a search. Every search engine on the

World Wide Web has its own rules for how to find things, so visitors to your FrontPage Web site might need some guidance on how to compose a search query.

The search page includes a comment at the top of the page that explains what the page does. At any time, you can delete this comment by clicking any of the text in the comment once and then pressing the `Delete` key. Comments, which appear in a different color than the other text on a page, are invisible to your visitors—they are displayed only when the page is being edited in FrontPage.

## Customize How Results Are Displayed

After you have created the search page, you can publish your site and begin using it immediately.

After a search is requested, the search form component creates a results page. Search results are displayed on a page that's very similar to the search page. It has the same theme, graphics, and layout; a search form component; and a table of results.

Figure 17.3 shows how the results of a search are displayed on a Web page.

**FIGURE 17.3**

*Viewing the results of a Web search.*

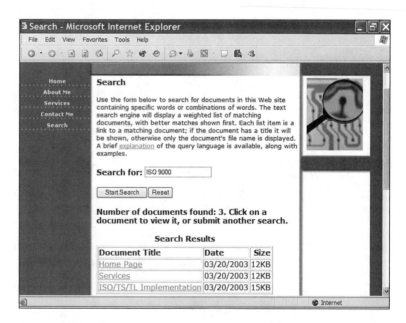

Searches are ranked in order of their "score," a number that represents how often the search term is found on a page. The higher the number is, the more likely it is that the result matches what you were searching for.

When a FrontPage Web site contains a search component, a special file is created that contains a text index of the words used on each page in your site. With the exception of 300 common words such as *a*, *an*, and *the*, this index contains all words that appear within your pages.

You can customize how a search is performed by modifying the search form component. This component is the portion of the page located within a dotted line (just like any other form in FrontPage). It includes a Search For text box and two buttons: Start Search and Reset.

Although this component looks like any other form, you can't add or remove buttons, move buttons around, or do anything else that's possible when you're working with forms.

Instead, it's edited like the Web components described in Hour 12, "Use Web Components to Jazz Up a Site."

To edit the search form component, follow these steps:

1. Open the search page for editing and double-click inside the component's dotted lines.

   The Search Form Properties dialog box opens with the Search Form Properties tab on top. You can use this to change the text of the buttons and the Search For label.

2. Click the Search Results tab to bring it to the front, as shown in Figure 17.4.

**FIGURE 17.4**

*Use the Search Form Properties dialog box to change how search results are reported.*

The Search Results tab is used to format the search results page and customize how a search is performed. You can pick the information that is displayed about each page that comes up in a search—the size of the page, the date and time it was last updated, and the page's score.

**17**

3. In the Display Options section, select the boxes for anything that you want to display along with search results.

## Limit the Pages That Are Searched

When you add a search form component to a site, it is set up to look for the matching text in every document in the site, with one exception—files in the _private folder are ignored.

You also can set up the component to limit a search to a specific folder in your site.

To do this, follow these steps:

1. Double-click the search form component. The Search Form Properties dialog box appears.
2. Click the **Search Results** tab to bring it to the front.
3. In the **Word List to Search** text field, enter the name of the folder that should be searched (or leave it as All to look through the entire site).
4. Click **OK**.

FrontPage rebuilds the word index used by the search form component to find and display results.

Whenever you modify a search form component, you should choose Tools, Recalculate Hyperlinks so that the word index is rebuilt.

As described in the last hour, "Learn More About Your Site's Audience," this tool checks all the hyperlinks in your site for validity and handles other housekeeping tasks. One of these is the re-creation of the searchable word index. Every noncommon word that shows up on a page shows up in the index.

This process can take five minutes or longer, depending on how many hyperlinks on your pages link to sites on the World Wide Web.

## Add a Search Form to an Existing Web Page

If you're publishing a large Web site, you can offer several targeted searches by placing more than one search form component on the same page.

To add a search form component to an existing Web page, follow these steps:

1. Open the page for editing and click the spot where the component should be placed.

2. Choose **Insert, Web Component** to open the Insert Web Component dialog box.

3. In the Component type list, choose **Web Search**.

   The pane to the right changes to display the kinds of searches that can be added.

4. Choose **Current Web** and click **Finish**.

   The Search Form Properties dialog box opens. Use this dialog box to configure the appearance of the search form and the search results page, and specify whether to search all of the site or just a specified folder.

5. When you're done, click **OK**.

   A search form then is added to the page. Unlike the search page, it does not contain any text explaining how to use the form.

A search form component added in this manner can be customized at any time, just like the one included in the search page template. To tinker with it, double-click the component.

# Add an MSN Search

The search form component looks at only the pages and other documents on your Web site. Another service that you can offer to visitors is a way to search the entire World Wide Web using MSN—Microsoft's Web portal.

FrontPage includes an MSN Search Web component that can be added to a page in a few minutes. Figure 17.5 shows an example of how it looks.

**FIGURE 17.5**

*Adding MSN Search capabilities to a Web site.*

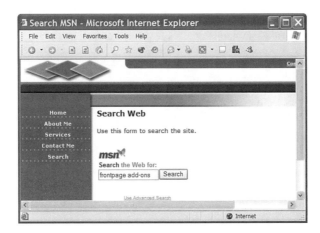

When the Search button is clicked, a page on MSN is opened displaying matching results.

To add an MSN Search component, follow these steps:

1. Open the page that will contain the MSN Search component (or create a new one).

2. Click the spot where the component should be placed.

3. Choose **Insert, Web Component**.

   The Insert Web Component dialog box opens.

4. In the Component type list box, scroll down and choose **MSN Components**.

   The pane to the right of the box displays a list of MSN features that can be added to your FrontPage sites.

5. Choose **Search the Web with MSN** and click **Finish**.

An MSN Search form is added to the page.

> Although the MSN Search component is a nice addition to a site, the most popular search engine by far these days is Google. You'll learn how to add Google searching to your site in Hour 21, "Create and Edit Pages Using HTML."

## Add a Site Map

A recurring theme in this hour has been the need to help visitors find what they're looking for on your site. Another way to provide some assistance is to create a site map, a table of contents that links to every page that your site offers. An example is shown in Figure 17.6.

This might seem like overkill, but when you consider the alternative—visitors give up and look for it on someone else's site—it's better to be thorough.

Besides, the FrontPage Table of Contents component can create a site map from the same navigational structure used on your link bars.

To create a site map, follow these steps:

1. Open the page that will contain the site map and click your cursor at the spot the map should be placed.

2. Choose **Insert, Web Component**.

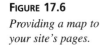

**Figure 17.6**

*Providing a map to your site's pages.*

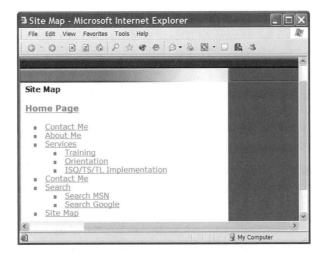

**17**

3. In the Component type list box, choose **Table of Contents**.

4. In the Choose a Table of Contents pane, choose **For This Web Site** and click **Finish**.

   The Table of Contents Properties dialog box appears, as seen in Figure 17.7.

**Figure 17.7**

*Creating a site map.*

In this dialog box, Page URL for Starting Point of Table identifies the home page for the site map. By default, this is the site's home page, which makes sense. To choose a different page click **Browse**. The Current Web Site dialog box opens. Select the home page for the map and click **OK**.

5. Choose the display options that you want using the Options check boxes.

The Recompute Table of Contents check box makes sure that pages aren't left out when you work on the site later. This gives FrontPage more to do and might slow its performance a bit, but it's unlikely to be a problem (unless you're already having trouble running FrontPage on your computer because of processor speed or memory issues).

6. Click **OK**.

A "dummy" version of the site map is displayed on the page in the editing window. To see the real thing, click the Preview button below the page, or preview the site in a Web browser.

To make changes to the site map, open the page for editing and double-click it. The Table of Contents Properties dialog box opens.

The site map has the added advantage of making your site easier to index in Google and other popular search engines. Make sure there's a prominent link to the map on your site's home page, which Web-crawling software that is run by the search engines will quickly find and scan for hyperlinks to visit.

# Summary

Any FrontPage Web site of more than a dozen pages can benefit from a search engine. Even if you create a well-designed site, some visitors will be unable to find what they want and will look for a Search button on your Web's link bar.

In this hour, you learned how to create a search engine that's specific to your Web site. This is one features that makes it worthwhile to seek out a hosting service that offers FrontPage Server Extensions.

You also learned how to offer a site map and an MSN Search page, two FrontPage Web components that take a few minutes to create and benefit your visitors.

# Q&A

**Q  A book I have on FrontPage 2002 suggests that keywords can be added to Web pages to make them easier to find in a search. How can I do this?**

A  It's relatively easy to add keywords to a page using a hidden `keywords` meta tag. However, because this feature has been abused by unethical Web publishers, most search engines ignore them (including Google and Altavista). Inktomi is the last large search portal to support them, and it contributes only a small amount of traffic to most sites, so it isn't usually worth the effort.

To add keywords to a page, right-click an empty area of the page and click Page Properties from the context menu. On the Page Properties dialog box that appears, choose the Custom tab to bring it to the front.

Two different Add buttons are shown—one for system variables and another below it for user variables. Click the User Variables Add button. The User Meta Variable dialog box opens.

In the Name text box, enter the text keywords.

In the Value text box, enter a list of keywords that describe the page (or site), separated by commas. Here's an example:

```
drill, driller, drilling, contractor, contract, TSS, Texas,
Oklahoma, New Mexico, Louisiana, Arkansas, Dallas, Austin,
OSHA, OSHA certified, OSHA medical monitored, level D PPE,
level B safety, CME 55 ATV track rig, CME 55 ATV, Mobil B 59,
B 59, Mobil B 57, B 57, Mobil B 53, B 53, Simco Earthprobe 200,
Hilti core drill, Stow slicer, Ford Super Duty support,
Ford Super Duty truck, 3500 PSI steam cleaning unit,
down hole tool, down hole tooling decontamination, cleanup,
clean, removal, environmental drilling, geotechnical drilling,
direct-push sampling, ORC injection, inject ORC, remediation,
Bombadier track unit, safe, high quality, reliable
```

The keywords in this list describe an environmental cleanup company and the services and equipment it offers. Because the feature is falling into disuse, a better way to promote a site for search engine users is to use descriptive words and phrases often in page titles, hyperlinks, and on the pages themselves.

**Q  Is there a way to change the text that appears when my page shows up in a search engine?**

A  There is—add a hidden `description` meta tag to each page in a manner similar to adding the `keywords` tag. Right-click a page, choose Page Properties, and click the Custom tab to bring it to the front. Then add a user variable named `description` with a value of 100 words or less explaining what's on the page in sentence form (rather than a bunch of keywords that identify its topics). Here's an example:

```
An environmental, geotechnical, and direct-push drilling contractor
licensed in Texas, Oklahoma, New Mexico, Louisiana, and Arkansas.
```

**17**

Some Web publishers use a page's main heading and the first few sentences that appear on it for the description. If you use description, it's important to make a different one for each page of your Web site. Some search engines conclude that pages with the same title and the same descriptive summary are duplicates of each other, and list only one of them in its database.

# HOUR 18

# Turn Your Site into a Community

Keeping a Web site from getting stale is a challenge. After you've designed and published the site, you're not done. Adding new content that keeps visitors coming back takes continued effort.

Sometimes the best solution is to let your visitors do the work.

Thousands of successful sites on the World Wide Web offer discussion groups where visitors can read and write public articles to each other. Some sites offer nothing *but* this service. These groups, which are comparable to mailing lists, Usenet newsgroups, and Web guestbooks, are a great way to keep people coming back to your site.

If you're using a Web server that has FrontPage Server Extensions, you can add a discussion group to a site and create discussion-centered sites.

In this hour, you will learn

- How to create a discussion Web site
- How to add a discussion group to an existing site
- How to set up a membership policy
- How to select a format for articles posted by members
- How to delete old (or inappropriate) articles

# Create a Discussion Site with a Wizard

Using FrontPage 2003, discussion groups are implemented with the Discussion Web Wizard, one of the built-in wizards you can choose when creating a new site.

The wizard creates a discussion group where visitors can read articles and post their own replies, which immediately are published on the Web site.

An example is shown in Figure 18.1.

**FIGURE 18.1**

*Viewing a discussion group created with FrontPage.*

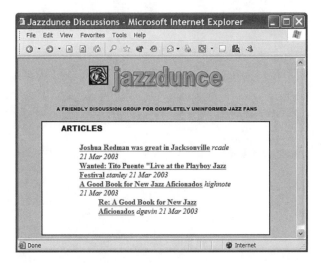

Articles in the discussion can be threaded so that each article and all of its replies are grouped together. This makes it easier for participants to read about the topics they're interested in.

They also can be nonthreaded, causing articles to be listed in order of the date and time they were written.

A discussion group can be added to an existing Web site or created as a new site of its own.

To create a discussion group, follow these steps:

1. If you are adding it to an existing Web site, open the site for editing.
2. Choose **File, New**. The New pane opens next to the editing window.
3. In the pane, click the **More Web Site Templates** hyperlink.

    The Web Site Templates dialog box appears (see Figure 18.2).

FIGURE **18.2**

*Creating a new discussion group.*

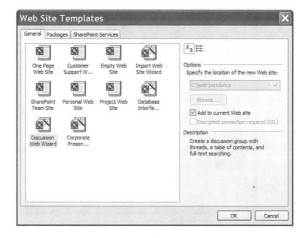

FIGURE **18.2**

*Creating a new discussion group.*

4. Choose one of these options:

   • If you are adding the discussion to an existing site, select the **Add to Current Web Site** check box.

   • If it's a new site, click the **Browse** button and choose a folder (preferably empty) where the site should be stored. (As an alternative, you can type a folder's location in the **Specify the Location** text box.)

5. Select the **Discussion Web Wizard** icon and click **OK**. The Discussion Web Wizard opens. Like other FrontPage wizards, it asks a series of questions that determine how the discussion group will be created.

6. Click **Next** to begin the wizard.

The options offered by the wizard are described in the next several sections.

## Choose the Pages to Include

The Discussion Web Wizard asks a series of questions about how you want the discussion group to be structured. The first thing you must decide is which features to offer, as shown in Figure 18.3.

A discussion group must have a submission form so that visitors can post articles. You also can include the following features:

   • **Table of contents**—A page, which can be the home page of a discussion site, that links to articles that have been written.

   • **Search form**—A search form component that can be used to look through the articles for specific text.

18

FIGURE 18.3

*Picking your discussion group's pages.*

- **Threaded replies**—The grouping of related articles together. If one visitor posts an article and other people reply to it, they are listed in the same thread.

- **Confirmation page**—A page indicating that an article has been posted.

Most of these features are standard for discussion groups on the World Wide Web. The search form component, which was discussed in the previous hour, requires FrontPage Server Extensions.

Check the boxes of the features that you want to enable for your discussion group and click Next.

## Pick a Name and Folder

After you choose the features that your discussion will include, you must decide what to call your discussion group and where its articles should be stored, as seen in Figure 18.4.

FIGURE 18.4

*Choosing a folder and name for the group.*

The name will appear atop most pages and articles on discussion group pages, so it should be reasonably short, such as "Current Events," "Recipe Exchange," or "FrontPage 2003 Tips."

The folder name determines where articles are placed in the Web site. The Discussion Web Wizard recommends a name that begins with an underscore character (_) because it causes discussion articles to be ignored by a site's search form component.

By excluding articles from an overall site search, you prevent the pages you have created from being overlooked among dozens of discussion articles.

With the exception of the _private folder, all folder names that begin with an underscore are hidden when you work on a Web site in FrontPage. Hidden folders exist in the site but are not listed when you display the Folders view or click View, Folder List.

If you choose to begin your discussion group's folder name with an underscore, you'll need a search form as part of the discussion site to make it searchable. As you learned in the previous hour, a search page can be created quickly from a template. (If you change your mind about your choice of a folder, click Back, change your answer, and then click Next to come back to this question.)

18

To see a Web site's hidden folders, choose Tools, Site Settings, then click the Advanced tab, and then check the box next to Show Hidden Files and Folders. You'll see all folders you created that begin with the _ character, along with several other hidden folders created by FrontPage to manage your site.

To continue with this step of the wizard, do the following:

1. Type the discussion group's name in the **Enter a Descriptive Title for This Discussion** text field. Type a folder name in the **Enter the Name for the Discussion Folder** field.

2. When you're done, click **Next**.

## Select a Format for Articles

Next, the wizard asks which text boxes should appear on the discussion's submission form (see Figure 18.5).

FIGURE 18.5

*Choosing the information contained in each article.*

Your answer to this question determines how many things you'll be asking visitors to provide in each article that they post. You can select one of the following configurations:

- Article subject and comments
- Article subject, category name, and comments
- Article subject, product, and comments

If you choose to include a category name or product in articles, a list box will be provided where visitors can provide this information by selecting from a list of possible responses. (You'll set this up later after the wizard has created the discussion group.)

Choose one of the options and click Next.

## Establish a Membership Policy

The Discussion Web Wizard next asks for the membership policy of your discussion group, as seen in Figure 18.6.

FIGURE 18.6

*Setting up a discussion group for public or restricted access.*

You can make your group available to all people who visit your Web site or limit it to members only—people who have registered for a username and password.

The second option takes more time up front because you'll be receiving requests to set up accounts.

> Requiring a username and password also reduces the amount of participation in the discussion group—many Web-based discussion sites don't require registration before someone can post an article.

Making your discussion group open to all participants requires more maintenance. You'll be checking the group more often to remove articles that aren't consistent with your editorial goals for the Web site, and there also might be articles that contain illegal or objectionable material.

Choose either Yes or No on the membership policy question and click Next to go on.

## Offer a Table of Contents

If you have opted to include a table of contents in the discussion group, the wizard asks whether to present articles in oldest-to-newest order or vice versa.

If the oldest messages appear on top, your visitors will need to scroll to the bottom of the table of contents page to see new articles.

Although this is the default setting, it's often more convenient to present the newest articles first.

Choose an option and click Next.

If you are creating a discussion site rather than adding one to an existing site, the wizard asks whether the table of contents should be the home page of the site.

Click Yes to save the table of contents page as `index.htm`, overwriting the site's existing home page if one exists.

Click No to save the page under a different name.

After choosing an option, click Next.

## Set Up Search Results

When a discussion group includes a search form, the wizard asks for the information to present in search results, as shown in Figure 18.7.

FIGURE **18.7**
*Set up search results*
*for a discussion group.*

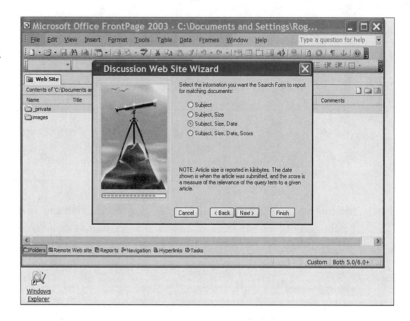

When a search is conducted, four things can be presented about each page that contains the search term:

- The subject of the article
- The size of the article's Web page
- The date and time the article was posted
- A numeric score that reflects how well the article matches the search term

Choose one of the four options and click Next.

## Choose a Layout

The final question asked by the wizard is the desired layout for the discussion group, as shown in Figure 18.8.

You can present the discussion using frames, no frames, or a "dual interface" combination that supports both.

Frames divide a browser window into smaller sections that each holds its own Web page. You learn how to create your own frames in Hour 24, "Divide a Page into Separate Frames."

FIGURE **18.8**

*Choosing a design for the discussion group.*

In a discussion group, the no-frames option places the list of articles and the articles on separate pages. Participants must jump back and forth between these pages as they read and write articles.

The two frames-only options show the list of articles in one section of the Web browser and an article in another section.

Using frames for a discussion Web site makes it easier to read articles at the expense of some browser room. The area devoted to each article will be half as large as it would be on a no-frames Web site, forcing readers to scroll more often. A frame-based FrontPage discussion Web site is shown in Figure 18.9.

18

FIGURE **18.9**

*Presenting a discussion group within two frames.*

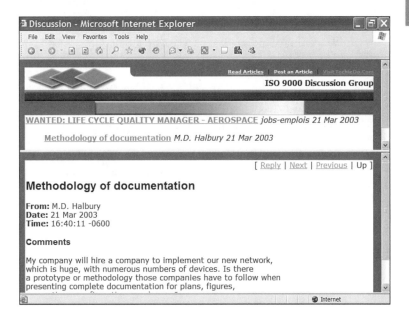

A frames-only Web site can't be viewed on text-based Web browsers or extremely old browsers, such as version 1 of Netscape Navigator or versions 1 and 2 of Internet Explorer.

Although most of your visitors are likely to be capable of using frames, you can serve everyone by offering frames and a no-frames alternative.

The dual interface option offers the no-frames discussion group to people whose browsers don't support them and one of the frames options to everyone else.

Choose one of the site design options and click Next. The Discussion Web Wizard presents a summary of your answers—use Back to go back and change an answer, if needed, or Finish if you're ready to create the discussion group.

## Complete the Discussion Site

After you click Finish, Web pages are added to a Web site for reading, posting, and listing articles.

These pages are named according to the title of the discussion Web site and the purpose of the page. For example, if you're creating a Web site called frontpage that supports searching, a table of contents, and article confirmation, the following pages would be added:

- **frontpage_cfrm**—The confirmation page, sent after an article is submitted
- **frontpage_frm**—The main frame of a frame-based discussion Web site
- **frontpage_post**—The page where articles are posted
- **frontpage_srch**—The page for searching articles
- **frontpage_tocf**—The table of contents page, listing all articles

If the table of contents had been chosen as a site's home page, it would be named index.htm instead of frontpage_tocf.

You can edit the text on each of the discussion Web site's pages, adding graphics, using themes, and aligning the FrontPage components for posting, listing, and searching discussion articles.

A discussion Web site can be created and edited on your computer, but you can't post or read articles until they has been published on a Web server that supports FrontPage Server Extensions.

# Maintain a Discussion Site

Your work is not over when a discussion Web site has been published and tested. After users start posting articles to your discussion group, you might want to monitor articles and delete any that contain inappropriate content (depending, of course, on your own definition of what's appropriate).

To review articles posted in your discussion, open your Web site on the server that hosts it (not the copy of your site that's on your own computer): Choose File, Open Site; type the site's Web address in the Site Name field; and then click Open. The site opens in Folders view.

Articles are stored as individual pages in the folder named after your Web site. If you named the discussion jaguars, articles will be in a jaguars folder. If the name is _security, articles will be in a folder called _security.

When your discussion group's article folder is visible, you can open each article page for editing. To delete an article, follow these steps:

1. Right-click the article in the Folders view.
2. Choose **Delete** from the context menu that appears.

FrontPage discussions do not have a feature that automatically deletes old articles after a specific period of time. The only way to remove old articles is to do it yourself.

18

# Summary

In this hour, you learned how to encourage visitors to create their own content on your Web site.

The Discussion Web Wizard makes it easy to create a place for articles to be read, posted, and searched. The real work comes afterward, when visitors start using the discussion group.

Inviting discussion is an effective way to attract visitors to a Web site, but it often requires maintenance work to delete inappropriate content and keep the list of articles from getting too large.

Discussions on World Wide Web sites tend to build their own momentum—the more people participate, the more likely it is that other people will find the place.

Hosting an area for Web-based discussion will give you a close look at the World Wide Web's capability to foster community. As you manage the discussions that take place and the inevitable controversies that will occur in any forum where ideas are freely debated, you might find yourself with a new job title: community leader.

# Q&A

**Q  Whenever I try to publish my discussion Web site, I get an error message stating that FrontPage Server Extensions are not installed. Do I need these on my computer?**

**A**  To use a discussion Web site, you must be on a Web server that is equipped with FrontPage Server Extensions. If you are receiving that error, it normally means that your server does not currently support extensions. You should contact your Web hosting service to see if server extensions are installed and working properly.

# Hour **19**

# Connect a Database to Your Site

FrontPage 2003 is part of Microsoft Office System, the family of products that includes products such as Office, Publisher, InfoPath, and Project. In this hour, you'll get a strong idea of how close-knit this family has become.

Using FrontPage, you can create a Web page that interacts directly with a database. This could be used to take orders from customers, display an address book, present a current events calendar, and the like.

Without leaving FrontPage, you can read and store information in a database or even create a new database. These features are coordinated with Microsoft Access and Microsoft Excel, the database and spreadsheet programs in the Office suite.

In this hour, you will learn

- How to use the Database Results Wizard to choose records from a database
- How to present records on a Web page
- How to create an Access database based on a Web form

These tasks can be conducted entirely within FrontPage, so you can use these features even if you don't own Access or Excel.

# Make Use of Existing Database Files

FrontPage 2003 is closely integrated with the other programs in the Microsoft Office productivity suite. You can easily exchange data among these programs and use some Office features within FrontPage.

If you've never used a database, the terminology might throw you a bit, but a database is simply an extremely well-organized way to structure information in a file.

A *database* is a file that is used to store large amounts of related information together. Each item in a database is called a *record*, and each part of a record is called a *field*. Databases are structured in a way that makes it quick to retrieve records based on any needed criteria.

A *table* in a database is a grouping of records containing the same type of information.

To see this another way, an event calendar database for a music-related Web site could have a table for festivals and another table for performers, as shown in Table 19.1.

**TABLE 19.1**   An Event Database

| Event Database | Festival Table | Record for Jacksonville Jazz Fest |
| --- | --- | --- |
| | | **When field:** 4/11/2003 |
| | | **Where field:** Jacksonville, FL |
| | | **Who field:** Tony Bennett, Joshua Redman, and Boney James headline this three-day event, organized by local NPR affiliate WJCT. |
| | | **Link field:** `http://www.wjct.org/jazz/jazz_fest.html` |
| | | Record for Great Hawaiian Jazz Blowout |
| | | **When field:** 5/3/2003 |
| | | **Where field:** Honolulu, HI |
| | | **Who field:** Local jazz musicians cover the full range of jazz styles, from early American and gospel to blues, Dixieland swing, big band, Latin, world beat, mainstream and contemporary. |
| | | **Link field:** `http://www.honolulujazzscene.net` |

| Performer Table | Record for Joshua Redman |
| --- | --- |
| | Home page field: `http://www.joshuaredman.com` |
| | Birthdate field: 2/1/1969 |
| | Birthplace field: Berkeley, CA |
| | Record for Tony Bennett |
| | Home page field: `http://www.tonybennett.net` |
| | Birthdate field: 8/3/1926 |
| | Birthplace field: Astoria, NY |

The records in each table contain different kinds of fields. The festival table has records with fields that hold a date (WHEN), place (WHERE), hyperlink (LINK), and description (WHO). The performer table has records with fields that contain a hyperlink (HOMEPAGE), date (BIRTHDATE), and place (BIRTHPLACE).

When you have information stored in a database, you can select records to display, modify, or delete (although FrontPage is primarily used to display records).

For example, a Web site displaying an event database could present a page listing all festivals that are taking place during the next three months. Instead of laboriously creating that page by hand on a weekly or monthly basis, records would be retrieved from a database.

Web sites designed with FrontPage can interact directly with database files created in Microsoft Access and Microsoft Excel.

You can use them together in several different ways:

- Create a new Access database to hold the information collected on a Web form
- Display the contents of an Access or Excel database as a Web page
- Search an Access or Excel database from a FrontPage Web site

To make use of a database on a Web site designed with FrontPage, you must be hosting the site on a Web server that is equipped with FrontPage Server Extensions and Active Server Pages (ASP).

Active Server Pages is a scripting language that enables Web pages to contain programming code in addition to HTML formatting. An Active Server Page, which ends with the .asp filename extension instead of .html, contains scripts that are run by a Web server as

19

the page is loaded, producing output that can change constantly. Most e-commerce sites use technology such as this to present products, offer discounts, and take orders.

> Although Active Server Pages is a programming language, don't let that keep you from using databases if you're not a programmer. FrontPage takes care of all the programming behind the scenes, as it does with VBScript, JavaScript, and other expert features of Web design.

The primary way to employ Active Server Pages is to subscribe to a Web hosting service that uses Microsoft Internet Information Server (IIS).

# Add an Existing Database to a Site

With the assistance of server extensions, FrontPage 2003 can display database records on a Web page from any Access or Excel database file. The easiest way to incorporate a database into your site is to import the file and then set up a database connection.

To add an existing database file to your site, follow these steps:

1. Choose **File**, **Import**. The Import dialog box appears.
2. Click the **Add File** button. The Add File to Import List dialog box opens, as shown in Figure 19.1.

**FIGURE 19.1**

*Adding a database file to a Web site.*

3. Find and select the database file and click **Open**. The file is listed in the Import dialog box.

4. Click **OK**. If the database is in one of the formats that FrontPage recognizes (primarily Access or Excel), the Add Database Connection dialog box opens, as shown in Figure 19.2.

**Figure 19.2**

*Creating a connection for a new database.*

To access an imported database in your site, that database must be associated with a database connection. When you retrieve or create records, you refer to this connection instead of the database file's name.

5. Give the database a name that describes its contents in the **Name** field, and then click **Yes**.

If the database is not stored in a folder of your Web site called fpdb, FrontPage asks if the file can be moved to a new folder of that name. Click **Yes** to take the suggestion, which is a good idea.

FrontPage adds the database to the Web site and adds four files that are required for it to function: global.asa (in the site's main folder) and fpdblib.inc, fpdbrgn1.inc, and fpdbrgn2.inc (in a new folder named _fpclass). You don't have to do anything with these files, aside from taking care not to delete them.

19

After importing a database and creating a new database connection, FrontPage opens the _fpclass folder in Folders view. The way to get back to the site's main folder is a bit tough to find: Click the Up One Level button, which is one of the icons in the top-right corner of Folders view, not far below the red X on the FrontPage title bar.

# Display Database Records on a Page

After a database has been imported and a connection has been created for it, you're ready to start displaying records from the database on your Web site.

To accomplish this, database results can be added to a Web page using the Database Results Wizard.

The wizard asks a series of questions about the database that you want to use, the parts of the database to display, and how they should be formatted on a Web page.

Here's how to call on the wizard:

1. Open the Web page that will contain the database results (or create a new one). This page should have the file extension .asp because it uses Active Server Pages. If it doesn't, right-click the file in Folders view, click **Rename** from the context menu that appears, and rename it.

2. Choose **Insert**, **Database**, **Results**. The Database Results Wizard opens (see Figure 19.3). The first step is to choose the database connection associated with the database.

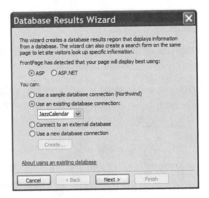

**FIGURE 19.3**

*Choosing a database connection to use.*

The following database connections can be used:

- A connection to a sample database
- An existing connection that has already been associated with a file contained in the current Web site
- A new database connection

3. Because you're working with a database that you have imported into the site, select the **Use an Existing Database Connection** option and, in the list box below it, choose that database's connection. Then click **Next**.

4. The wizard's next screen, which is shown in Figure 19.4, asks for the database records that should be displayed.

**FIGURE 19.4**

*Choosing the table to display.*

Records from the database can be displayed in several ways, depending on how well versed you are in database use:

- To retrieve records from a table or some other source set up in the database, choose the **Record Source** option; then select the source from the list box right below it.

- To retrieve records using Structured Query Language (a programming language used to work with database files), choose the **Custom Query** option and click the **Edit Query** button.

  The Custom Query dialog box opens. (You must be familiar with SQL to make use of this option.)

  In this dialog box, type your SQL programming statement in the SQL Statement field and test it by clicking **Verify Query**. When FrontPage reports that the statement works, click **OK**.

Click **Next** to go on.

5. The next step in using the Database Results Wizard is to choose which record fields to display.

   By default, all fields in a record are shown. To choose which fields to display, click the **Edit List** button. The Displayed Fields dialog box appears, as shown in Figure 19.5.

6. To hide a field, select it in the Displayed Fields list box and click the **Remove** button. Contrary to the name, this doesn't delete the field—it simply hides it when results are displayed on the Web page. (If you change your mind, select it in the Available fields list box and click **Add**.)

**19**

FIGURE **19.5**

*Choosing the record fields to display.*

7. When database records are shown on a page, fields are displayed in the order they are listed in the Displayed Fields list box. To move a field to a different spot in the order, select it and click either the **Move Up** or **Move Down** buttons.

8. Click **OK**. The Displayed Fields dialog box closes, returning you to the wizard's last screen.

9. Displaying database records on a Web page can take too much time if hundreds of records are being shown. One way to guard against this problem is to lower the maximum number of displayed records.

   To take this preventative measure, click the **More Options** button. The More Options dialog box appears.

   In this dialog box, change the **Limit Number of Returned Records** field from 256 to a lower number—32 or 64 is reasonable—and make sure that the adjacent check box is selected. Then click **OK**.

10. Click **Next**. The wizard asks how the records will be displayed on a Web page, as shown in Figure 19.6.

FIGURE **19.6**

*Choosing how to display database records.*

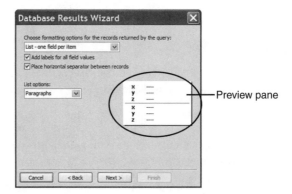

Records can be shown as a table that resembles an Excel spreadsheet, in a list with one record field per line, or in a drop-down list box (this last choice produces a page that's pretty hard-to-read, so keep that in mind).

To see a preview of each format, change the value of the list box **Choose Formatting Options for the Records Returned By the Query**. In a preview pane, the wizard displays a graphic that depicts how records will be displayed.

Then choose a format. The wizard responds by changing the dialog box to add additional options that fine-tune the display. Several dozen different choices are available, so you may want to start with one of these:

- If you're displaying records from an Access database, a good choice is a list customized with the List Options selection of either **Paragraphs** or **Bullet List**.

- If you're displaying an Excel spreadsheet, a good choice is a table customized by selecting the check boxes **Use Table Border** and **Expand Table to Width of Page**.

After selecting and customizing a format, click **Next**.

11. The wizard's last question is whether to display all the records at one time or split them into groups that will be divided over several pages.

    Choose one of the options. If you pick the Split Records into Groups option, in the Records Per Group field, type the number of records to display at one time.

10. Click **Finish**.

That's it (whew!). The Database Results Wizard has run out of questions and is ready to add database results to the page.

As you work on a page that contains database results, a placeholder is displayed in place of the actual results, as shown in Figure 19.7.

This placeholder consists of highlighted text at the top and bottom of a sample record. This sample doesn't contain database information; instead, it shows you the names of each field that will be displayed (surrounded by << and >> characters). For example, the page shown in Figure 19.7 will display each record as a bulleted list of the fields When, What, Where, Who, and Link.

Like other Web components that can be placed on a page, this one can be modified—to make changes to how database results are displayed, double-click the highlighted text. The Database Results Wizard appears again, enabling you to review your answers and make changes to them.

**19**

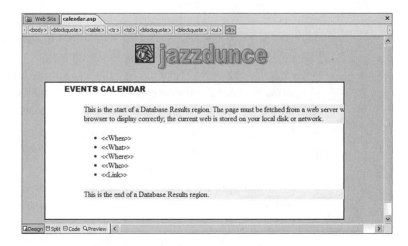

FIGURE 19.7

*Editing a Web page
containing database
results.*

You also can modify the display of records in Design view simply by editing the page.

The way you format the sample record in the placeholder determines how each database record is displayed. Any formatting that can be done to text—alignment, font selection, sizing, and the like—can be applied to the fields in the sample record.

To remove a field, delete its name and the << and >> marks around it.

To add a field, follow these steps:

1. Click your cursor at the spot the field should be displayed. This must be somewhere within the top and bottom highlighted text of the placeholder.

2. Choose **Insert**, **Database**, **Column Value**. The Database Column Value dialog box appears.

3. In the **Column to Display** list box, select the field that should be displayed.

4. Click **OK**.

   The name of that field is added to the page between << and >> marks. When database results are displayed, the contents of that field are shown at that position.

When you have added database results to a Web page and formatted them as desired, you can't see the page until you publish the Web site to your Web server.

Figure 19.8 shows an example page that uses this wizard to display records from a database of music events.

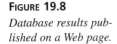

**FIGURE 19.8**

*Database results published on a Web page.*

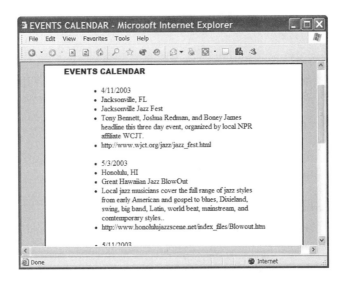

The database used to prepare this example is the same one described in Table 19.1.

After you have created a Web page that displays database results, it will be updated any time you make changes to the database and republish that file to the Web.

# Save Information to a New Database

When you collect information from a form on a Web page, you have several ways to store that data. You can send it to an email address, save it as a Web page, or save it as a text or XML file—options that are all covered in the next hour, "Use Your Site to Gather Information."

Another way to save information collected on a form is to store it in a database. This database doesn't even have to exist; FrontPage can create one based on the things you're asking for on the form.

To create a new database based on a form, follow these steps:

1. Open a form that you created with the Form Page Wizard (or the techniques described in the next hour).

2. If the page containing the form does not have the .asp file extension, rename it: Open the site in Folders view, right-click the page, and choose **Rename**.

3. Right-click an empty area within the form's dotted-line borders and choose **Form Properties** from the context menu that appears. The Form Properties dialog box opens (see Figure 19.9).

19

FIGURE 19.9

*Saving form data to a database.*

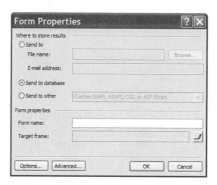

4. Select the **Send to Database** option and click **OK**.

   Because this form has never been associated with a database, FrontPage displays a warning that the form settings are invalid and asks if they should be edited.

5. Click **Yes**. The Options for Saving Results to Database dialog box is displayed. If you had an existing database that was designed to hold the contents of this form, you could use this dialog box to associate that database's connection with the form.

6. Because you're creating a new database based on the form, click the **Create Database** button.

   FrontPage creates a new Access database, storing it in the Web site's fpdb folder. It also creates a connection to that database.

7. Click **OK** to close the dialog box.

The new database will hold the information that's collected from the form. FrontPage will use what's on the form to determine how the Access database should be structured, giving it the same name as the page but replacing the .asp file extension with .mdb. It also gives the connection a similar name. (For example, if you named the page address.asp, the database would be named address.mdb and its connection would be named address.)

After you publish the Web site, you can use the form to add records to the new database. This database file can be loaded with Microsoft Access, or you can use the aforementioned Database Results Wizard to display records from the database on a Web page.

To find and open this database after your visitors have begun to use it, open the Web site directly on the Web server:

1. Choose **File**, **Open Site**. The Open Site dialog box appears.

2. In the **Site Name** field, enter the same address you would use to view your site in a Web browser.

You may be asked for the username and password you use when publishing the site. Provide this information and click **OK**.

The Web site opens in Folders view, where you can find and double-click the database to open it in Microsoft Access.

# Summary

If your Web hosting service supports Active Server Pages and FrontPage Server Extensions, you can create, edit, and display the contents of an Access database or Excel spreadsheet from your FrontPage Webs.

Working directly with a database often makes more sense than offering its contents as text on Web pages. Manually editing text is a time-consuming task, especially if the database is updated frequently. Displaying database results on a Web page offers immediate access to that data.

In Hour 23, "Share Information with XML," you'll learn how to use FrontPage with another popular format for storing data—Extensible Markup Language (XML).

# Q&A

**Q Is there a way to rename a database connection? The default new_page_1 isn't very descriptive of what the connection is used for.**

**A** You can't change the name, but it's relatively easy to create a new database connection to replace it.

When a new Access database is created from a form page, FrontPage 2003 uses the filename of the page to name the connection. Because the filename of a new page is called something like new_page_1.htm when you create it, the connection ends up with a name like new_page_1.

To prevent this from happening, give the page a better name before you use it to create a new database.

19

# HOUR 20

# Use Your Site to Gather Information

Forms gather information from the people who visit a Web site. You can use forms to solicit feedback, conduct surveys, play games, and interact with an audience in ways that aren't possible with other media.

In Hour 9, "Collect Information from Your Visitors," you used the Form Page Wizard, which is well suited to many forms. For the times it isn't, you can create a form manually by designing it on a Web page.

In this hour, you will learn

- How to design a form
- How to collect keyboard input using text boxes
- How to collect other kinds of input with check boxes, option buttons, and drop-down boxes
- How to label parts of a form with text
- How to limit form responses to a range of possible choices

When the form is completed, you'll determine how to use the information it has collected—saving it to a text file, sending it as email, or calling special Web server programs that can decode the form.

You'll also be able to modify existing forms, which is useful even if they were originally created by a wizard.

## Create a Form by Hand

To add a form to a Web page, follow these steps:

1. Open the page for editing in Design mode.

2. Click your mouse at the spot on the page where the form should be placed.

3. Choose **Insert**, **Form**, **Form**. A form is added to the page with two buttons: Submit and Reset. The boundaries of the form are marked by a dotted outline, which will not appear when the page is displayed by a Web browser (see Figure 20.1).

**FIGURE 20.1**

*Editing a newly added form on a page.*

Form boundaries

Every form is added to a page with two built-in elements:

- A Submit button for transmitting the information collected on the form
- A Reset button for clearing all answers on a form and starting over

These two buttons are placed at the bottom of a form, but you can move them anywhere within the form's border.

In my experience, the Reset button is a little-needed feature that has the potential to make some of your visitors very, very unhappy. The button is useful only if a user fills out a form and decides for some reason to start over, which I can't recall doing myself in eight years using the World Wide Web.

There's also a risk associated with the button: If a visitor fills out a form and clicks Reset by mistake, all of the person's responses disappear and can't be brought back. To delete this button from a form, click it in Design mode and press the Delete key.

All information that is collected on a form must come from elements located within its border in Design mode. This border is used only for that purpose—a page can contain more than one form, so these borders make sure an element is associated with the correct form.

If you put a form element on a page outside of a form boundary, a new form is created to hold that element, complete with its own Submit and Reset buttons.

Forms are made up of several different kinds of buttons, boxes, labels, pictures, text areas, and text boxes.

Figure 20.2 shows most of these elements on a Web page.

**FIGURE 20.2**

*Collecting input in several different ways on a form.*

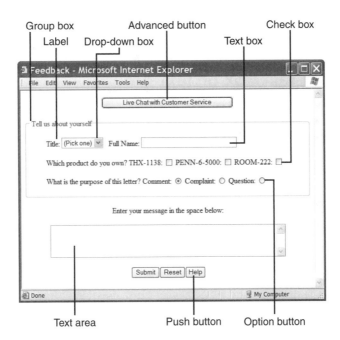

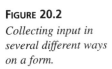

# Add Elements to a Form

Every form element is added by using a command on the Insert, Form menu. To add an element to a form, follow these steps:

1. Open the page for editing.
2. Click the mouse at the spot where the element should appear, which must be within the form's boundaries.
3. Choose **Insert**, **Form** and the element you want to add.

Form elements can be arranged just like anything else on a Web page. You can drag them around, center them, put them into tables, add pictures, and so on. The only rule is that form elements must stay within its border.

You can add more forms to a page by adding a new form or form elements outside of that border.

FrontPage offers a shortcut that's handy if you are working on a form with a lot of elements— a Form toolbar.

To open the Form toolbar, follow these steps:

1. Choose **Insert**, **Form** and then place your mouse over the dotted edge at the top of the menu, above all the commands. The dotted edge turns into a button, and a four-pointed arrow appears in place of your cursor, as shown in Figure 20.3.
2. Drag this edge off the menu to any spot over your page. The Form toolbar opens.

Hover your mouse over each button to see a ScreenTip containing its name.

## Add a Text Box or Text Area

Text boxes and text areas enable your Web site visitors to enter keyboard input on a Web page. A text box can hold a single line of input, so it's convenient for things like a user's name, street address, and ZIP code. A text area can hold an unlimited number of lines, making it useful for longer input, such as a user's comments about your site.

To add a text box to a form, follow these steps:

1. Place your cursor within the form in the editing window, at the spot where the text box should appear.
2. Choose **Insert**, **Form**, **Textbox**. The text box is added to the page.

Click and drag to open the Form toolbar

FIGURE 20.3

*Viewing the Form
toolbar.*

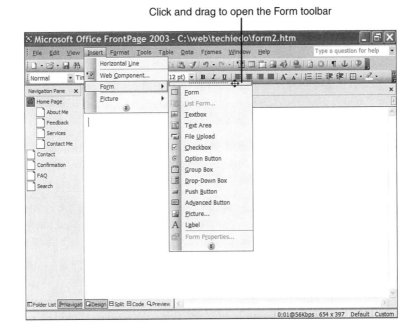

FrontPage gives each box a default name and width (as it does with other form elements).

FrontPage assigns the box a default width that approximates the number of characters that can be displayed in the box. More characters can be entered, but they won't all appear within the box.

To rename the element or make other changes, double-click the element. The Text Box Properties dialog box appears, as shown in Figure 20.4.

FIGURE 20.4

*Editing a text box.*

**20**

Change the name of the element by editing the Name text field. Every form element should be given a descriptive name that explains its purpose. This name will be used when the element's information is stored in a file, saved in a database, or sent to you via email.

The name given to a form element should contain only alphanumeric characters and the underscore character (_). If you use anything else, such as spaces, FrontPage will warn you that the form might not work correctly in a browser.

The Initial Value text field gives the text box a default value. If anything is in this field, it will appear when the form is first loaded by a Web browser or the Reset button is clicked.

If the text box is being used to enter a password, click the Password field option Yes. Asterisks will appear in place of what's really being typed into the field, keeping snoops from seeing the password. The real text will be sent when the form is submitted.

When a single line of text is not enough room for input, a text area can be employed.

To add a textarea to a form, follow these steps:

1. Click within the form at the spot the text area should be placed.
2. Choose **Insert**, **Form**, **Text Area**.

A text area then is added that is 2 lines tall and roughly 20 characters wide. Unlike a text box, a text area can receive more than one line of input from a user.

To change the name, size, and default value of the text area, double-click the element in the editing window. The TextArea Box Properties dialog box appears (see Figure 20.5).

**FIGURE 20.5**

*Editing a text area.*

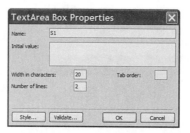

Text areas are edited like text boxes, with one added feature. To change the height of the box, type a new value in the Number of Lines field.

# Add a Label

A *label* is text that describes the purpose of another form element. When form elements are used to collect the answer to a question, a label can ask the question.

To add a label to a form, follow these steps:

1. Add the element that will be labeled (such as a text box or text area).

2. To the right or left of that element, type the text that should be used as a label.

3. Select both the text and the form element, either by dragging your mouse over them or by holding down the Shift key as you press the right arrow or left arrow keys. The elements appear highlighted.

4. Choose **Insert**, **Form**, **Label**. A border appears around the text to indicate that it's now a label.

Turning text into a label makes it easier for people to use a form. In many cases, they can click the label in addition to the form element. Clicking a check box's label is the same as clicking the check box, for instance.

> Labels also provide assistance to visitors using your site with text-only Web browsers and technology for differently abled people such as screen readers. Assistive software can use the label to explain the purpose of a form element. For example, an audio-only Web browser could speak each label aloud as a user moves a control to that element.

Another form element can be used to group several elements under a common label: the group box.

A group box is a thin black rectangle with a text label on its top edge. Refer back to Figure 20.2 to see what one looks like.

To add a group box, follow these steps:

1. Click the mouse within the form's borders.

2. Choose **Insert**, **Form**, **Group Box**. A group box appears with the label Group Box.

3. To change the label, click anywhere within the label and begin typing.

4. Press **Enter** to finish renaming the label.

5. To place form elements within the box, drag them inside it and release the mouse.

**20**

On the Insert, Form menu, the Group Box command may be disabled.

FrontPage allows group boxes to be added to a form only if the software has been configured to target Internet Explorer Only as its desired audience. This appears to be a bug; group boxes are supported by Netscape Navigator, Mozilla, and other browsers.

To see the target audience for the site, choose Tools, Page Options and click the Authoring tab. The Browsers and Browser Versions sections of the tab show which browsers are included in the audience.

## Add a Check Box or Option Button

Check boxes and option buttons are form elements that have only two possible values: selected or not selected. You can set these elements to either value when the page is first loaded.

Check boxes and option buttons differ in appearance. They also differ in how they can be used: Option buttons can be grouped to prevent more than one from being selected at one time. Check boxes do not have this characteristic.

A check box appears with a check mark if it's selected and appears empty otherwise. Each box is given a name and a value—ON by default—that is sent for each selected check box when the form is submitted. Nothing is sent for a check box that is not selected.

An option button is a circle that has a dot in it if it's selected. Option buttons are given a group name rather than naming each button—this common name is what groups them together. When the form is submitted, the value of the selected option button in the group is sent and the others are ignored.

A sample use for check boxes and option buttons may make their differences more clear:

Using check boxes, a user could be asked what political party he or she voted for in the past decade. If the question is for citizens of the United States, there could be check boxes for the Republican, Democratic, Libertarian, Green, and Reform parties. Between zero and five boxes could be checked, depending on how often the person jumped across party lines at the ballot box. An appropriate value for these boxes would be YES because it's transmitted only for boxes that are selected.

Using option buttons, a user could be asked what political party he or she voted for in the past election. If there were option buttons for the Republican, Democratic, Libertarian, Green, and Reform parties, and all of these buttons had the same name, only one of them could be checked. By using option buttons instead of check boxes, the user would be limited to a single answer.

To add a check box or option button to a form, follow these steps:

1. Click your mouse at the spot where the element should be placed.

2. Choose **Insert**, **Form**, **Checkbox** or **Insert**, **Form**, **Option Button**. The element is added to the page without any text that describes its purpose.

3. To add some descriptive text, place your cursor alongside the element in the editing window and begin typing.

To change the name and default value of a check box or option button, double-click the box. The element's Properties dialog box appears. Figure 20.6 shows the Option Button Properties dialog box. The Check Box Properties dialog box has the same fields with Name in place of Group Name.

**FIGURE 20.6**

*Modifying an option button.*

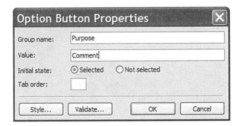

Type a name in the Group Name field (for option buttons) or Name field (for check boxes), remembering that option buttons in the same group should have the same name.

In the Value field, give the field a value that shows what it means when a user selects that check box or option button.

For example, on a form with Send More Information next to a check box, a suitable value for the box would be Yes. On a form with the option buttons Mail Only, Email Only, and Mail and Email, suitable values would be Mail, Email, and Both, respectively.

The Initial State option determines whether the field is selected when the form is first displayed. Choose Selected to put a check mark or dot in the field. For option buttons, remember that only one can be selected at any time, so the others should be set to the Not Selected option.

## Add a Drop-Down Box

Drop-down boxes serve a similar purpose to option buttons: They enable the user to choose from several possible responses. However, instead of these possible choices being

**20**

divided into buttons, they're placed in a menu. Drop-down boxes also differ in another way—they can be configured to allow more than one choice to be selected.

To add a drop-down box to a form, follow these steps:

1. Click the spot on the form where the drop-down box belongs.
2. Choose **Insert**, **Form**, **Drop-Down Box**. A small drop-down box is added to the form without any text in it.

A new drop-down box is set up without any possible responses. The list of responses is added by editing the drop-down box. Double-click it to open the Drop-Down Box Properties dialog box, shown in Figure 20.7.

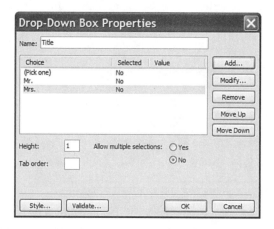

To add responses to a drop-down box, follow these steps:

1. Double-click the box. The Drop-Down Box Properties dialog box opens.
2. Click the **Add** button. The Add Choice dialog box appears.
3. In the **Choice** text field, type the text that should appear on the drop-down box for this choice.

   For example, the box being edited in Figure 20.6 is missing another popular choice for a person's title: Ms. That text could be entered in the Choice text field.
4. To make the choice the default value for the element, (which causes the value to appear in the box when the form is first loaded), click the **Selected** option button. If you change your mind about the value, click **Not Selected**.
5. Click **OK**. The Add Choice dialog closes and the new response is added to the list in the Drop-Down Box Properties dialog box shown in Figure 20.7. Responses appear in the same top-to-bottom order as they do in the list.

6. To move a response, select it in the list and click **Move Up** or **Move Down**.

7. To delete a response entirely, select it and click **Remove**.

8. To make changes to a response, select it and click **Modify**.

9. The default behavior of a drop-down box is to allow only one choice to be selected. To allow the user to make multiple selections from the list, click the **Yes** option button in the Allow Multiple Selections option.

10. Another default is to display one line of the drop-down box when it isn't being used (in other words, when its drop-down arrow has not been clicked to open the box). To display additional lines, change the value of the Height text field.

11. Click **OK** to save the drop-down box.

> The first choice in a drop-down box is sometimes used like a label by giving it a value such as (Pick One) or (Click Here to Select). This makes the box easier to use and has an added advantage: It makes it clear that the user filling out the form did not choose an answer for this element.

## Add a Pushbutton

Pushbuttons are form elements that look just like the Submit and Reset buttons placed automatically on forms by FrontPage.

The Submit button is used when a form has been filled out and is ready to be transmitted.

The Reset button clears all of the answers provided on a form and restores elements to their default values.

Pushbuttons can be associated with hyperlinks, so you can add them to a form with links to other pages. One possible use is a Help button that loads a page describing how to use the form.

To add a push button to a form you are editing, follow these steps:

1. Click the mouse where the button should be placed.

2. Choose **Insert**, **Form**, **Pushbutton**. A button is added with the label Button.

3. To change the name and label of the button, double-click the button. The Pushbutton Properties dialog box appears.

4. Type a name for the button in the **Name** text field.

5. The Value/Label text field establishes the text that will appear on the button. Delete Button from this field and type another label in this field.

20

6. Choose one of the Button Type option buttons: **Normal**, **Submit**, or **Reset**.

The Submit and Reset button types can be used to add one of the standard buttons to the form, which is helpful if you accidentally delete one while working on it. There also can be more than one Submit button in a form, each of which transmits the form responses when it is clicked.

The Normal button type is for buttons that will be associated with hyperlinks.

7. Click **OK**. The button changes to reflect the new label.

8. After a button has been added to a form, it can be associated with a hyperlink like any other element of a page. To add a hyperlink, click the button to select it and then click the **Insert Hyperlink** button to open the Insert Hyperlink dialog box, which can be used to select a link for the button.

Hyperlinks should not be associated with a form's Submit or Reset buttons because it will interfere with their primary purpose of submitting or clearing the form.

FrontPage also can be used to add "advanced buttons" to a page. These buttons look like pushbuttons but can be set to a different height and width. To create one, first choose **Insert, Form, Advanced Button** to add the button. Type the label directly on the button in Design mode. To modify its size, right-click the button to open a context menu, and then choose **Advanced Button Properties**.

## Add a Graphical Submit Button

Because pushbuttons are so plain-looking, they're likely to stick out like a sore thumb on a Web page that's colorful and visually appealing.

The picture form element can be used to turn a graphic into a Submit button. To add a picture to a form, follow these steps:

1. Click the spot on the form where the graphic should appear.

2. Choose **Insert, Form, Picture**.

Take care not to choose the similar-looking command of Insert, Picture.

The Picture dialog box appears. Use this to find the graphic that should be added to the page as a button.

3. Click the graphic.

The graphic is added to the form and set up as a Submit button.

4. To give the picture element a descriptive name, double-click it in the editing window to open the Picture Properties dialog box. Type a name in the **Name** field and click **OK**.

When a picture is used to submit a form, the position that was clicked on its surface will be transmitted.

# Receive Information from a Form

All of the information gathered on a form won't amount to much unless it is sent somewhere. Form responses can be saved to a file, saved to a database, sent to you via email, or sent to a form-handling program on a Web server.

When a form is created in FrontPage, it is set up to save responses in a file named form_results.csv in the site's _private folder. *CSV* stands for "comma-separated values," and it's a text format that can be read easily by Microsoft Excel or imported into a database. (You also can take a look at it with a text editor such as Windows Notepad, although it'll be hard to read that way.)

If you send form responses to a file, database, or email, you must be publishing the site on a Web server that supports FrontPage Server Extensions.

Sending form data to a database was covered in Hour 19, "Connect a Database to Your Site." The other methods are covered in the next three sections.

## Save Form Responses to a File

The information collected on a form can be stored in a file on your Web server, in one of the folders used by your site.

The file can take one of three formats:

- **Text**—A plain format that can be viewed in a text editor or loaded in some database and spreadsheet programs
- **HTML**—The format of Web pages, making it possible to view the responses with a browser
- **XML**—A universal format for data exchange that's being widely supported in Office 2003 and hundreds of software programs from Microsoft and other companies

20

To save form responses to a file, follow these steps:

1. Right-click anywhere within the form's borders and choose **Form Properties** from the context menu. The Form Properties dialog box appears, as shown in Figure 20.8.

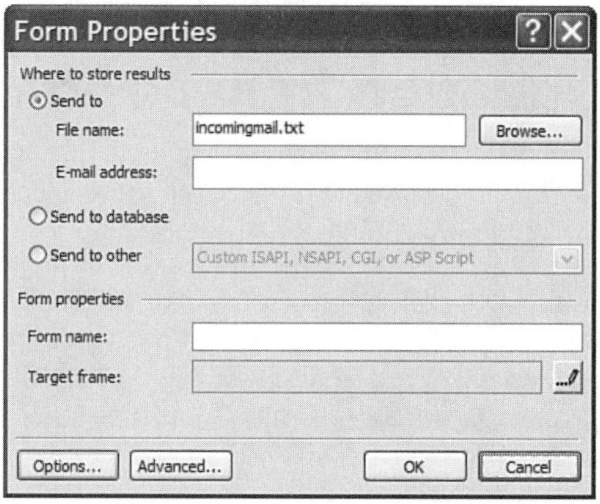

**FIGURE 20.8**

*Determining how form
responses are saved.*

2. Type a name for the file in the **Filename** text field.

   Form responses are saved in this file on the Web server hosting the site. If this file doesn't exist when a user fills out the form for the first time, the file will be created.

   This file can be saved in the _private folder of the Web site, which prevents other people from viewing the file if your site is hosted on a server equipped with FrontPage Server Extensions.

   To save it in this folder, in the File Name text field, preface the name with the text _private/. (For example, using _private/email.txt saves form responses in the _private folder in a file named email.txt.)

   The file can be viewed by opening the Web site directly on the Web server: Choose File, Open Site, and then enter the site's address in the Site Name field.

3. The form is saved as text, formatted one element to a line. To choose a different format, click the **Options** button.

   The Saving Results dialog box appears (see Figure 20.9).

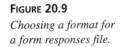

**FIGURE 20.9**

*Choosing a format for a form responses file.*

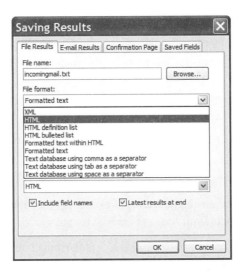

5. Use the **File Format** drop-down box to select a format for the data:

   - To save the data in CSV format and make it easy to read with Microsoft Excel and other database programs, choose **Text Database Using Comma as a Separator** or one of the other Text Database formats.

   - To save the data so that it can be viewed with a Web browser, a good choice is either **HTML** or **Formatted Text Within HTML**.

   - To save the data as XML, choose **XML**.

     This last option is a new feature of FrontPage 2003. XML is a universal data format designed to make information reusable in other programs, such as those in the Office suite.

     Because it is a new feature, it won't work unless the server hosting your site supports FrontPage Server Extensions that have been extended to support FrontPage 2003.

   The file's name will be changed to reflect the format of the file: .htm for HTML, .xml for XML, and either .txt or .csv for text.

6. Click **OK** to close the Saving Results dialog box, and click **OK** again to close the Form Properties dialog box.

The form is set up to store responses in the designated file. This file will be readable on the Web by anyone who knows its name, so it should not be used to store confidential information such as a credit card number.

**20**

## Send Form Responses via Email

Form data that is mailed will arrive like any other email. The name and value of each form element will be displayed in the body of the email, as in the following example:

```
Name:      Sam Snett
Company:   Sams Publishing
Address1:  201 W. 103rd St.
Address2:
City:      Indianapolis
State:     IN
Zip:       46290
Email:     snett@samspublishing.com
```

The mail will come from an automated reply-to address established by your Web host—my server sends form data from webmaster@frontpage24.com.

If one of the responses on a form represents a person's email address, as in the preceding example, the form can be set up to use it as the reply-to address of the mail.

What does this accomplish? When you click Reply to send a letter to the person who filled out your form, that person's address appears in the To line of the email (instead of your server's automated address). This new feature of FrontPage 2003 eliminates one of the major sources of grumbling for users of past versions of the software—it was cumbersome to reply to visitor mail.

To send form responses to an email address, follow these steps:

1. Right-click anywhere on the form and choose **Form Properties** from the context menu that opens. The Form Properties dialog box appears.

2. Type the email address that will receive data in the **Email Address** text field.

   As you probably have guessed, this should be your own email address or one for someone who expects the mail. FrontPage will deliver the data to any email address you specify. Make sure it's correct.

3. If the **Filename** box is not empty, remove the text from it. Otherwise, FrontPage will store responses in the file rather than emailing them.

4. Form email will be sent using the format displayed earlier in this section—an element's name followed by its value. To choose another format, click the **Options** button. The Saving Results dialog box opens.

5. Click the **Email Results** tag to bring it to the front.

6. Choose a format with the **Email Format** drop-down box. The same options offered with files are offered here.

7. To set a subject line for the email, making it easier to spot these responses in your inbox, type it in the **Subject** field.

8. To use an email form element for replies, enter the element's name in the **Reply-To Line** text field and enable its **Form Field Name** check box (as shown in Figure 20.10).

**FIGURE 20.10**

*Setting the reply-to address for emailed form responses.*

9. Click **OK** to close the Saving Results dialog box, and click **OK** again to close the Form Properties dialog box.

Test the form after publishing it with a Web browser to make sure the email arrives in the right place.

If your Web site includes a "contact me" form, you can reduce the amount of spam that you receive by never putting your email address on the site.

This is a pretty drastic step—some visitors don't like using forms—but by keeping your address off the Web site, you prevent spammers from finding it with Web-exploring software and adding it to their databases.

Software used by bulk email senders automatically scours the Web for email addresses, adding them to mailing lists. This is a depressingly common occurrence, as any Web publisher can attest. There's even a name for the problem: email harvesting.

By making yourself available only through a Web form, you can prevent these programs from finding your email address.

**20**

If you'd really like to include your email address on a site, another alternative is to create a graphic that contains the address and use this instead of text. Email harvesting software can't find text on a graphic.

## Sending Form Responses to a CGI Program

The last way to handle forms is to send responses to a program on your Web server that can receive form data and do something with it.

Most of these programs simply email the data to a specified address, but there also are programs for polls, surveys, e-commerce, and other services.

Before you can use a CGI program with a form, you may need to rename elements of the form to names required by the program. You also will need the address of the program— a Web URL—and the delivery method that it uses, which is called either GET or POST. All of this should be explained by the program's documentation.

Form-handling programs rely on the Common Gateway Interface (CGI), a protocol that determines how a Web server exchanges information with other programs on the same computer. CGI programs require special access to a Web server, and most Web hosting services don't grant it to their customers for security reasons. Some hosting services do install CGI programs that can be shared by all customers.

If you have a CGI program that handles forms, here's how to use it:

1. Right-click somewhere on the form and choose **Form Properties** from the context menu. The Form Properties dialog box is displayed.
2. Choose the **Send to Other** option button. The drop-down box next to the item should change from gray to white.
3. If the box contains the Custom ISAPI, NSAPI, CGI, or ASP Script option, leave it alone. Otherwise, open the drop-down box and choose that option.
4. Click the **Options** button. The Options for Custom Form Handler dialog box opens.
5. Type the Web address of the CGI program in the **Action** text field. If you don't know this, contact your Web host for this information.
6. Choose the delivery method POST or GET from the **Method** drop-down list box.

   These methods are dependent on the CGI program—another piece of information you may need from your host.

7. Click **OK** to close this dialog box, and click **OK** to close the Form Properties dialog box.

# Create a Confirmation Page

After visitors submit a form, a Web page is displayed that can be used to let them know it was handled successfully. This is called a confirmation page because it confirms that everything went okay.

If you are sending form responses to a file, email address, or database, FrontPage can use its own default confirmation page—a very plain-looking page that lists the information submitted from the form.

A better technique is to create your own page, using the theme and design of your site that will be displayed upon the submission of a form.

To do this, follow these steps:

1. Create the page, with text that explains that the form has been received.
2. Open the page that contains the form.
3. Right-click within the form's borders and hoose **Form Properties**. The Form Properties dialog box opens.
4. Click the **Options** button. The Saving Results dialog box opens.
5. Click the **Confirmation Page** tab to display it on top.
6. Click the **Browse** button. The Current Web Site dialog box appears. Use this to find and select your newly created confirmation page.
7. Click the **OK** button to close the Saving Results dialog box, and click **OK** again on the Form Properties dialog box.

When you publish and test the form, you should see the confirmation page after the form has been submitted.

**20**

# Summary

Forms are an essential feature of the World Wide Web because they immediately connect a publisher with the people who visit the site.

You can create forms quickly with FrontPage 2003's Form Page Wizard. You also can take more control over a form by adding its elements to a Web page directly.

By using text boxes, check boxes, option buttons, and other parts of a form, you can ask questions in a variety of different ways. A multiple-choice question can be limited to a single answer with option buttons or multiple answers on a drop-down box. More open-ended answers can be typed in as one or more lines of text.

After spending two hours on the subject of Web forms, you should be able to ask anything of the visitors to your site. Getting them to actually *answer* is another matter.

# Q&A

**Q** **FrontPage saves form data to a `.csv` file, but Yahoo! GeoCities won't let me publish it. How can I fix this?**

**A** GeoCities and some other hosting providers limit the file extensions that can be used on their server for security reasons. In the Form Properties dialog box, change the file extension from `.csv` to `.txt`.

A CSV file is a text file containing data that is separated by commas. Using `.txt` as the extension instead of `.csv` does not change the contents of the file in any way.

**Q** **On each of these form elements, what does the Tab Order do?**

**A** When a form is being filled out, pressing the Tab key skips to the next form element, and pressing Shift+Tab key skips to the previous one. The form's *tab order* determines where to go in response to these keys. By default, the browser uses the top-to-bottom order of elements on the page for this purpose.

When you want to set up a different order, values can be entered in the Tab Order field of each element on the form. Give the first element the number 1, the second 2, and so on, all the way to the final element on the page.

# Part VI

# Creating Web Sites Like a Pro

## Hour

21  Create and Edit Pages Using HTML

22  Format Your Site with Cascading Style Sheets

23  Share Information with XML

24  Divide a Page into Separate Frames

# HOUR 21

# Create and Edit Pages Using HTML

All World Wide Web pages are created using Hypertext Markup Language (HTML), a set of formatting commands that are added to text documents.

These commands, which are called *tags*, turn normal text into headings, hyperlinks, paragraphs, images, and anything else you can put on a page.

When you create a Web page in FrontPage 2003, the software marks it up with HTML tags behind the scenes. You see how it's going to look in a Web browser and can avoid learning HTML entirely.

Well, almost entirely.

Sometimes you might need to add something to a page using HTML tags instead of doing your own editing.

In this hour, you will learn

- How to add HTML to a Web page
- How to view the markup tags that make up a document
- How to create Web pages with HTML
- How to use advertising networks and other services that require the placement of HTML on your pages

# Get Started with HTML

It's possible to use FrontPage entirely as an HTML editor. You can take advantage of its Web management and maintenance features while marking up pages strictly in HTML mode, as if you were using Windows Notepad or another plain-text word processor.

However, it makes sense to let FrontPage write its own HTML because the software does a good job at a task that's often complex and tedious.

You can avoid HTML completely and develop professional, sophisticated Web sites with FrontPage. However, if you ever decide to offer a Web enhancement developed by another site, you might need to work directly with HTML.

For example, if you host banner ads on your Web site, the service delivering the ads might provide HTML-tagged text that presents the ads. If you can't place the HTML on the pages of your site, you can't use the service.

The World Wide Web has numerous site-enhancing offerings, including free hit counters, guest books, and banner-advertising exchanges. Many of these programs offer their services through HTML that must be placed on your pages.

Although HTML text looks intimidating at first glance, a primer on the basics of the language can lessen its "fear factor."

A Web page is actually an ordinary text file that you can load with any text editor, such as Windows Notepad. HTML tags are added to the text to achieve different effects like these:

- Creating a hyperlink to a favorite Web site:

  ```
  <a href="http://www.cnn.com">CNN</a>
  ```

- Turning text into a heading:

  ```
  <h1>News from the Trip</h1>
  ```

- Making several lines of text into a bulleted list:

  ```
  <ul>
    <li>4 cups flour
    <li>1 cup salt
    <li>4 cups water
    <li>4 tablespoons oil
    <li>1/2 cup cream of tartar
  </ul>
  ```

- Displaying a digital photo:

  ```
  <img src="epcot1.jpg" alt="Visiting Epcot" height="420" width="360">
  ```

# Using HTML Tags

Text is "marked up" in HTML by putting tags around it. All HTML tags begin with the < character and end with the > character. The following tag adds a horizontal line to a Web page:

```
<hr>
```

The text hr stands for "horizontal rule." You can place an <hr> tag on a Web page anywhere you want a line to appear.

Two kinds of tags exist: opening tags and closing tags. An *opening tag* indicates where some kind of formatting should begin. A *closing tag* indicates where it should end.

Consider the following marked-up text from a Web page:

```
<h1>Today's Top Story</h1>
```

This text uses the HTML tag <h1> to turn the text "Today's Top Story" into a size 1 heading. There also are <h2>, <h3>, <h4>, <h5>, and <h6> tags for headings with five additional sizes—they range from 1 (largest) to 6 (smallest).

Two HTML tags are used in this example: the opening tag, <h1>, and its closing tag, </h1>. The names of all closing tags are preceded by the slash character (/).

Most HTML tags require opening and closing tags to function correctly. For headings, you must use both tags to show where the heading begins and where it ends.

The <hr> tag is one of several opening tags that do not require a corresponding closing tag. The horizontal line appears on a page exactly where the <hr> opening tag is placed.

 HTML tags aren't case sensitive, so you could place <H1>, </H1>, and <HR> on a Web page and achieve the same effects as <h1>, </h1>, and <hr>.

# Work with HTML Tags

An HTML tag also can contain extra information to control two things:

- How the tag is displayed on a page
- What the tag can be used to do

All this extra information is placed before the > character at the end of a tag, as in the following example:

```
<hr width="50%">
```

21

This <hr> tag has the added text width="50%". This is a tag attribute that causes the horizontal line to be displayed 50% as wide as it would appear normally. A tag can have more than one attribute, as long as they're set apart from each other by blank spaces.

After you understand the way HTML tags are structured, it becomes easier to understand what they're being used to accomplish. Even if this is your first exposure to HTML, you might be able to figure out what the following tagged text does:

<a href="http://www.samspublishing.com">Visit Sams</a>

In this example, HTML turns the text "Visit Sams" into a hyperlink pointing to http://www.samspublishing.com, the address of the Sams Publishing Web site. The <a> tag stands for "anchor"—hyperlinks are also called *anchors*—and the href attribute is short for "Hypertext Reference."

# Tag a Page with HTML Commands

When you work on a page in Design mode, the normal editing mode in FrontPage, you can't edit the HTML. If you typed the text <hr> on a page, FrontPage would assume that you wanted to display that actual text—in other words, the text "<hr>"—not a horizontal line.

To work directly with HTML in FrontPage, open a Web document and click the Code button at the bottom of the FrontPage editing window, as shown in Figure 21.1.

The buttons along the bottom edge of the FrontPage editing window enable you to shift among four different modes:

- **Design**—See how the document looks as you work on it, letting FrontPage write its own HTML behind the scenes.
- **Code**—See how the HTML is used to create the document and make your own changes using markup tags.
- **Split**—See both Design and Code modes at the same time.
- **Preview**—See how the document will appear in a Web browser. You cannot edit the document while it is in this mode.

As you are working on a Web document, you can click the Code button at any time to view or edit the Code used to create the document. Figure 21.2 shows what FrontPage looks like in Code editing mode.

**FIGURE 21.1**

*Switching to HTML editing mode.*

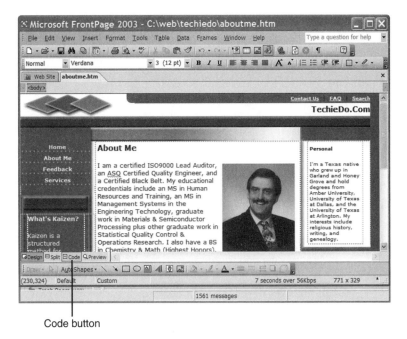

Code button

**FIGURE 21.2**

*Viewing a Web page's HTML formatting.*

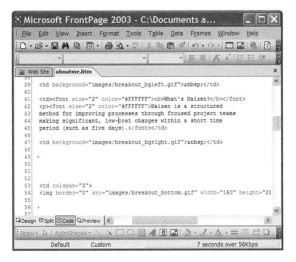

If you're looking at the HTML of a page that was created in FrontPage, don't expect to make much sense of it unless you're experienced with HTML. The software uses some sophisticated HTML to produce the presentation, formatting, and effects that you have learned about in the past 20 hours.

**21**

If you'd like to experiment with HTML, the easiest way to do that in FrontPage is to start a new Web site that has no theme. Pages added to the site will contain the simplest possible HTML that FrontPage can create.

FrontPage starts every Web page with a minimal amount of HTML formatting:

- <html> tags show where the Web page begins and ends (in other words, the entire document).
- <head> tags indicate the page's header—information about the page that isn't displayed in the main browser window.
- A <title> tag gives the page a title in the browser's title bar.
- <body> tags indicate the page's body—the area that will show up in the main browser window.

FrontPage also uses <meta> tags in the header of the page that describe the document and how it was created.

Anything you want to display on a Web page should be placed between the existing <body> tags.

Paragraphs of text are formatted with the <p> tag.

 FrontPage uses different colors for text, HTML tags, attributes, and other elements on a page. To customize the colors that are used, choose Tools, Page Options to open the Page Options dialog box; then click the Color Coding tab to bring it to the front. Pick the colors that you want, and click OK to make your changes permanent.

## Change a Page's Title

A Web page's title is denoted by the <title> tag, which is easy to change in FrontPage's Design mode:

1. Right-click the page and choose **Page Properties** from the pop-up menu that appears. The Page Properties dialog box opens.
2. If the **General** tab is not visible, click it to bring the tab to the front.
3. Type a title for the page in the **Title** field.
4. Click **OK** to close the dialog box.

The same thing can be accomplished by editing the HTML used to present the page, and it's a worthwhile exercise if you'd like a little practice with HTML.

To change a page's title using HTML markup, follow these steps:

1. Open the page for editing.
2. Click the **Code** button to switch to Code editing mode (Code view) and display all of the page's HTML.
3. Scroll to the top of the document and look for <title> and </title> tags.
4. Highlight the text between these two tags.
5. Type a new title.

Your newly revised title will be shown in any of the editing modes and when the page is previewed in a Web browser.

A good way to discover things about HTML is to create an empty page and open it for editing in Split mode. Any change that you make in the Design pane of the editing window will be reflected instantly in the Code pane, as shown in Figure 21.3.

**FIGURE 21.3**

*Here the title of the page also includes a link to the IMAPS Web site.*

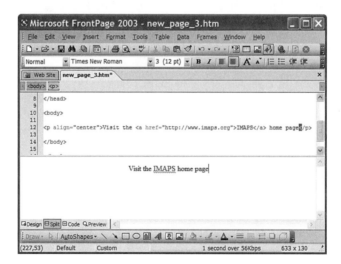

# Leave Existing HTML Untouched

When Web designers evaluate Web publishing software, one of the most important features they look for is whether the program will reformat existing HTML when a document is edited for the first time.

This feature, which is often called "round-trip HTML," is supported in FrontPage.

**21**

This is important is because of quirks in how browsers interpret HTML tags. To see an example of this, two Web pages are displayed by Microsoft Internet Explorer 6 in Figure 21.4.

The two pages in Figure 21.4 display a group of five images that are pushed together. The goal is to make them look like a single image—a television playing a program. Dividing images this way is a common technique used by professional Web designers when they are creating a complex, visually appealing page.

The TV on the left in Figure 21.4 was created with this HTML:

```
<p><div align="center"><img src="tvtop.gif" width=239 height=18
align=bottom><br><img src="tvleft.gif" width=15 height=120
align=bottom><img src="tvscreen.jpg" width=160
height=120><img src="tvright.gif" width=64 height=120
align=bottom><br><img src="tvbottom.gif" width=239 height=30
align=bottom></div></p>
```

The TV on the right was created with this HTML:

```
<p>
<div align="center">
<img SRC="tvtop.gif" ALIGN="bottom" width="239" height="18">
<br>
<img SRC="tvleft.gif" ALIGN="bottom" width="15" height="120">
<img SRC="tvscreen.jpg" width="160" height="120">
<img SRC="tvright.gif" ALIGN="bottom" width="64" height="120">
<br>
<img SRC="tvbottom.gif" ALIGN="bottom" width="239" height="30">
</div>
</p>
```

Both of these televisions are displayed using the same HTML tags in the same order, but only one of them is displayed correctly. The TV on the right in Figure 21.4 contains white lines around the movie, making it obvious that the television is made up of separate images.

The only difference between these pages is that one of them puts each HTML tag on its own line, and the other does not. The placement of tags on different lines often leads to display glitches like this in Internet Explorer, Mozilla, and other browsers.

For this reason, when a designer finally gets the HTML tags on a page to produce the desired effect, an editing tool can introduce errors by rearranging the placement and spacing of tags.

FrontPage 2003 leaves existing HTML alone when it loads a Web page that was created using other software. If a portion of a page relies on specific HTML formatting, as the television example did, it isn't touched unless you edit that portion with Code view in FrontPage.

# Clean Up the HTML on a Page

**NEW 2003** As you poke around the HTML of a Web site created with FrontPage, you're likely to find some things that are confusing, redundant, or completely unnecessary—especially if you cut and paste content onto a page that was created by other Office products such as Microsoft Word.

Word can be used to create material for the World Wide Web. The text will contain special HTML formatting so that it can be edited again later with Word; this HTML doesn't affect how it is presented in a Web browser.

A new feature of FrontPage 2003 is the capability to clean up a page's HTML, removing things such as these Word-specific features.

The cleaning process makes the Web page load faster by removing HTML formatting that doesn't affect the presentation or content of the page. It also makes the HTML simpler to understand if you need to edit it later. This process is called *optimizing* the HTML.

To optimize a page, follow these steps:

1. Open a page for editing.
2. Choose **Tools**, **Optimize HTML** to open the Optimize HTML dialog box (see Figure 21.5).

   Four kinds of HTML can be removed:

   - **Comments**—Hidden text that shows up only when the HTML formatting of the page is viewed. These comments describe the contents of the page in some way, usually for the benefit of the people who work on it.

   - **Whitespace**—Indentation and blank lines that don't affect the presentation of the page.

**21**

- **Unused content**—HTML tags and Cascading Style Sheet styles that are unnecessary because they will be disregarded by Web browsers. As an example, browsers ignore repeated <p> tags. They display only one paragraph break, regardless of the number of <p> tags that appear between paragraphs.

- **Generated HTML**—Application-specific HTML such as that created by Microsoft Word for its own purposes that does not affect the display of the page in a Web browser.

3. To clean a particular kind of HTML, check its box.

**FIGURE 21.5**

*Choose from the various options to clean up a page's HTML formatting.*

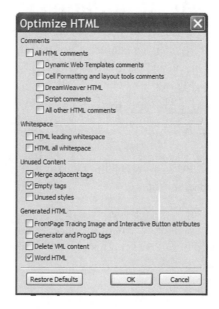

4. Click **OK** to optimize the page, or click **Cancel** to leave it alone.

When in doubt about what you might be optimizing, leave a box blank—some of the formatting that can be removed is useful.

For example, although you can remove all HTML comments from a page, it's not a good idea when you are collaborating with others. There could be important information about how the page was developed.

The Web page will be changed to reflect any of the optimizations you have selected. Switch to Code mode to see the results.

# Add HTML to a Web Page

As a Web publisher, you have a large number of advertising, promotional, and other site-enhancement services to choose from, including many that are free or that offer to pay you money.

Some of my favorites are these:

- Google AdSense, a text advertising service that pays publishers each time ads are clicked. See www.google.com/adsense.
- Commission Junction, an e-commerce program that pays publishers for referring customers to online stores. See www.cj.com.
- Amazon.Com, which pays publishers for referring customers to its site who buy one or more products during the visit. See http://associates.amazon.com.
- WebRing, a site that can be used to exchange links with publishers whose sites are similar to your own. See www.webring.com.
- Google Site Search, a free service that adds the capability to search your site using the Google search engine. See www.google.com/services/free.html.

> Looking for more services like these? The Adbility site reviews Web site enhancement services, offering advice on which ones to consider and which ones to avoid. Visit the site at http://www.adbility.com.

Some of these kinds of services can be implemented on a site using FrontPage Web components, as described in Hour 12, "Use Web Components to Jazz Up a Site."

When that option is available, take it—these components are easy to implement and tinker with later.

Other services, such as the ones I've just listed, require HTML to be placed directly on one or more pages of your site. The HTML presents content from the service—such as a constantly changing banner ad—so that it will be displayed correctly on your site.

Usually, you aren't given the HTML to use until you've been approved for membership at one of these sites. This is always true of services offering to pay you—these affiliate programs, as they are called, require your address and other information before you can receive any money.

Any service that requires the use of HTML makes this a condition of membership, so it's important to do this correctly.

**21**

When you have the right HTML, you can switch to Code mode in FrontPage and add it yourself, but there's another method that's a bit easier:

1. Open the page where the HTML should be placed.

2. In either Design or Code editing mode, click your cursor at the spot where the HTML should appear.

3. Choose **Insert, Web Component**. The Insert Web Component dialog box opens.

4. Scroll the **Component Type** list to the bottom and choose **Advanced Controls**. The Choose a Control box displays the advanced components that can be added to the page (as shown in Figure 21.6).

**FIGURE 21.6**

*Adding an HTML component to a Web page.*

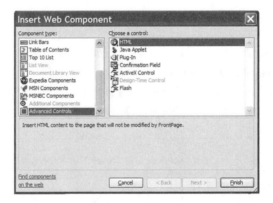

5. In that box, choose **HTML** and click **Finish**. The HTML Markup dialog box opens.

6. In your Web browser, select the HTML you need and press **Ctrl+C** to copy it to the Clipboard.

7. Return to the HTML Markup dialog box and paste the HTML into its text area (see Figure 21.7).

 This HTML will not be reformatted or checked in any way before it is placed on a page. If the service gives you HTML that doesn't display correctly in a Web browser, it's not a problem introduced by FrontPage.

8. Click **OK**.

The dialog box closes and a question-mark icon is added to the page where the HTML has been placed.

**FIGURE 21.7**

*Copying HTML for placement on the page.*

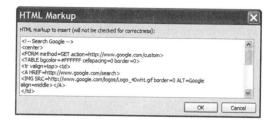

To see what this HTML code produces (and make sure that it works), connect to the Internet and preview the Web page. Double-click the question-mark icon to make changes in the HTML Markup dialog box.

If you decide to remove the HTML code, click the question-mark icon and hit the Delete key.

# Summary

If using FrontPage 2003 is your first experience creating Web sites, you'll probably hear some "in my day, things were different" stories about HTML from old fogies like me.

Before the development of software like FrontPage, Web sites were created by marking up text with HTML tags in simple text editors such as Windows Notepad. Many developers still prefer working directly with HTML, believing that you get more control over the finished product by coding it yourself.

You can be both old-fashioned and newfangled with FrontPage. View HTML when you want, and hide it when you use the software's graphical user interface to design sites. You also can avoid HTML entirely and let FrontPage do all of the work for you.

# Q&A

**Q Why doesn't any of the text from an included page show up in HTML mode?**

**A** FrontPage 2003 saves the contents of included Web pages separately from the rest of each page in a site. These elements, which are usually shared by more than one page, are saved to their own Web pages—common practice is to create an _includes folder and store them there. Everything is combined when you publish.

In the _includes folder, you can open and edit these pages like any other pages in your Web site.

**21**

**Q Is there any reason I should work directly with HTML instead of using FrontPage 2003 to create the HTML for me?**

**A** One of the main purposes of software like FrontPage is to make it easier to create Web pages. Many people who don't have a technical background will find it easier to develop Web pages if they don't have to learn the tags and syntax of HTML— and as you've seen during the last 20 hours, you can accomplish a lot without knowing the language.

The main advantage of learning and using HTML is that you can implement everything in the language as it's introduced. FrontPage 2003 supports most features that are currently implemented by Microsoft Internet Explorer, Netscape Navigator, and the other popular Web browsers, but as new features are introduced by the World Wide Web Consortium and browser developers, you might need to rely on HTML to implement them.

**Q Can I add an advertising network's HTML in Code mode, or do I have to use the HTML Web component?**

**A** If you are comfortable editing HTML, you can add a Web enhancement service's HTML code directly in Code view. However, you'll be missing out on one of the benefits of the HTML component—it remembers exactly which HTML was placed on a page to support a specific service.

When you paste HTML directly on a page, it might not contain comments that show where the service's HTML begins and ends. Later when you need to update or remove the code, it can be difficult to distinguish it from the formatting for the surrounding page.

Changing or deleting the code is much easier with the HTML component. Double-click the question-mark icon to edit the code, or click it once and press the Delete key to remove it.

# Hour **22**

# Format Your Site with Cascading Style Sheets

Although more than 90% of Web users employ popular Web browsers such as Internet Explorer, Netscape Navigator, and Mozilla, many other kinds of software can present a public Web site. There are text-only browsers such as Lynx, nonvisual browsers for differently abled people, Internet-enabled cell phones, and alternative browsers such as Opera and Safari.

Coping with this varied audience is made easier through a Web technology called Cascading Style Sheets (CSS).

Using CSS, you can modify the appearance of a Web site in dramatic ways, saving all of the presentation-related formatting separately in its own file, which is called a *style sheet*. Changing the style sheet changes every page in the site that uses it.

In this hour, you will learn

- How to create a Cascading Style Sheet
- How to add new styles
- How to modify existing styles
- How to apply styles to specific elements of a Web page, such as paragraphs, hyperlinks, and bold text

# Use Styles to Design a Site

Popular word processors such as Microsoft Word have a feature called *styles* that enables you to define the presentation of elements that appear in a document, such as headlines, body text, and pictures.

For example, you could establish a style making all body text in your document 12-point Courier text, indented a quarter inch from the left margin.

After you have set up this rule for body text, every paragraph in the document that has been defined as body text will be displayed in 12-point Courier font and will be indented a quarter inch to the right.

Later, if you decide to pick a different font or font size, you can modify the body text style, which is much easier than changing each paragraph in the document directly.

This idea has been introduced to the World Wide Web through *Cascading Style Sheets (CSS)*, a language that specifies how the contents of a Web page should be presented. Cascading Style Sheets are an extension of HTML rather than a replacement.

The biggest push in World Wide Web design today is to separate the appearance of a page—its fonts, colors, and alignment—from the information that it offers.

This change makes a Web publisher's life much easier when the site needs to be redesigned. It also makes a Web site more available to a diverse audience.

The best way to accomplish this is to make use of Cascading Style Sheets.

A *style sheet* is a set of commands that define how a Web document will be presented. A Web page can incorporate a style sheet in two ways:

- Placing the style sheet on the page along with HTML tags
- Storing the style sheet separately in its own file and linking to that file within Web pages

A style sheet contains commands to set the fonts, colors, and formatting of text, hyperlinks, and other parts of a page.

Currently, four popular Web browsers offer complete support for CSS 1.0 and significant partial support for CSS 2.0, the first two versions of the standard: Microsoft Internet Explorer, Netscape Navigator, Mozilla, and Opera.

Although CSS support is now available to most Web users, some incompatibilities still exist between its implementation on different browsers and other obstacles to consider. The biggest is the propensity of Netscape Navigator 4 versions to crash when a few style sheet features are employed.

Today, fewer than 2% of Web users are still using that browser, which is more than four versions old. However, you might want to test your site with that browser to make sure that it's still presentable to those visitors.

FrontPage includes *themes*, a feature that enables you to choose an entire Web site's appearance at one time. You can modify parts of a theme, such as a text font, and all selected Web pages will be updated to reflect the change.

When you apply a theme to a Web page (or site) in FrontPage 2003, the software uses CSS to apply the graphics, fonts, and colors.

Themes are similar to Cascading Style Sheets but are much more limited. They are used only to define some overall aspects of a page's presentation: the color and font of text, hyperlinks, and headings; the background of each page; and the appearance of link bars, buttons, and bullets. Everything you use a theme for can be handled manually by editing a page in Design mode. You can set the background, establish all fonts, and create your own link bar graphics.

Unlike themes, Cascading Style Sheets can be used for techniques that are completely impossible in HTML. Take a look at Figure 22.1.

**FIGURE 22.1**

*Viewing a Web page that uses Cascading Style Sheets.*

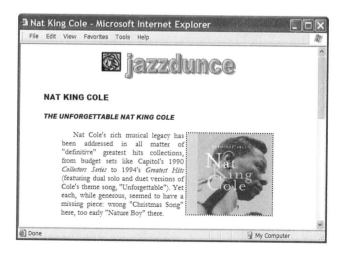

This Web page uses CSS to do several unusual things:

- Indent the start of each paragraph
- Justify paragraphs along the right margin
- Give a picture a dotted-line border

Style sheets enable you to take control over formatting decisions that are normally handled by a Web browser, such as the background color of each paragraph. They also give you many more options for determining the appearance of the different page elements.

## Create a Style Sheet

Style sheets can be implemented as part of a Web page or on a separate document that's linked to the page.

The second technique is preferable because it makes it possible to use the same style sheet on several different Web pages, establishing a common style for them all.

To create a style sheet, follow these steps:

1. Choose **File**, **New** to open the New pane.
2. Click the **More Page Templates** link. The Page Templates dialog box appears.
3. Click the **Style Sheets** tab to bring it to the front.

   This tab displays 13 templates that can be used to create a new style sheet. There's a Normal Style Sheet template that's empty and 12 templates with formatting selections similar to themes of the same name.
4. Select the **Normal Style Sheet** icon (by clicking it once), and then click the **OK** button.

   FrontPage creates a blank style sheet, opens it for editing, and opens the Style toolbar, as shown in Figure 22.2.

Style sheets are given the filename extension .css. When you save the new sheet for the first time, be sure to keep this file extension when picking a name for the file. You can place style sheets in any folder of your Web site.

If you can't see the Style toolbar, choose View, Toolbars, Style. To hide it, click the X button on its title bar.

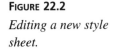

**FIGURE 22.2**

*Editing a new style sheet.*

**22**

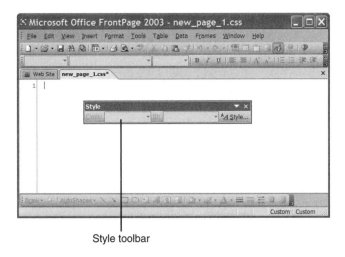

Style toolbar

# Edit a Style Sheet

After a style sheet has been created, you can edit it to define new styles and modify existing ones.

Styles can be associated with specific HTML tags, which alter how the tag is displayed on a Web page. The style is displayed only when the page is loaded by a Web browser that supports Cascading Style Sheets. Other browsers will display the page as if no styles were applied to it.

As described in the preceding hour, "Create and Edit Pages Using HTML," HTML markup is what FrontPage uses behind the scenes to present the contents of a Web page. Defining styles requires knowledge of HTML tags and what they accomplish.

Styles also can be defined that are not associated with any existing HTML tags. These styles do not change the appearance of existing elements of a Web page (such as paragraphs, links, or headings). Instead, they are applied to specific portions of a page.

This will make more sense if you consider an example—a newspaper Web site that defines a style sheet for each news story page. Several user-defined styles could be applied to things that appear in a story:

- The story's headline
- The reporter's name
- The location where the story was filed

- The text of the story

- The caption of a photo that appears with the story

If the story was being prepared in FrontPage, an editor could apply specific styles to different elements of the page. For example, if the headline was selected in the editing window, applying the headline style would format the text according to the style sheet.

One of the most popular uses of style sheets is to display text that is justified along the right margin. Browsers cannot support this formatting without style sheets.

To edit a style sheet, follow these steps:

1. Open the style sheet for editing.

2. Choose **Format**, **Style**. The Style dialog boxappears, as shown in Figure 22.3.

**FIGURE 22.3**

*Creating and modifying styles on a style sheet.*

3. To see the HTML tags that can have styles applied to them, in the List list box, choose **HTML Tags**.

   The Styles list box displays all of the HTML tags that can be styled. The ones you'll probably be using most often are these:

   - a: A hyperlink that has not been visited

   - a:active: A hyperlink that is being clicked

   - a:hover: A hyperlink that the cursor is passing over

   - a:visited: A hyperlink that has been visited

   - h1 through h6: Headings in sizes 1 through 6

   - ol: A numbered list

**22**

- p: Paragraphs of text
- ul: An unnumbered list

4. To see styles that are present on this style sheet, in the List list box, choose **User-Defined Styles**.

 The Styles list displays these styles (or nothing, if you're working on a new sheet for the first time).

5. Choose one of these options:

 - To create a new user-defined style, click the **New** button. The New Style dialog box opens.

 - To modify a tag's style, select it in the Styles list and click the **Modify** button. The Modify Style dialog box opens.

 The New and Modify Style dialog boxes display a preview of what text will look like when the style is applied to it. Because no changes have been made yet, there's nothing to see.

6. To make a change to a style, click the **Format** button, which causes a drop-down menu to appear, as shown in Figure 22.4.

**FIGURE 22.4**

*Modifying how a style is formatted.*

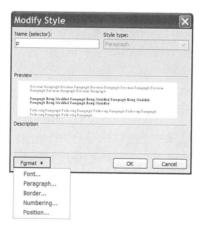

You can use these menu commands to make the following changes to how a tag is displayed on a Web page:

- **Font**—The font, size, color, and other attributes of text
- **Paragraph**—The spacing and indentation of paragraphs containing this text
- **Border**—The border and shading that appear

- **Numbering**—The way lists of text are numbered and indented, and the icons used with each item
- **Position**—The placement of the item in relation to other items that are either adjacent to or overlapping on the page

When you select one of these commands from the Format menu, a dialog box opens that can be used to define the style. The techniques are the same ones used when working on a page and using commands of the main FrontPage Format menu.

7. After a style has been defined, click **OK** to close the dialog box, and repeat steps 5–6 if you want to define additional formatting for that style.
8. When you're done working on a style, click **OK** to return to the Style box.
9. You can apply a style to another tag or finish working on the style sheet by clicking **OK**.

After a style sheet has been created, it must be linked to any Web page on which its formatting will be applied.

## Change the Appearance of Text

When you are editing text on a Web page, you can use two menu commands to change the font and appearance of the text: Format, Font opens the Font dialog box; Format, Paragraph opens the Paragraph dialog box. Both of these were covered in Hour 1, "Create a Web Page."

The style of text can be defined using the same techniques. Here's how to set up a font style for individual lines of text:

1. Choose **Format, Style** to open the Style dialog box.
2. Choose either HTML Tags or User-Defined Styles in the **List** list box, depending on the style being worked on.
3. Select the tag or style from the **Styles** list and click **Modify**.
4. Click **Format, Font**. The Font dialog box opens, as shown in Figure 22.5. You can define as much or as little about the font as desired using this dialog box. As you're defining the style, a preview of the finished product appears in the Preview pane.
5. To select a particular font, choose it from the **Font** list box or type its name in the box. To specify more than one font—a good idea because your visitors might not have your first choice on their computer—type the names of several fonts, separated by commas (for example, Verdana, Arial Black, san-serif).

**FIGURE 22.5**

*Setting up a font style.*

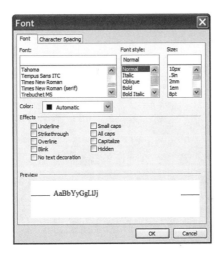

If you list several fonts, when a visitor views the page, the first installed font will be used with any text associated with the style.

6. Use the **Font Style** and **Size** list boxes to define more about the font used with this style.

7. To select a color for text, change the **Color** list box from Automatic to another value.

8. If you want to apply a special effect, such as underlining, capitalization, or blinking, select its box in the **Effects** pane.

9. The spacing between characters also can be changed: Click the **Character Spacing** tab to bring it the front. In that tab, choose a **Spacing** value. For even more customization, change the value of the **By** list box.

10. When you're done defining the font style, click **OK**.

You also can create a style that applies to paragraphs of text rather than individual lines, like so:

1. While working on the style, click **Format**, **Paragraph**.

   The Paragraph dialog box appears (see Figure 22.6). As with font styles, you can define as much or as little as needed.

FIGURE 22.6

2. To affect how text is aligned, select one of the values from the Alignment list box. The options are the same ones as on the Formatting toolbar: Left, Center, Right, and Justify.

3. Use the Indentation section to move the margins of paragraphs inward (by selecting a positive value) or outward (by selecting a negative value).

   The example text in the Preview pane moves to show you the effect of this change.

4. The Line Spacing list box can be used to set up single spacing, double spacing, and 1.5 spacing. For more precise spacing, use the Before, After, and Word list boxes.

5. When you're done, click **OK**.

After you have defined a style for a tag, the Modify Style dialog box displays a new description for that tag. For example, if you set up the Alignment of an HTML tag to justify text, this description appears in the Description pane:

```
text-align: justify
```

This description is a Cascading Style Sheets formatting command. FrontPage creates these commands for you, so you don't have to learn the particulars of the CSS language to make use of it on your Web sites.

# Apply a Style to a Web Page

When you modify a style by editing a style sheet, FrontPage displays that style using the Cascading Style Sheets language in the editing window, as shown in Figure 22.7.

**FIGURE 22.7**

*Viewing a Cascading Style Sheet.*

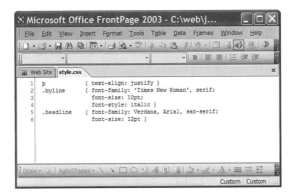

```
1  p            { text-align: justify }
2  .byline      { font-family: 'Times New Roman', serif;
3               font-size: 10pt;
4               font-style: italic }
5  .headline    { font-family: Verdana, Arial, san-serif;
6               font-size: 12pt }
```

Don't edit this document manually unless you're familiar with CSS—instead, click Format, Style to open the Style dialog box and make changes.

Editing styles in a .css file enables you to make changes that apply to all Web pages linked to the style sheet.

At this point, you have worked with style sheets by saving them in a separate file. You can also edit a style sheet while editing a Web page, which causes the style to apply only to that page.

Because styles can be defined on a Web page or on a style sheet linked to the page, you might wonder what happens when both are present at the same time. Does the page use the style in the style sheet or the one on the page itself?

The "cascading" part of Cascading Style Sheets refers to how styles can be defined in more than one place. These styles cascade together, forming a single set of style rules in which rules of precedence determine which formatting to use.

When two different styles affect the same Web page element, the one closer to the element is used. A style defined on a page is closer than one defined in a style sheet; a style defined in a style sheet is closer than one defined by a Web browser.

After you create a style sheet, you must link it to any Web page that will make use of its styles.

To link a style sheet to a page, follow these steps:

1. Open the page for editing, and choose **Format**, **Style Sheet Links**. The Link Style Sheet dialog box is displayed.
2. Click the **Add** button. The Select Style Sheet dialog box appears.
3. Use the dialog box to find and select the style sheet file; then click **OK**.

   The style sheet appears in the URL list box. You can add style sheets at this point—a page can be linked to more than one sheet.
4. Click **OK**. The style sheet is linked to the page.

When you've associated a style sheet with a page, your styles appear in the Formatting toolbar in the Style list box.

To apply a style to part of a Web page, follow these steps:

1. Open the page for editing.
2. Select the portion of the page that should have the style applied to it.
3. Choose the style from the **Style** list box of the Formatting toolbar, as shown in Figure 22.8.

   The style is applied to that portion of the page, changing its appearance using any of the formatting you have designated with that style.

**FIGURE 22.8**

*Applying a style on a Web page.*

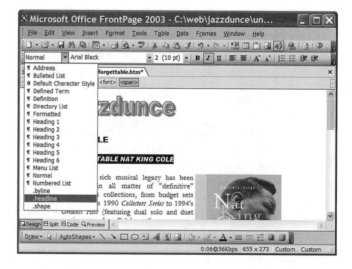

# Match HTML Tags with FrontPage Features

Style sheets use HTML tags to identify elements of a Web page. If you're not familiar with HTML, you might not know how these tags are used on a Web page.

When you choose Format, Font to add a special effect, the following HTML tags are used:

- blink: Blink effect
- cite: Citation effect
- code: Code effect
- dfn: Definition effect
- em: Emphasis effect
- kbd: Keyboard effect
- samp: Sample effect
- strike: Strikethrough effect
- strong: Strong effect
- sub: Subscript effect
- sup: Superscript effect
- u: Underline effect
- var: Variable effect

Several buttons on the Formatting toolbar can be used to format text. They're associated with the following HTML tags:

- b is associated with the Boldface button.
- i is associated with the Italics button.
- u is associated with the Underline button.
- blockquote is associated with the Increase Indent button.

The Formatting toolbar also has a pull-down menu with several formatting options that apply to entire paragraphs. They use the following HTML tags:

- p: Normal
- pre: Formatted
- address: Address
- h1 through h6: Heading 1 through Heading 6
- ol: Before and after a numbered list

- `ul`: Before and after a bulleted list
- `dir`: Before and after a directory list
- `menu`: Before and after a menu list
- `li`: For each item in a numbered, bulleted, directory, or menu list
- `dl`: Before and after a definition list
- `dt`: For each term in a defined term list
- `dd`: For each definition in a definition list

FrontPage uses other HTML tags as you create Web pages, including a for hyperlinks, `img` for pictures, and `applet` for Java applets.

 One way to determine the tags that are being used by FrontPage is to take advantage of Split mode, a new feature of FrontPage 2003.

Create a new page and click the Split button below the editing window. You'll be able to add something to the page in a Design window and look below it in the Code window to see the HTML tag—or tags—used to create it.

## Summary

Cascading Style Sheets give a Web designer amazing control over the appearance of a site. The kinds of effects that are common in print but have never before been available on the World Wide Web now are possible with the use of style sheets.

Style sheets help designers in another way: They make it possible to separate the visual appearance of a Web page from its content, making it simpler to change and update the appearance of the pages.

Although this might be more than you care to do as you're beginning to develop your own Web sites, it makes the work of keeping a site up-to-date easier. You don't have to edit pages by hand if you redesign the appearance of a site—instead, edit a style sheet that's linked to all of the pages of the site, and republish that file. The whole site changes its appearance instantly.

CSS also makes the content of your Web site viewable by a wider audience—in addition to the popular Web browsers, your site can make use of CSS to be seen in unusual places such as all-text browsers, cell phones, and browsers for the differently abled.

# Q&A

**Q** **I've created a new style based on the keyboard tag. How do I apply this style to a Web page?**

**A** Earlier versions of FrontPage did not display all user-defined styles in the Formatting toolbar, which made it difficult to use any of the Character styles you created. There was no place in FrontPage from which you could select those styles.

FrontPage 2003 displays all styles you create in the Formatting menu. Paragraph styles are displayed next to a paragraph icon, and character styles are displayed with an underlined *a* icon.

**22**

# Hour **23**

# Share Information with XML

The newest version of Microsoft Office, the software system that includes FrontPage 2003, is the first to offer full support for Extensible Markup Language (XML), a standard for data exchange that has become enormously popular in the last five years.

Office programs such as Microsoft Word, Microsoft Access, and the new Microsoft InfoPath can produce files that are structured using the rules of XML. In turn, these files can be read by any software that supports XML.

The same is true in reverse: XML data produced by any software or service can be read by the programs in the Office suite.

In this hour, you will learn

- How to edit XML files with FrontPage
- How to display XML data on a Web page
- How to save form responses in the format

## View and Edit XML Files

One of the biggest frustrations for any software user is the lack of portable data. Files that you create using one program are often readable only by that program or successive versions of the same software.

If you ever want to switch to a new program, you must either abandon or convert your old files, if that's even possible.

Even more of a hassle is the circumstance of losing the old program entirely, which leaves you with a bunch of files that might no longer be possible to read.

*Extensible Markup Language (XML)* was created to eliminate this concern and make it easier for software to share information.

Although you don't need to learn XML to use it in FrontPage 2003, a brief introduction will help explain why it's so useful.

XML is a standard for the creation of formats that structure information in a reliable, easy-to-read way. When you use a program such as Microsoft Word to produce an XML file, you can be assured that your data will always be available for use, even if you stop using the program that created it.

An XML file is a text file that is formatted—or "marked up"—in a way that should be familiar to people who know Hypertext Markup Language (HTML), the language used to present Web pages.

In the file, elements of information are organized and identified by wrapping them in tags that begin with a < character and end with a > character. For instance, a `<fullName>` tag could denote a person's full name in an XML file that stores a contact book.

The actual data in the file is placed between a start tag and an end tag. A start tag begins with the < character and ends with the > character. An end tag begins with the `</` characters and ends with a > character.

For example, here's an XML element:

```
<fullName>Sam Snett</fullName>
```

When several elements are related to each other, they can be grouped together by putting them inside another element, as in this extended example:

```
<address>
   <fullName>Sam Snett</fullName>
   <streetAddress>201 W. 103rd. St.</streetAddress>
   <city>Indianapolis</city>
   <state>IN</state>
   <zipCode>46290</zipCode>
</address>
```

This snippet of XML data contains one address in a file of addresses. Each element within the `<address>` start tag and `</address>` end tag is part of the same mailing address.

FrontPage can be used as an XML editor, so you can open XML files in the editing window and make changes, import them into a Web site, and use them in other ways.

Because XML was designed to be as human-readable as possible, you'll often find that you can understand the contents of an XML file with which you are unfamiliar.

Figure 23.1 shows FrontPage being used to edit an XML file.

**FIGURE 23.1**

*Editing an XML file with FrontPage.*

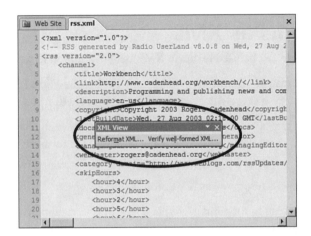

**23**

As you can tell by looking at the figure, the XML file being edited is some kind of Web-related database that contains a site title, an address, a copyright statement, and other information.

You can view and edit an XML file in FrontPage as you would other documents:

1. Choose **File, Import**, and then use the Import dialog box to add the XML file to the site.

2. If you aren't in Folders view, click the **Web Site** tab or choose **View, Folders**.

3. Double-click the XML file. The file opens in the editing window, which displays the full contents of the file. An XML View toolbar, which is circled in Figure 23.1, also opens.

4. To make sure that the XML file is *well-formed*, which means that it is structured correctly and follows all of the rules of XML, click the **Verify Well-Formed XML** button on the XML View toolbar.

5. FrontPage also can reformat the XML file so that it is more readable (to you, not to computers). Click the **Reformat XML** button on the XML View toolbar to improve the readability of the file.

If you want to see the XML View toolbar again after it has been closed, choose View, Toolbars, XML View. You also can move the toolbar so that it isn't floating in its own window: Drag the title bar of the XML View window to one of the edges of the FrontPage user interface, such as the top edge where the Standard and Formatting toolbars are usually displayed.

# Save Forms as XML

Your Web site can be used to create XML data in addition to reading it.

When you create a form, either by hand or by using the Form Page Wizard, you can configure the form to save visitor responses to a file in XML format.

FrontPage uses the names of form elements to identify each element in the XML data as well, so you should choose descriptive names for each form element that's being saved to the file.

To save a form's responses as XML, follow these steps:

1. After creating the form, right-click an empty area within the form's borders and, on the context menu that appears, choose **Form Properties**.

   The Form Properties dialog box opens. You can use this to determine how and where form responses are saved.

2. Choose the **Send to File name** option, if it isn't already selected.

3. Click the **Options** button. The Saving Results dialog box appears, enabling you to choose the format of the file.

4. In the File Format drop-down menu, choose **XML** (see Figure 23.2).

**FIGURE 23.2**

*Saving form responses in XML format.*

5. By default, FrontPage uses the form element's name twice in the XML data—as part of an XML tag and as part of the response itself.

For example:

```
<address>address: 201 W. 103rd. St.</address>
```

To remove form element names when they accompany the visitor's response (the `address: 201 W. 103rd. St.` portion of the preceding example), remove the check mark from the **Include Field Names** box in the top half of the dialog box (above the Optional Second File section).

6. Visitor responses are stored in the file in chronological order, with the most recent response at the bottom. To reverse this order, remove the check mark from the adjacent **Latest Results at End** box.

FrontPage saves form data to a file only if a file name has been specified. The software may have chosen a default name and folder location for you, such as `_private/form_results.xml`.

7. In the **File name** text field, provide a name for the XML file. If you precede the name with a folder, such as `_private`, it must be one of the folders in your site.

> If you're hosting the file on an extended server, the `_private` folder is a good choice for form responses because it hides the file from your visitors. (On other servers, this file may be readable unless you configure the `_private` folder to prevent this access.)

8. XML data is easy for computers to handle but is not quite as readable for humans. If you want to look over form responses as they are collected on your Web site, you can specify a second file where they should be saved in a more readable format.

By saving responses as HTML, the same format as Web pages, you can read them with your Web browser.

In the Optional Second File section of the dialog box, use the **File name** text field and the **File Format** drop-down menu to set up this file.

9. Click **OK**.

Form responses are saved to the designated file, or files, on your Web site. You can view them by opening the copy of your site that's stored on your Web server.

Another way to read the XML file containing visitor responses is to synchronize the site: Open the site on your computer and choose File, Publish Site. Then set the Save All Changed Pages option to Synchronize.

When you click Publish Web Site, you're asked whether to save the Web server's copy of the form responses file (or files) to your computer. Click Yes to save the same file in both places.

# Display XML Data with a Data View

With the help of an extended server equipped with Windows SharePoint Services 2.0, FrontPage 2003 can be used to produce sites that draw data from a wide range of sources, including XML documents, Web services, and databases.

Most Web sites that offer this kind of functionality are created with programming languages such as Java Server Pages or Active Server Pages.

FrontPage makes this possible with no programming through the use of *data views*— Web components that display information retrieved from a data source and that keep themselves up-to-date.

Data views can extract and display information from the following sources:

- XML files
- Web services
- Databases such as DB2, Microsoft SQL Server, and Oracle

Web sites created with FrontPage keep track of all the data sources from which they can draw information. The group of sources is called the *data catalog*.

A data view is updated any time its underlying data source changes. For example, if you create a Web page that displays names and addresses from an XML-formatted contact book file, when a new contact is added to the file, the data view ensures that the addition shows up automatically on the page.

Working with a data view on a Web page is similar to working with a database, which was described in Hour 19, "Connect a Database to Your Site." Some of the same terminology applies here: A data view presents records from a data source; each of those records is divided into individual fields.

One useful application of data views is to display elements from an XML file, sorted to your specifications and filtered so that specific records are displayed and others are omitted.

A site that contains data views must be hosted on a Web server equipped with Windows SharePoint Services 2.0. You must work on the site directly on the Web server—FrontPage prevents data views from being created on pages stored on your computer.

As described in Hour 13, "Publish Your Site," Windows SharePoint Services 2.0 is a server enhancement from Microsoft that can be used to create dynamic Web sites. It extends the functionality of FrontPage Server Extensions.

**23**

Before creating a data view for an XML file, the file should be imported to your site: Choose File, Import and then use the Import dialog box to select the file. (Alternatively, you can retrieve it over the Internet: Type the file's Web address in the File name field.)

Next, a page should be created (or opened) that will be used to hold the data view.

Before you can put a data view on the page, it must be saved under the file extension .aspx, which indicates that the page makes use of ASP.NET, an improved version of Active Server Pages. Choose File, Save As, and then rename the page to end with that extension.

To insert a data view on an existing Web page:

1. Click the spot on the page where the XML data should be displayed.
2. Choose **Data**, **Insert Data View**. One of the following two things happens:
    - If you are editing a site on your computer or on a Web server that does not offer SharePoint Services 2.0, FrontPage reports that this feature is unavailable.
    - On a SharePoint-equipped host, the Data Source Catalog task pane opens, displaying the catalog of sources from which data can be displayed (see Figure 23.3).
3. Click the **+** next to the XML Files item to see the list of XML data sources, which includes the file that you just imported.

A data view can be created by simply dragging a source from the Data Source Catalog task pane to a Web page. However, this causes FrontPage to guess which of the source's records and fields should be displayed. In my experience using this feature with XML files, most guesses are wildly off the mark.

FIGURE 23.3

*Choosing a source for a data view.*

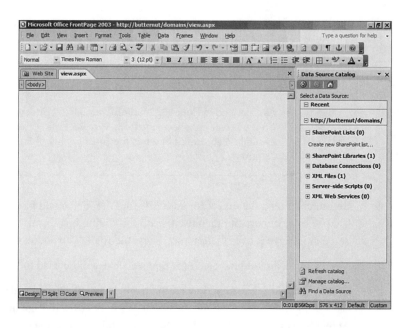

4. Hover over the XML file's name until an arrow appears next to it; then click the arrow and choose **Show Data** from the drop-down menu that appears. The Data View Details pane opens (see Figure 23.4).

FIGURE 23.4

*Viewing the contents of a data source.*

5. In the Work with Data section of the pane, records from the XML file are displayed along with the name of each field in the record. To choose the records and fields to present on the Web page, hold down the **Shift** key and click items to display in the order they should be presented.

6. Click the **Insert Data View** link on the task pane.

The data view appears on the Web page, showing the selected contents of the XML file. Preview the page to see the results of your handiwork. Whenever the XML file is updated, every page that contains a data view associated with the file will be updated automatically.

A data view of an XML file is shown in Figure 23.5. FrontPage presents the data as a table with a tag name atop each column. This, like every other aspect of the presentation, can be modified.

**FIGURE 23.5**

*Displaying the contents of an XML file with a data view.*

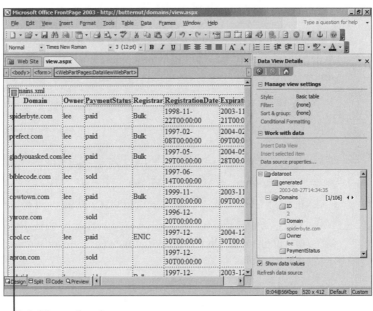

Data View options icon

## Choose How Many Records to Display

If a data source contains more than 10 records, FrontPage divides the display into 10-record pages, offering a link at the bottom of the view that can be clicked to see more.

The number of displayed records can be changed by editing the data view:

1. Click anywhere within the data view. A Data View Options icon appears at one of its edges (one was shown in Figure 23.5).
2. Click the **Data View Options** icon and choose **Style** from the drop-down menu that appears. The View Styles dialog box opens.
3. Click the **Options** tab to bring it to the front.
4. In the Record Sets section, choose an option:
   - Choose **Display All Items** to present all records on one page.
   - To display more (but not all) of the records on each page, edit the **Display Items in Sets of This Size** field.
5. Click **OK**.

The data view is updated to reflect the change.

## Filter Records on Different Criteria

A data view doesn't have to display the entire contents of an XML file or any other data source. One or more filters can be applied based on the value of record fields.

To apply filters to an existing data view, follow these steps:

1. Click the **Data View Options** icon and then choose **Filter** from the drop-down menu. The Filter Criteria dialog box appears.
2. Click the **Click Here to Add a New Clause** button. A list box appears in the Field Name column, as shown in Figure 23.6.
3. In the **Field** list box, choose a field that will be used to filter data.
4. The Comparison column sets up the filtering criteria. By default, it is set to Equals. To change this, click **Equals** and then choose a different criteria from the list box that is displayed.
5. Complete this filter: Provide a value in the **Value** column.
6. To add another filter, repeat steps 2–5.
7. When you're done, click **OK**.

The data view is updated so that only the records matching all of the filters are presented.

## Format the Data View

The records presented in a data view can be formatted with styles, the buttons of the Formatting toolbar, and the like.

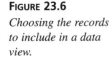

**FIGURE 23.6**

*Choosing the records to include in a data view.*

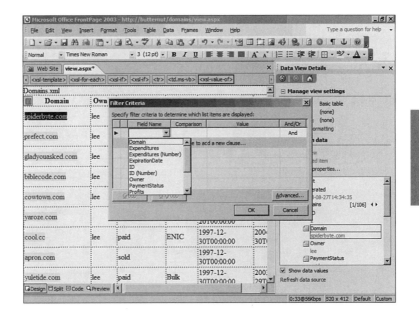

When a view is structured as a table, changing the appearance of one field of a record causes all other fields in the same column to be similarly formatted: For example, applying italics to an item causes all values in that column to be italicized.

Fields also can be formatted based on the data that they hold. Numeric values can be changed to currency, date and timestamps can be displayed as dates, and Web addresses can be presented as hyperlinks.

To change the presentation format of a column in a data view, right-click one of the values in that column. Then on the context menu that appears, choose Format Item As and one of the options (see Figure 23.7).

Changing how a field is presented does not alter the data in the XML file: All data views can only read data and present it in different ways; they can't be used to modify it.

## Sort Records and Group Them Together

Records presented in a data view can be sorted in ascending or descending order and can be grouped. Both of these features are keyed to a field that's present in the data.

To organize a data view by sorting or grouping, follow these steps:

1. Click the **Data View Options** icon and choose **Sort and Group**. The Sort and Group dialog box opens (see Figure 23.8).

FIGURE 23.7

*Changing the presentation format of a column in a data view.*

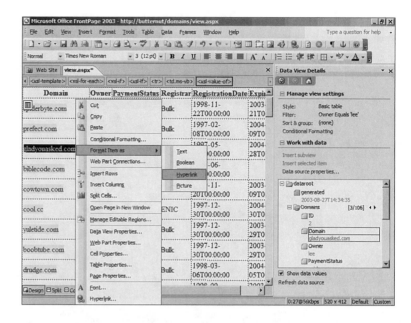

FIGURE 23.8

*Sorting records in a data view.*

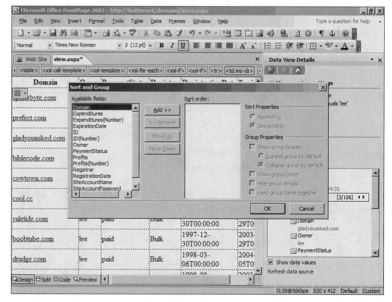

2. Choose the field that will determine the sorting order and click **Add**. The field appears in the Sort Order column.

3. A second sorting field determines the order when the first sorting field is shared by two or more records. To choose one, click it in the **Available Fields** column and click **Add**.

4. Any of the sorted fields can be used to group records. Choose the field in the **Sort Order** column and click the **Show Group Header** option.

5. Groups can be displayed when the page is loaded (expanded) or hidden (collapsed). Choose one of these options in the **Group Properties** section and click **OK**.

**23**

Data views are a sophisticated example of a *Web part*, a new kind of Web component introduced with FrontPage 2003.

The table-based views detailed in this section are one of more than a dozen formats that the Data view can employ. To convert a view to another view, click its Data View Options icon and choose Style from the drop-down menu.

In addition to presenting data from sources such as XML files and databases, Web parts can be used to collect input from visitors, share content from a SharePoint-based collaboration site, and present dynamic Web content in other novel ways.

# Summary

The most important improvement to Microsoft FrontPage and the other programs of the Office suite may be their support for Extensible Markup Language (XML).

XML frees information from the software used to create it. You can create and produce XML files and other data with the comfort of knowing that the data won't disappear if you lose or replace the program used to create it.

Although FrontPage 2003 can be used as an XML editor, the more significant support is offered in the presentation and creation of XML data with the software.

If you're using a Web-hosting service equipped with the most current version of SharePoint Services, you can use a data view Web component to present data from an XML file on a Web page.

You also can save responses from a form page as XML, making it available easily for use in other software.

# Q&A

**Q** **Some XML tags include more than just a name—such as a name followed by an equals sign and something in quotes, as in `<book edition="Paperback">`. What are these?**

**A** XML elements can be modified by one or more attributes, which take the form `name="value"` and provide additional information about that particular element.

In the example you provided, the attribute `edition` has the value `Paperback`, and it's an extra bit of information related to the publication data of a book.

XML is a complex language that's beyond the scope of this book to describe in detail. Because FrontPage can produce and consume XML on its own in the same manner that it works with HTML behind the scenes, you don't need to know much about XML to benefit from its use.

To learn more about the concepts embodied by XML and how you can make use of them, Sams Publishing offers *Sams Teach Yourself XML in 10 Minutes*, by Andrew Watt (ISBN 0-672-32471-7), and *Sams Teach Yourself XML in 24 Hours*, by Michael Morrison (ISBN 0-672-32213-7).

# Hour 24

# Divide a Page into Separate Frames

A challenging part of Web site design is determining how to organize your site so that it is easy to use. This is determined primarily by the choices you make in page content, link bars, and navigational hyperlinks.

Web designers have another tool in their belt that lets them venture outside of the typical page-oriented design: a special feature called frames.

Frames divide a single browser window into smaller sections, each holding its own Web page, making it possible for visitors to view more than one page simultaneously.

Although frames are one of the more complicated aspects of Web design, FrontPage 2003 takes the pain out of the process, making them as easy to work with as tables.

In this hour, you will learn

- How to create and resize frames
- How to put a Web page into a frame
- How to add and remove scrollbars from a frame
- How to create an inline frame and place it on a Web page

# Create a Frame

Frames divide a browser window into two or more separate windows, each separated by a thin gray border. This will make more sense after you take a look at one—Figure 24.1 contains a Web page divided into several frames.

**FIGURE 24.1**

*Using frames to display family photos.*

FrontPage 2003 includes 10 page templates with the most common frame arrangements. The page shown in Figure 24.1 was created from the Banner and Contents template and has three frames: a banner frame with the title Family Photo Album, a left frame with a list of hyperlinks, and a right frame containing a digital photo. (If you're curious, those prices are what my grandfather charged at his gas station in 1960!)

You can configure frames in several ways:

- Frames can be set to a specific size.
- Frames can be resized when site visitors change the size of their browsers.
- Frames can have vertical and horizontal scrollbars or no scrollbars at all

When you're working with frames, a hyperlink in one frame can open in that frame or any other frame on the page. It also can open in a new window or fill the entire Web browser window. The frame in which the linked document loads is called the *target frame*.

In Figure 24.1, the frame on the left contains a list of hyperlinks to pages that display digital photos. The target frame is the one on the right, so when one of the links is clicked, a photo page opens in the right frame.

You can determine the target frame of a hyperlink in two different ways:

- Set up the hyperlink so that it includes a reference to a target frame
- Set up the page containing the hyperlink so that it has a default target frame

## Add a Frames Page to a Site

The easiest way to work with frames in FrontPage is to create a new Web page from 1 of the 10 frame templates. After you have created a frames page from a template, you can make adjustments so that it fits your desired design.

Create a frames page by following these steps:

1. Open the Web site you are working on (or create a new one).
2. Choose **File, New** to open the New pane if it isn't already open.
3. The pane displays a few of the pages and Web sites you can create using templates and wizards. To see all of them, click the **More Page Templates** link. The Page Templates dialog box appears.
4. Click the **Frames Pages** tab to bring it to the front, as shown in Figure 24.2.

**FIGURE 24.2**

*Choosing a frames page template.*

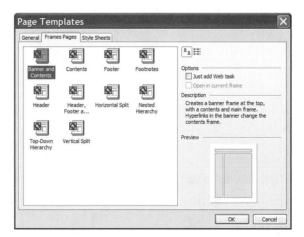

5. To select a frames page template, choose its icon.

   The Page Templates dialog box displays the approximate size and arrangement of the different frames. Look at the Description and Preview sections to find out what the template contains.

6. Make sure the **Open in Current Frame** check box is not selected.

7. Click **OK**.

FrontPage creates a framed Web page by placing two or more empty frames in a page, each with Set Initial Page and New Page buttons (see Figure 24.3).

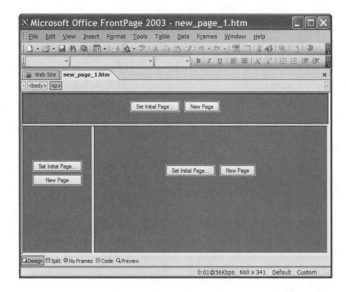

As you can see, FrontPage creates the frames page without putting any content in the frames.

This illustrates a fundamental concept of frames that's important to understand as you begin working on them: Frames are designed using a frames page that contains the formatting and size of the frames, but little else.

The actual content of each frame is a separate Web page—to display something in a frame, you must create a new page or use an existing one.

## Put a Page in a Frame

The Web pages that you display in a frame continue to exist as separate pages, even though you can edit them while working on the frames page. If you open one of these pages directly for editing and make changes, your edits are reflected on the frames page.

When a frames page is created from a template, the Set Initial Page and New Page buttons are displayed in each frame until you have assigned a page to it.

To create a blank page in the frame, click New Page. A new blank page based on the Web site's current theme opens in the frame.

To put an existing page in a frame, follow these steps:

1. Click **Set Initial Page**. The Insert Hyperlink dialog box opens. Use this to find and select the page that should appear in the frame.

2. Click **OK**. The frames page is reloaded with the selected page inside the frame (see Figure 24.4).

FIGURE **24.4**

*Setting a frame's initial page.*

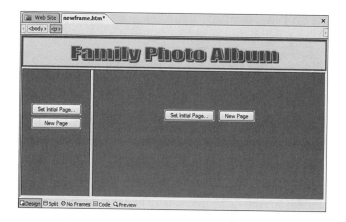

 The page that you display within a frame doesn't have to be part of your Web site; it can be any page on the World Wide Web. However, many Web publishers object to their work being "framed" in this way because it makes you appear to be the author of their work. There have even been some lawsuits over the issue. For this reason, the most prudent course is to frame only your own pages or secure permission from others before using their page in this way.

After pages have been placed in frames, they can be edited within their frames. Click your cursor on the page to begin working on it.

# Work on a Framed Page

Any Web page displayed within a frame can be edited in two ways: You can work on it within the frames page or open the page separately.

Editing a framed page is like working on any other, with one exception: You must decide where hyperlinks on the page will be opened.

A hyperlink can open its linked document in four places:

- Within the same frame
- Within a different frame on the same page
- In the entire Web browser window, replacing the frames page
- In a new Web browser window, leaving the existing frames page open in another window

The place where a linked page loads is called the *target frame*. You can designate a target frame whenever you create or edit a hyperlink.

When you are working with hyperlinks, you can specify the target frame by name or use one of five standard targets:

- **Same Frame**—The linked page opens in the same frame as the hyperlink.
- **Whole Page**—The linked page fills the entire browser window.
- **New Window**—The linked page opens in a new browser window, leaving the existing browser window alone.
- **Parent Frame**—The linked page replaces the entire frames page.
- **Page Default**—The linked page opens to the default target frame set up for the entire page.

The standard targets are useful when you want to break out of the currently displayed frame in some way, either to open new frames or to open a page that doesn't contain any frames.

Here's how to create a hyperlink that specifies a target frame:

1. While editing a page, select the text or graphic that will be associated with the hyperlink, and click **Insert Hyperlink** to open the Insert Hyperlink dialog box.
2. Choose the page to which you're linking:
    - If the page is part of your site, use the dialog box to find and select it (but don't click OK yet).
    - If the page is not part of your site, enter the URL (Web address) of the page in the Address field.

3. Click the **Target Frame** button. The Target Frame dialog box appears, as shown in Figure 24.5. You can use this dialog box to select the frame in several different ways:

**FIGURE 24.5**

*Selecting a hyperlink's target frame.*

24

- To choose one of the frames on the page, click it in the Current Frames Page panel. The frame becomes darker in the pane, and its name appears in the Target Setting field.
- To choose one of the standard targets, select it in the Common Targets list box.
- To choose the frame by its name, enter it in the Target Setting field.

4. After selecting a target, you can make it the default for all links on the same page. To do this, select the **Set as Page Default** check box.

5. Click **OK**. The Target Frame dialog box closes.

6. To finish creating the hyperlink, click **OK**.

> To edit a hyperlink and change its target frame, right-click the link and choose Hyperlink Properties from the context menu. The Edit Hyperlink dialog box is displayed, which can be used just like the Insert Hyperlink box in steps 2–6 of the preceding list.

All of the frame templates in FrontPage set a default target for each page contained in a frame. If most or all of a page's links should go to a different target frame, it's easier to change the default target than to pick a target for each link.

You change the default target by editing one of the properties of that framed page:

1. Right-click an empty area in the framed page and choose **Page Properties** from the context menu that appears.

   The Page Properties dialog box is displayed (see Figure 24.6). If a default target frame has been set for the page, its name is displayed in the Default Target Frame text field.

**FIGURE 24.6**

*Choosing a default target frame.*

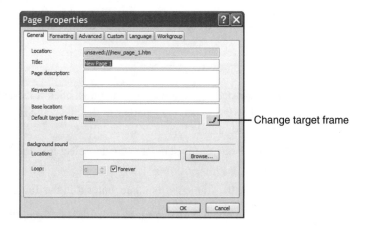

Change target frame

2. To set a default, click the Change Target Frame button shown in Figure 24.6.

3. Select the target using Target Frame dialog box, and click **OK**.

You can use most of the target frame options with any hyperlink, regardless of whether your Web site contains frames. The Whole Page target is useful when you want to make sure that a page in your site is displayed in a full browser window (rather than in an existing frame). The New Window option opens a separate browser window.

## Create an Alternative to Frames

Frames were introduced by Netscape for its Navigator Web browser in late 1995 and are standard in all five popular browsers today: Navigator, Internet Explorer, Mozilla, Opera, and Safari.

However, people who use text-based browsers and extremely old Web browsers (such as version 1 of Netscape Navigator or versions 1 or 2 of Internet Explorer) won't be able to use a Web site that's reliant on frames.

For these reasons, some Web developers create both a frames page and a nonframes alternative for their sites.

In FrontPage, when you are editing frames, an extra button appears at the bottom edge of the editing window: No Frames.

Click this button to see what frame-deprived visitors will see when they visit your frames page. The default is a very plain page with text that reads "This page uses frames, but your browser doesn't support them."

To create a more friendly and useful alternative to frames, follow these steps:

1. With the frames page open for editing, click **No Frames**.
2. Replace the existing text with a description (and even some of the content) of the pages that were presented in those frames.
3. Apply your site's theme to the page, if you're using themes.
4. Add links to each of the important pages on your site. They will load in the entire browser window.
5. Open one of the Web pages in your site that's being displayed in a frame.
6. Make sure that the page also contains links to your main pages.

   Many Web designers put these links at the bottom of the page. (The links are redundant for any visitor using frames, so you don't want to devote too much emphasis to them.)
7. Repeat steps 5–6 until you've hit all of the framed pages in the site.

Creating a no-frames alternative is a time-consuming task, so you might question whether to undertake it for an audience that's likely to comprise less than 5% of your site's visitors.

There's an additional reason to do this: Popular search engines such as Google and Altavista might not be able to find and index all of your site's contents without a no-frames alternative.

After you have created a frames page, filled it with pages, and set up the links and a no-frames alternative, you're ready to save the page.

## Save a Frames Page for the First Time

When you work on a frames page, you'll be editing that page along with all of the pages displayed in its frames.

For this reason, FrontPage responds differently when you save the frames page.

To save a frames page and all of the pages it contains, follow these steps:

1. Click the **Save** button.

   The Save As dialog box opens, looking a little different than it would otherwise: A large panel on the right side shows the arrangement of the frames on the page (see Figure 24.7).

**FIGURE 24.7**

*Saving a frames page and its contents.*

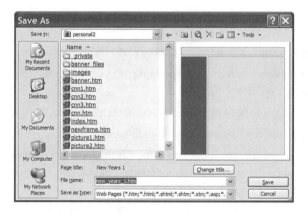

The dark frame in that panel is the one that will be saved next.

2. Type a name for this page in the **Filename** field, making sure to keep the .htm filename extension at the end.

3. The page's title appears in the **Page Title** field. Although the title will not appear on the frames page, it will be seen by people (and search engines) who are not using frames. Click **Change Title** to choose a better title.

4. The Set Page Title dialog box opens. Enter a title in the Page Title field, and click **OK**.

5. If you're happy with the filename and title, click **Save**. (If the page contains unsaved photos or clip art, a Save Embedded Files dialog box opens. Use this to choose a filename and folder for these files.)

What happens next depends on whether there are any other framed pages left to save. If there are, you return to the Save As dialog box. You might see a different dark frame in the panel on the right side; if so, repeat steps 2–4.

If you're done, FrontPage saves the frames page and returns to the editing window.

## Make Adjustments to a Frame

Because frames are created from standard templates, you will probably need to make adjustments as you're working on a frame-based page.

As you have seen, a frames page requires one Web page for each frame and an extra page that is used to configure the frames.

You can do several things to adjust a frames page to your liking:

- The height or width of a frame can be changed.
- Scrollbars can be added, removed, or displayed only if they are needed.
- Visitors can be allowed to adjust a frame's size, or can be prevented from moving borders.

Changing the size of a frame is easy: Drag its border to a new location.

To add and remove scrollbars and make more precise size adjustments, follow these steps:

1. Right-click one of the pages affected by the frame and choose **Frame Properties** from the context menu.

   The Frame Properties dialog box opens, as seen in Figure 24.8.

**FIGURE 24.8**

*Setting up a frame's size and scrollbars.*

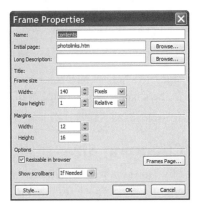

24

2. To set the width of the page, adjust the Width field (in the Frame Size area, not the Margins area):

   • To set the width in pixels, choose the width value and **Pixels** from the adjacent list box.

   • To set the width as a percentage of the page size, choose the value and **Percent** from the adjacent list box.

3. To set the height, follow the same procedure as in step 2 in the Row Height field.

4. If you want to prevent visitors from resizing a frame, deselect the **Resizable in Browser** check box. Otherwise, select this box.

Most Web designers prefer to prevent resizing because a visitor can turn a lovingly crafted page into an unreadable mess with a few movements of the frame borders.

5. Use the Show Scrollbars list box to determine whether scrollbars will be viewed within that page:

   • Choose **If Needed** to hide scrollbars unless the page's contents are bigger than the size of the frame.

   • Choose **Always** to always display a scrollbar.

   • Choose **Never** to never display a scrollbar.

One word of caution when choosing Never: This choice could prevent your visitors from seeing some of the content on a framed page, depending on their particular screen resolution and browser window size.

6. Every frame is given a name by default, which can be used as a target frame for hyperlinks. To change a frame's name, type it in the **Name** field.

7. Click **OK**. The frames page reloads to reflect the changed dimensions.

## Create a Frame of Changing Size

Because Web pages are viewed by browsers at many different screen sizes, it's not a good idea to set up a precise width for every frame from left to right or top to bottom.

Instead, at least one of the frames in each direction should have an unspecified size. That way, the frame will take up all of the room that's left over from the other frames.

To give a framed page an unspecified size, follow these steps:

1. Right-click the framed page and choose **Frame Properties**.

2. Set the **Width** and **Height** to 1.

3. Set both of the adjacent list boxes to **Relative** instead of Pixels or Percent.

4. Click **OK**.

# Add an Inline Frame

Another way to make use of frames is to place one frame entirely inside a page. These are called *inline frames*, and they have been supported by Web browsers since version 4 of Internet Explorer and version 6 of Netscape Navigator.

Figure 24.9 shows an inline frame that displays headlines from one site on another.

**FIGURE 24.9**

*A Web page that uses an inline frame.*

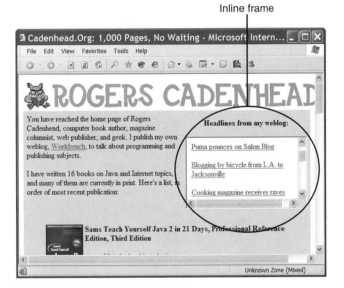

Inline frame

If you have used FrontPage's browser compatibility feature to indicate that the site works with earlier versions of those browsers, you won't be able to add inline frames to it.

To add an inline frame to a page, follow these steps:

1. With the page open for editing, click the spot on the page where the frame should be added.

2. Open the page and choose **Insert, Inline Frame**.

   A new frame opens in the page with Set Initial Page and New Page buttons.

3. Choose a page to display in the frame:
   - To put a new, blank page in that spot, click **New Page**.
   - To place an existing page in the inline frame, click **Set Initial Page**.

The selected page is displayed at that position on the frames page, in a window 300 pixels wide and 150 pixels tall.

You can edit the frame to change its size and appearance:

1. Double-click one of the edges of the frame. The Inline Frame Properties dialog box opens (see Figure 24.10).

FIGURE 24.10

*Changing inline frame properties.*

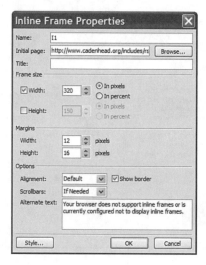

2. To set the width of the frame, check the Width check box in the Frame Size section of the dialog box (not the Margins section). Choose **In Pixels** if the width will be expressed in pixels, or **In Percent** if it will be a percentage of the page's total width. Use the adjacent list box to select a value.

3. To set the height, repeat step 2 in the **Height** area of the Frame Size section.

4. An inline frame's border can be hidden, making it appear as if it were part of the frames page. To accomplish this feat, deselect the **Show Border** check box.

5. Choose a scrollbar policy for the frame with the Scrollbars list box: **Always**, **If Needed**, or **Never**.

6. To offer text for nonframes visitors, type it in the **Alternate Text** field.

> There's less of a need to do this for an inline frame than there is for other frames because inline frames don't usually affect navigation.

7. Click **OK**.

After an inline frame has been added to a Web page, it always remains in sync with that page. That's why it's useful for a headline-sharing page such as the one shown in Figure 24.9: Headlines change constantly, so it's easy to keep them up-to-date within an inline frame.

24

# Summary

Frames are a great example of how FrontPage 2003 can simplify Web development. Working with frames by directly editing HTML tags on a Web page can be cumbersome, especially if your Web contains frames contained within other frames and other complex arrangements.

In this hour, you added frames to a Web, opened links in different frames, and edited frames by adding and removing scrollbars. You also worked with inline frames—frames that are located entirely within another Web page.

FrontPage's frame templates make it easy to add 10 different frame layouts to a page.

Now that you have hands-on skills with each of the essential features of FrontPage, you can benefit from the software's sophisticated editing, publishing, and Web site-maintenance capabilities.

As you have learned, FrontPage makes it possible for Web publishers of any skill level to make use of Web design languages and technologies such as Hypertext Markup Language (HTML), Cascading Style Sheets (CSS), Dynamic HTML, JavaScript, and Active Server Pages (ASP). By this point, you can create sites with features that rival those of Web design experts.

Whether you're using FrontPage 2003 for work, school, or fun, you can now add your contribution to the World Wide Web's astoundingly immense repository of information, communication, and commerce.

As the author of this book and a longtime FrontPage user, I'm eager to see what readers are doing with the software. When you publish your own FrontPage site, tell me about it by visiting my Web site at www.frontpage24.com.

# Q&A

**Q  Why aren't frames created using cells, as tables can be?**

**A**  Unlike tables, frames must be defined strictly in one direction: horizontal or vertical. It's a different way to subdivide a rectangular area than tables use, but it can be just as effective.

Unless you start with a frames page template, you will create a page with multiple frames one frame at a time. The first two-page frame is loaded, one of those frames splits into two, and so on, until all frames have been developed.

**Q  I created a Web with frames. When I preview it in Internet Explorer, the Address bar does not change when I load different pages in my Web. What's wrong?**

**A**  The Address bar of a Web browser is not supposed to change as you load pages into different frames. This prevents a user from bookmarking a page contained within a frame rather than loading all the frames. To get a better understanding of why this is important, open the Web that you finished during this hour's workshop. Preview the index.htm page in a browser and then preview the sections.htm page.

The only way for the Web to work correctly is if index.htm is loaded. Loading one of the other pages causes the Web to be displayed without any frames.

# PART VII

# Appendices

A   FrontPage Internet Resources

# APPENDIX A

# FrontPage Internet Resources

According to the World Wide Web search engine Google, more than 670,000 Web pages mention Microsoft FrontPage in some manner. Unless you have a few decades to kill, you might not want to sift through all those pages to find useful FrontPage sites.

This appendix covers the best Internet resources currently available for Microsoft FrontPage. You can find tips, bug-troubleshooting help, discussion forums, and many other useful bits of information that aren't in the official Microsoft FrontPage 2003 documentation. You'll also come across some good examples of Web sites designed with FrontPage.

## Web Sites and Discussion Groups

Dozens of Web sites exist for FrontPage users seeking help, themes, product add-ons, and other offerings.

The first place you should go, in our admittedly biased opinion, is this book's official World Wide Web site:

`http://www.frontpage24.com`

Visit this Web site for the latest details on corrections, clarifications, and other information that supplements this book. You also can use it to send email to author Rogers Cadenhead.

Sams Publishing offers support for this book and all of its other titles on its Web site:

`http://www.samspublishing.com`

To find the section devoted to this book, search for the ISBN 0672325527.

# Web Sites

## Microsoft FrontPage

`http://www.microsoft.com/frontpage`

This is Microsoft's official home page for FrontPage 2003 and past versions of the software. Go here first for product specifications, technical support, and online ordering. You can search through Microsoft's support database for information on bug fixes related to FrontPage, find out about free offers that you're eligible for, download new templates and other FrontPage add-ins, and subscribe to *Microsoft FrontPage FanZine*, an email newsletter. There's also a gallery of Web sites designed by FrontPage users.

## Chris's FrontPage Info

`http://www.webworkshop.org/frontpage`

If you'd like the perspective of an experienced FrontPage site designer, try Chris Calabrese's FrontPage Info Web site. A FrontPage user since January 1997, Calabrese has compiled quick tips, problem solutions, and a guide to Internet resources for FrontPage users. He also offers an active community discussion forum where users can help each other.

## FrontPage Technical Support

`http://www.msfrontpage.net`

Dynamic Net FrontPage Technical Support, a site run by a Web hosting company that provides FrontPage hosting, offers links to useful documents published by Microsoft and tips on newsgroups, Web sites, and other information. It's one of the only sites that focuses on Active Server Pages in addition to FrontPage.

## FrontPage World

`http://www.frontpageworld.com`

FrontPage World is an extensive guide to the software that's published by Paul Colligan, the author of the "FrontPage Tips" weekly email newsletter. The site offers a "FrontPage Secrets" online course, dozens of great-looking FrontPage themes for sale at prices ranging from $15 to $59, an active discussion forum, and lots of other features.

## Microsoft Web Presence Providers

`http://www.microsoftwpp.com`

This is a database of Web hosting providers that support FrontPage 2003 and previous versions of the software. This can be viewed by state or in alphabetical order, and there's an associated database for international providers.

## Acme Internet

`http://www.acmeinfo.com`

Acme Internet, a Web hosting provider in Minneapolis, Minnesota, is one of the first companies to offer FrontPage 2003 hosting and is a longtime specialist in Microsoft Web hosting. It's experienced with the issues that can arise in hosting and publishing FrontPage Web sites.

## AccessFP FrontPage Resource Centre

`http://accessfp.net`

The AccessFP FrontPage Resource Center is a site published in Stockport, England, that offers resources for each version, from FrontPage 97 to FrontPage 2003. There are community forums, links to free and for-sale FrontPage themes and templates, and a tutorial "ezine" called "AnyFrontPage Bytes."

## Outfront Templates and Tools

`http://www.frontpagecommerce.com`

Thomas Brunt, a FrontPage add-on developer and provider of FrontPage Web hosting, offers several dozen FrontPage templates that can be put to use on your own sites. Prices range from $15 to $30 and include the graphics files and Flash animations featured in each template.

**A**

### At-FrontPage

http://www.at-frontpage.com

A long-time FrontPage support site published by Tiffany K. Edmonds, At-FrontPage features several dozen tutorials on specific aspects of each FrontPage version, including some on incorporating databases into your Web sites.

### FrontPage Developer Resources

http://msdn.microsoft.com/library/default.asp?url=/nhp/default.asp?
➥contentid=28001170

In FrontPage 2003, choose the menu command Help, Microsoft FrontPage Developer Resources to visit Microsoft's FrontPage Developer Resources site. Documentation and development kits are available for extending the software with custom themes and new wizards written with Visual Basic, Visual C++, and other languages.

## Discussion Groups

Several of the FrontPage Web sites mentioned previously offer their own email newsletters, mailing lists, and discussion groups.

The most popular, hosted by Microsoft, is on Usenet, a widely distributed community of discussion groups on different topics.

### Microsoft FrontPage Client Newsgroup

news://microsoft.public.frontpage.client

If you can handle the large number of messages posted each day, this Usenet newsgroup is a great way to get personal support from other FrontPage users. If you don't have access to a news server that carries Microsoft newsgroups like this one, you can read it with your Web browser on Google Groups at http://groups.google.com or the Microsoft Web site at http://communities.microsoft.com/newsgroups.

# GLOSSARY

**access log**   A file saved by a Web server that tracks requests for Web pages and other files.

**access number**   The phone number dialed to connect to the Internet.

**accessibility**   The considerations involved with ensuring that individuals with special needs can access Web pages and navigate Web sites.

**action**   In Dynamic HTML, the thing that happens in response to an event. *See also* event and object.

**active graphics**   In FrontPage themes, graphical link bars that change in appearance when a Web user passes the mouse pointer over them.

**Active Server Pages (ASP)**   A technology developed by Microsoft that enables programming code to be placed on Web pages and executed whenever the page is presented by an extended server.

**active Web pages**   *See* dynamic Web pages.

**ActiveX**   A Microsoft technology that enables Web developers to place executable programs on Web pages. The programs, which are called ActiveX controls, run within their own windows on a page.

**ActiveX control**   An ActiveX program that loads in a Web browser.

**address bar**    The text field along the top edge of a Web browser where you can type a Web page's URL and press Enter to load the page.

**agent log**    A file saved by a Web server that keeps track of Web browser identification tags that were sent along with each request.

**alternative text**    Text that appears when a visitor's Web browser cannot display a picture or embedded object.

**animated GIF**    A GIF graphics that displays a series of images in sequence to produce animation. The format that makes this possible is called GIF89a.

**antialiasing**    A graphic design term for adjusting the edges of a graphic so that it blends more smoothly with the background.

**article**    A message posted to a discussion Web site.

**aspect ratio**    The width-to-height ratio of a picture. Most image programs have an aspect ratio feature to ensure that pictures are resized proportionally.

**audio**    Sound on your computer. Common audio file formats include AU, MP3, WAV, and MIDI.

**autostretch**    In a layout table, the capacity of a row or column to expand so that it fills the space that's left over by the rest of the table.

**AVI**    Audio Video Interleaved, a video format introduced by Microsoft.

**background graphic**    An image that is displayed as the background of a Web page.

**background sound**    An audio file that plays when a Web page loads in a Web browser.

**bandwidth**    The amount of data transferred over the Internet or via a particular connection. Bandwidth can be measured in kilobits per second or megabits per second. *See also* Kbps.

**banner**    *See* page banner.

**banner ad**    An advertisement that appears on a Web page across the top or bottom of the page.

**bookmarks**    Web browser shortcuts to your favorite sites, which are also called favorites. *See also* internal links and target.

**border**    In a table or graphic, the size of the whitespace that surrounds the element, in pixels.

**broadband connection**    A connection to the Internet that's at least 10–20 times faster than available with a dial-up modem. Most broadband connections are made using television cable or DSL telephone line technology and cost about $40 to $70 per month. Broadband connections require special hardware rather than a dial-up modem.

**browse**    To surf the Web.

**browser**    *See* Web browser.

**browser compatibility**    Issues involved in making sure pages appear correctly in different Web browsers and different versions of Web browsers.

**browser-safe colors**    *See* Web-safe colors.

**bulleted list**    An indented list of items preceded by a decorative character that calls attention to each item. Also called an unordered list.

**bulletin board**    A Web site that allows users to have ongoing discussions. Bulletin boards generally contain a table of contents page with links to individual messages, pages with the text for each message, and a page with a Web form so users can post and reply to messages. *See also* discussion site.

**cable connection**    *See* broadband connection.

**Cascading Style Sheets (CSS)**    A Web technology that establishes the formatting of Web page elements.

**cell**    An individual element of a table.

**cell padding**    In a table, the amount of empty space that surrounds the contents of each cell.

**cell spacing**    In a table, the amount of space in the grid border between each cell.

**CGI script**    A script that runs on a server and enables you to program a Web page. The most common example of a CGI script is a form processor that gathers data from a Web form. FrontPage components allow users to do things that used to require CGI scripting. *See also* scripting language.

**child level**    In objects and Web pages, child-level elements are lower in the hierarchy. For example, when you create FrontPage link bars in the Navigation view, child-level pages are represented as pages that fall under a main section page.

**client**    A computer that connects to a server to access a network, the Internet, or other data. Also refers to browsers, email programs, and other applications that allow users to get information and services from a server.

**client-side**    Refers to technologies such as DHTML, Cascading Style Sheets, Java applets, and ActiveX controls, which rely on a Web browser or other client application.

For example, only version 4.0 browsers and higher support DHTML.

**collapsible outlines**   Lists in which items can be hidden or displayed at the control of people visiting the page.

**color depth**   The number of colors that a computer screen can display or that an image can include. Options include millions of colors (16.7 million colors, true color, 24-bit color), thousands of colors (67,000 colors, high color, 16-bit color), and 256 colors (8-bit color). Higher color depths generally enable better-quality image displays.

**color scheme**   The colors of a Web page's background, text, and links.

**comments**   Text that appears on a Web page only as it is being edited. FrontPage offers a comments Web component that displays comments in purple text preceded by the word *Comment*.

**Common Gateway Interface (CGI)**   A set of commands and scripting languages that can run on most standard servers. Perl is a popular CGI scripting language. *See also* CGI script.

**continuous tone image**   An image with complex shading and gradation of colors, such as a photograph or an oil painting. On the Web, these images work best when formatted as JPEGs.

**cookie**   A special browser file that a Web site can use to personalize each visit to the site. Web sites can read the cookie files they have created, which enables a site to recognize who you are when you visit. By design, browsers send cookies only to the site that created them.

**cropping**   A photographic term that means to keep a portion of a graphic and discard the rest.

**CSS**   *See* Cascading Style Sheets.

**CSV**   Comma-separated values, a text format that can be read easily by spreadsheet and database programs such as Microsoft Excel and Microsoft Access.

**data**   Web pages, email messages, pictures, documents, and anything else that is stored on your computer or transferred over networks or over the Internet.

**data catalog**   In FrontPage, the data sources from which they can draw information.

**data views**   Web components that display information retrieved from a data source and keep themselves up-to-date.

**database**   A file that is used to store large amounts of related information together. Databases are structured in a way that makes it quick to retrieve records based on any needed criteria. *See also* field, record, and table.

**default**   The automatic setting that determines the behavior of an application or an element that is created or manipulated within an application. Most defaults can be changed by clicking a toolbar button, selecting a menu item, or changing settings in a dialog box. For example, FrontPage automatically aligns text and images to the left, but you can realign them to the center.

**definition description**   The indented text that follows a definition term in a definition list. *See also* definition list.

**definition list**   A list consisting of main entries followed by indented items with additional information. This type of list is generally used in tables of contents and other documents that contain titles or definitions followed by an explanation or description.

**definition term**   The main entry in a definition list, which is followed by a definition description in a definition list. *See also* definition list.

**delay**   In animation, the amount of time that elapses between frames; in video and audio, the amount of time that elapses between loops. *See also* loop.

**DHTML**   *See* Dynamic HTML.

**dial-up connection**   A way of connecting to the Internet using a phone modem and an ordinary phone line. The computer dials the number of an Internet service provider's modem and attempts to make a connection.

**dialog box**   A small window that opens on your computer as a program is running, often to ask a single question that can be answered by clicking a button containing a label such as Yes, No, or Cancel.

**directory path**   The location of a file in relation to a computer or Web.

**directory server**   A type of server that allows users to conference online with NetMeeting.

**discussion site**   A type of FrontPage Web where visitors can read and post messages to each other. *See also* bulletin board.

**display settings**   The resolution and color depth of a computer screen's display. Common settings are 640×480 at 256 colors (8-bit) or 800×600 at millions of colors (24-bit).

**docking a toolbar**   Anchoring a floating toolbar to the top, right, bottom, or left of the application window.

**domain name**   The address of a server or group of servers, as in `frontpage24.com`. *See also* virtual domain.

**double-click**   To click the mouse button twice in quick succession.

**download**   To copy a file from another computer to your system, using a network such as the Internet or another means of connecting computers. A word of caution: Downloaded files are a major source of computer viruses, so you should have up-to-date antivirus software on any computer to which you are actively downloading files. You also should download files only from sources you know and trust.

**DSL connection**   *See* broadband connection.

**Dynamic HTML (DHTML)**   A Web technology that enables Web developers to position, layer, and animate Web page elements; set up collapsible outlines; and load special fonts to a Web browser.

**dynamic Web pages**   Web pages enhanced with programs, scripts, and other Web technologies that respond to user input or contain animated special effects.

**dynamic Web template**   In FrontPage, a page template that serves as a master copy for other pages, making it easy to create different pages that contain many of the same things. *See also* editable regions.

**editable regions**   In a dynamic Web template, the parts of a page that will change.

**email link**   *See* mailto link.

**embedded files**   A file and plug-in application (complete with toolbar buttons) that appears as part of your Web page layout, such as a QuickTime movie with player controls. FrontPage also uses the term *embed* when you save Web pages that contain images that you've edited with the Picture toolbar. In this context, *embed* means adding the pictures to your Web page. *See also* inline files.

**encryption**   A way to encode data so that it remains confidential. Some Web servers can encrypt Web pages and other data so that you can enter confidential information on a site, such as when you are buying a product online and want to transmit your credit-card information.

**error log**   A file on a Web server that keeps track of errors generated by the server as it is used.

**event**   In DHTML, anything that happens to a Web page or object that triggers an action. *See also* action and object.

**extended server**   A Web server that offers either FrontPage Server Extensions or SharePoint Services. Many of the capabilities offered by FrontPage require the use of an extended server; the best choice is one that offers SharePoint Services 2.0.

**Extensible Markup Language (XML)**   A standard for the exchange of information through human-readable markup elements similar to HTML.

**external files**   Files that are launched separately from a Web page when a visitor clicks a link rather than appearing as embedded or inline files that are part of the Web page layout. *See also* inline files and embedded files.

**external links**   Hyperlinks to pages on other Web sites. *See also* hyperlinks.

**favorites**   *See* bookmarks.

**feedback page**   A Web page that site visitors can use to send email, usually to the publisher or someone else affiliated with the site.

**field**   In a database, an individual element in a record.

**filename extension**   A period and a string of characters added to a filename that tell computers and Web browsers the file type. For example, `image.jpeg` designates a JPEG file.

**flame**   An angry message sent by email or posted to a discussion site or newsgroup.

**floating toolbar**   A toolbar that floats in the middle of an application window when displayed. You can anchor a floating toolbar by dragging it to the top, bottom, left, or right of the application window. *See also* docking a toolbar.

**form**   On the Web, a page with form fields that allows users to enter information, select options, and post data to the server. When you collect information on your site, you use a Web page element called a *form*. Forms are made up of text boxes, lists, and other means of gathering information from visitors.

**form field**   A text box, scrolling list, button, or other page element that appears on a Web form so visitors can enter information, select options, and send data.

**form handler**   A CGI script or FrontPage component installed on a server that processes form data, such as by adding the information to a database or sending it to an email address.

**frames**   A way of dividing a single Web page into separate sections, each of which can have its own scrollbar and border. Clicking a hyperlink in one frame often causes a page to be opened in a different frame.

**frameset document**   A Web page that tells which pages to display in which frames.

**FrontPage navigation bar**   A type of navigation bar that you can generate automatically with FrontPage. *See also* navigation bar.

**FrontPage Server Extensions**  Software that extends a server's capabilities to offer FrontPage authoring features such as Web components and discussion sites. Unlike past versions of the software, FrontPage 2003 is not accompanied by its own version of FrontPage Server Extensions. Instead, extended server capabilities are supported by SharePoint Services.

**FrontPage Web**  A term used in past versions of FrontPage to describe a Web site created with the software.

**GIF**  Graphic Interchange Format, an image file format for the Web limited to 256 colors. The format works well for line art and flat-color pictures. The GIF format also allows you to create animations from GIF files and create transparent GIFs. *See also* animated GIF and transparent GIF.

**GIF animation**  *See* animated GIF.

**graphical bullets**  Bullets that are created as images rather than text.

**graphical text**  An image that contains text.

**heading**  An eye-catching headline that stands out from surrounding text.

**hit**  A request to a Web server for a file hosted by the site, such as a Web page or a graphics file.

**home page**  The main page of a Web site. Alternatively, the term refers to the first page a browser loads when it is started.

**horizontal line**  A Web page element that inserts a line on the Web page. Horizontal lines are commonly used to create separators for different types of information or sections on a Web page. Some people also use the terms *horizontal rule* or *page divider*.

**horizontal spacing**  The amount of space between the left and right sides of an image or other page.

**host**  In the context of the World Wide Web, to make pages and other documents (a Web site) available to users of the Internet. Many Internet service providers offer a limited amount of free space on their servers for you to publish your Web pages; companies are also available that will host sites for free. The provider's server then becomes the host for your site.

**hot spot**  An area on an image map that functions as a link.

**hover**  To position the mouse pointer over an area without clicking the mouse button. Hovering the mouse pointer over a hyperlink on a Web page displays the filename or the URL of the page that will load if you click that hyperlink. Hovering over an area in a program window frequently displays a ScreenTip or a ToolTip.

**hover button**   In FrontPage, an image or text link that changes in appearance when a visitor passes the mouse pointer over it or clicks it.

**HTML**   Hypertext Markup Language, the text-formatting and presentation language used to create most Web pages.

**HTTP**   Hypertext Transfer Protocol, the set of server, communications, and browser technologies that enables Web pages to be used on the Internet.

**hyperlink**   Text, graphics, or other elements of a Web page that you can click to load a new document into your Web browser. When you click a hyperlink, your browser loads the document to which the link refers; that document can be a Web page, a graphics file, or some other type of information. When you create your own Web page, you can include hyperlinks to any other file—whether that file is a graphics file on your local hard drive or a sound file on somebody else's Web site, for example.

**hyperlink rollover**   A piece of text or an image that changes its appearance when a visitor passes the cursor over it.

**hyperlinks**   Text or pictures on a Web page that you can click on to jump to another Web page or download a file.

**hypertext**   Text on a Web page that you can click to load a new document and jump to a particular location within that document.

**Hypertext Markup Language (HTML)**   *See* HTML.

**Hypertext Transfer Protocol**   *See* HTTP.

**icon**   A graphic that represents a concept or action. For example, in most computer applications, a folder icon represents a directory that contains files or a button that you can click to open a file.

**image map**   A graphic with clickable hot spots that function as hyperlinks. *See also* hot spot.

**inheritance**   A programming and Web concept in which child-level elements (objects that are lower in the hierarchy) inherit characteristics from parent elements. For example, level 2 headings are generally smaller than level 1 headings, but they still appear in the same font as the level 1 headings. *See also* child level and parent level.

**inline files**   Files that appear on a Web page, such as images or embedded movies or soundtracks. *See also* external files.

**inline frames**   A frame that is placed entirely within another Web page.

**input type**   On a form, the type of information being collected from a Web site visitor.

**internal links**   Links to targets within the same Web page. *See also* bookmarks and target.

**Internet**   A vast global network that allows people to view Web pages, send and receive email messages, participate in newsgroups, join chat rooms, and more.

**Internet service provider (ISP)**   A company that offers access to the Internet.

**intranet**   A private network of computers that are connected at a business, school, or another organization. If you are connecting to the Internet using a computer on an intranet, you may have to consult your network administrator for details on how to access the World Wide Web, email, and other services.

**ISP**   *See* Internet service provider.

**Java**   Sun Microsystems's programming language, which can be used to present interactive programs called applets that run in a Web browser.

**Java applets**   Programs written in Java that run as part of a Web page.

**JavaScript**   A client-side scripting language for programming Web pages. *See also* scripting language and client-side.

**JPEG**   Joint Picture Experts Group. A Web image file format that works well for photo-quality graphics that may contain thousands of different colors. To make the file size reasonable, making the graphics faster to download on the Web or be transferred by other means, JPEG uses a data-compression technique that makes the file size smaller at the expense of image quality. *See also* continuous tone image.

**JScript**   A scripting language similar to JavaScript.

**Kbps**   Kilobits per second, the unit of measurement for modem and connection speeds on the Internet, as in 56.6Kbps. The faster the modem is, the more quickly you can download data.

**key combination**   A shortcut that allows the user to press a combination of keys instead of selecting commands from a menu.

**keyword**   A descriptive word entered when using a search engine form to search for information on the Web or on an individual Web site.

**layer**   To arrange text and images so they overlap, or to position them one on top of one another.

**layout table**   A table whose purpose is to arrange elements of a Web page.

**line art**   Images with simple lines and solid colors. On the Web, these images work best when formatted as GIFs.

**link bar**   A FrontPage Web component that presents a group of graphics or text links used to navigate a site. They were called navigation bars in versions of FrontPage earlier than 2002.

**links**   *See* hyperlinks.

**lists**   groups of related information set apart by bullets, numbers, or other symbols.

**local files**   Files on the same computer, or on a computer on a local network to which you're directly connected.

**local links**   Links to pages on the same Web site. *See also* external links, internal links, and hyperlinks.

**local network**   A group of computers that are directly connected to each other, usually through a local server. Most offices and other organizations have local networks. *See also* intranet.

**local server**   A server that hosts a local network.

**loop**   In multimedia, a loop occurs each time the file plays.

**low-res image**   A low-quality image with a small file size that appears as a placeholder on a Web page until the larger, higher-quality image finishes loading.

**mailto link**   A hyperlink on a Web page that enables the visitor to send email to a specified address.

**main page**   The Web page that visitors automatically go to when they enter a URL that doesn't point to a specific document (as in `www.fp2k.com/24` rather than `www.fp2k.com/24/feedback.htm`.

**marquee**   An animated text message that scrolls on a Web page like a stock ticker.

**metatag**   Information about a Web page that describes something about the page. Metatags are not displayed in Web browsers. They gives search engine spiders and other applications important information, such as a summary of the page. *See also* spider.

**modem**   A device used to connect a computer to a telephone line.

**moderator**   The person who runs a discussion Web or newsgroup.

**monitor settings**   *See* display settings.

**mouse over**   When a visitor passes the mouse pointer over a text or image link. *See also* hyperlink rollover.

**mouseover graphic**   An image that changes when a visitor moves a mouse on top of it

**navigation bar**   *See* link bar.

**netiquette**   Commonly accepted standards for behavior on the Internet.

**numbered list**   An indented list of items, each preceded by a number.

**object**   In DHTML, a picture, block of text, or other Web page element that performs an action when an event occurs. *Object* is also used as a general term for a page element or a snippet of programming code. *See also* action, event, and page elements.

**offline viewing**   Looking at a Web document while not actually connected to the Internet.

**operating system**   The software that runs your computer and tells it how to work with other applications.

**optimizing**   Making the HTML formatting of a page simpler by removing unnecessary tags and spacing the elements consistently.

**overlay**   A page layout with overlapping or layered text and image elements. *See also* layer.

**page banner**   In FrontPage themes, the text graphic that appears near the top of a Web page that contains the page's topic.

**page elements**   A general term for Web files and things that you put on a Web page, including text, images, embedded files, scripts, and FrontPage components.

**page title**   Text that appears in the browser's title bar when a page appears in a Web browser.

**page transition**   An animated effect created with DHTML that changes what a Web browser displays when a visitor loads the page or leaves the page to load something else.

**parent level**   In Web pages and programming, the top elements in a hierarchy. In the FrontPage Navigation view, a parent-level page is generally the main page for a section, with child-level pages organized beneath it. *See also* child level and same level.

**Perl**   A popular CGI scripting language. *See also* CGI script and Common Gateway Interface.

**permissions**   In server administration, sets of passwords and access levels that allow co-workers to administer, edit, or view Web pages.

**photorealistic image**   *See* continuous tone image.

**pixel**   Short for "picture element." Computer screens display words, pictures, and other elements as little dots that blend together. Each dot is a pixel.

**plug-in**  An application that extends a Web browser's capabilities so it can launch files that browsers don't normally support. For example, the Shockwave plug-in allows you to view Shockwave movies on a Web page.

**PNG**  A graphical PNG format introduced to be a replacement and enhancement for GIF and JPEG graphics. It can be used to display images with 256 or fewer colors, such as a GIF (PNG-8 format), and images with thousands of colors, such as a JPEG (PNG-24 format). PNG graphics also can support transparency and other special effects.

**pop-under window**  An extra browser window that opens as you are visiting a Web page but is immediately minimized and out of view. The window shows up on your taskbar with other browser windows that have been opened but are not currently visible. Like pop-up windows, these are used most often for advertising purposes.

**pop-up window**  An extra browser window that opens as you are visiting a Web page, usually to display advertising. The name comes from the way they pop up on the screen in front of the page you're trying to view.

**Portable Document Format (PDF)**  Adobe's technology for creating online Acrobat documents that retain their fonts and layouts and that can be viewed with the Acrobat Reader plug-in.

**portal**  A commercial Web site that functions as a gateway to the Internet.

**positioning**  Placing an image or block of text in an exact location for a precise page layout.

**processor**  Another name for the central processing unit (CPU), the device that determines how quickly your computer runs.

**programming language**  A language such as C++, Java, or Visual Basic that allows programmers to write powerful software applications.

**prompt**  On a Web form, the wording of a question or a request for specific information from a site visitor.

**properties**  Details about a Web page, image, or other type of file or Web page element.

**publish**  To upload files to a Web server to make those files available to users of the Internet. One way to design Web pages is to create them on your computer and then publish the pages to a Web server that has direct access to the Internet. *See also* upload.

**QuickTime**  A video format introduced by Apple.

**ratings**  On the Web, metainformation intended for programs that block inappropriate Web pages. Web site ratings are somewhat like movie ratings.

**record**    An item in a database.

**referrer log**    A file on a Web server that keeps track of Web addresses that contain hyperlinks requesting pages from the server. Often spelled *referer log*.

**remote files**    Files on a computer that you can connect to by dialing up an Internet account. *See also* local files.

**remote server**    A server that you can connect to by dialing up your Internet account. *See also* local server.

**repeating page elements**    Pictures, links, and text that appear on pages throughout a Web site, such as a navigation bar.

**reports**    Lists of Web site details generated automatically by FrontPage in the Reports view.

**resample**    In FrontPage, the process of using the Picture toolbar to change the dimensions of the image itself rather than simply telling the Web browser to display the image at a different size through the Image Properties dialog box.

**resizing**    Modifying a graphic in FrontPage by changing its actual dimensions.

**resolution**    The number of dots (pixels) per inch used to render an image, or the display resolution for a computer screen. On the Web, images are formatted at 72 or 96 dots per inch (DPI). Standard computer display resolutions include 640×480, 800×600, and 1280×1024 (Super VGA). *See also* display settings and pixel.

**right-click**    To click an object on the computer screen with the right mouse button to display a shortcut menu.

**rollover**    *See* hyperlink rollover and mouse over.

**round-trip HTML**    Microsoft's term for FrontPage's capability to open Web pages created by other software without altering its formatting in any way.

**same level**    In Web pages and programming, elements that occupy the same level in a hierarchy. In the FrontPage Navigation view, parent-level pages appear on the same level, with child-level pages organized beneath them. *See also* child level and parent level.

**screen real estate**    The amount of available space on a computer screen for displaying application windows.

**ScreenTip**    A small pop-up box containing text that defines or describes a particular area of the screen. You can display a ScreenTip by hovering the mouse cursor over the area of the screen in question. Some applications call the ScreenTips that appear for toolbar buttons *ToolTips*.

**scripting language**    A simplified programming language that allows even nonprogrammers to create Web pages. Scripting languages rely on another application—such as a Web browser or a server application—to run. Popular scripting languages include JavaScript and Perl.

**search engines**    World Wide Web sites that use computers to catalog millions of Web pages, which you can use to search for specific text. Some of the most popular search engines are AltaVista (`www.altavista.com`) and Google (`www.google.com`).

**search form**    A text field with a Submit button. Visitors can type keywords and click the button to display a list of links that meet the search criteria. Some search forms also include pull-down lists or items with check boxes so users can select additional items to narrow down the search.

**search page**    A Web page with a search form.

**secure Web server**    Most often used for online shopping. A secure server encrypts information (such as a credit-card number) that is sent to the server and received from it so that confidential information is hidden from anyone who might try to view it. These servers make use of Secure Sockets Layer (SSL), a protocol for protecting private information over the Internet.

**security certificate**    A special browser window that vouches for the authenticity of a program's author. After you see the security certificate, you can decide whether you want to let the program run on your machine. A security certificate is required only when you're working with ActiveX technology; Java doesn't require this kind of direct action by the user.

**server**    A computer that sends information to other computers, either in response to a request or through an automated schedule. A popular type of server on the Internet is a Web server.

**server-side**    Technologies that rely on a server's capabilities. For example, many FrontPage features require a server with FrontPage extensions.

**shared borders**    A FrontPage feature in which regions of a page can be shared by all the pages of a site.

**Shockwave movie**    A multimedia file created with one of Macromedia's applications, including Director and Flash.

**shortcut menu**    A menu that appears when you click a page element with the right mouse button.

**site**    *See* Web site.

**site search engine**   A search engine that searches only the contents of a particular Web site rather than the entire Web. The FrontPage Search component allows users to create a searchable Web site.

**slow pages**   Pages that take a long time to load in the browser due to large (or many) images, large quantities of text, elaborate animations, and other factors. A Web page should take no longer than 20–30 seconds to load. The FrontPage status bar displays the estimated download time for the current Web page.

**source code**   The HTML code behind the Web pages. In FrontPage, you can click the HTML tab in Page view to see the source code. *See also* HTML.

**spam**   A kind of unsolicited Internet marketing in which thousands of email messages are sent to anyone with an email account. An electronic version of junk mail, spam often promotes unsavory businesses and is forged so that the sender's identity is hidden. Spam is a widely loathed practice that is illegal to send in a few jurisdictions. The name was inspired by a Monty Python comedy sketch and is unrelated to the Hormel spiced meat product of the same name.

**spider**   Programs used by search-engine companies such as Lycos and Altavista to automatically find and catalog Web pages. Spiders are also called *robots*.

**SSL**   *See* secure Web server.

**static database**   Information from a database that is formatted as a set of Web pages and that doesn't allow visitors to retrieve information or otherwise interact with the database itself.

**static Web pages**   Web pages that contain no animated elements, programmed components, collapsible lists, hover buttons, or other elements that the user interacts with. *See also* active Web pages.

**status area**   *See* system tray.

**streaming audio**   Sound on the Internet that begins playing as soon as the file is selected rather than at the end of a complete download of the sound file. This format is especially well suited for concerts and live radio.

**style sheets**   *See* Cascading Style Sheets. Using CSS, you can modify the appearance of a Web site in dramatic ways, saving all of the presentation-related formatting separately in its own file, which is called a *style sheet*. Changing the style sheet changes every page in the site that uses it.

**subsites**   Web sites that are contained within folders of another site

**system tray**   The part of your Windows taskbar that's next to the current time (usually in the lower-right corner of the display screen). This is also called the *status area*, and it may contain icons representing your Internet connection, speaker volume, antivirus software, and other programs that are running on your computer.

**tab order**   The order in which elements of a form will be accessed when a user hits the Tab key to move from one element to the next (or Shift+Tab, to move in the opposite direction).

**table**   On a Web page, a rectangular grid of rows and columns in which text and other Web page elements can be placed. Alternatively, a grouping of records in a database.

**tags**   In a markup language such as HTML or XML, a means of identifying content.

**target**   An area of a Web page that is defined so that you can create a link to it from within the same Web page. In FrontPage, targets are called bookmarks. *See also* bookmarks and internal links. The frame in which the linked document loads is called the *target frame*.

**taskbar**   The strip along the bottom or side of your Windows display screen in which appear the Start button, the buttons for all active programs, the current system time, and the system tray.

**tasks**   In FrontPage, items that appear in the Tasks view as reminders of work that needs to be done on a Web site.

**templates**   Built-in sites and pages that can be used to quickly create Web content in FrontPage.

**themes**   In FrontPage, a set of coordinated color choices and graphics that can be applied to a site's pages.

**thread**   Articles posted to a discussion site in response to a particular message.

**toolbar**   A row of buttons in an application window that users can click to perform tasks.

**ToolTip**   *See* ScreenTip.

**transparency**   A technique that makes a portion of a graphic blend in with the background of the page, which can be a solid color or a graphic.

**transparent GIF**   A GIF image with the background color removed so that it appears to float against the Web page's background.

**uniform resource locator (URL)**   *See* URL.

**upload**  To send files to a server or publish files to a FrontPage Web site. *See also* download and publish.

**URL (uniform resource locator)**  A unique address that identifies a document on the World Wide Web. You can direct your browser to a particular Web page by typing the page's URL in an address field and pressing Enter. A site's address can take many forms, but most of the largest Web sites have similar-looking and simple URLs, such as `www.yahoo.com`, `www.samspublishing.com`, and `www.metafilter.com`.

**user agent**  The Web browser used to view a Web page. *See also* agent log.

**variable**  a special storage place for information in a computer program.

**VBScript**  A scripting language for use on Web pages that's comparable to JavaScript.

**vertical spacing**  The amount of space between the top and bottom of a Web page element and the surrounding text.

**virtual domain**  A domain that is hosted on another server. Many people sign up for a domain name, as in `example.com`, but host it on their ISP or Web hosting company's server instead of their own.

**virus**  A program that creates copies of itself, usually without permission, and may cause damage to files on your computer or reveal personal data to others. Viruses can be spread on floppy disks and by email, so you should protect yourself by installing an antivirus program on your computer. You also should not open any attached file you receive in email unless you know the sender (especially if the file is a program or Microsoft Word document).

**Web**  *See* World Wide Web.

**Web browser**  The tool that lets you view pages on the World Wide Web. After you connect to the Internet, you load a browser; then you can see and interact with pages on the Web. Some of the most popular browsers are Microsoft Internet Explorer, Netscape Navigator, and Opera. Internet Explorer 6 is used in many of the tasks in this book.

**Web components**  In FrontPage, menu items that add features to a Web page that would otherwise require programming or scripting.

**Web directory**  World Wide Web sites that use human editors to categorize thousands of Web sites according to their content and make recommendations about the best sites. The main way to use these directories is to navigate to the categories you are interested in. Web directories include Yahoo! (`www.yahoo.com`) and the Open Directory Project (`www.dmoz.org`).

**Web hosting company**  A company that provides Web hosting services but not dial-up Internet access.

**Web part**  A new type of Web component introduced with FrontPage 2003 that can be used to collect data from sources such as XML and Web services, collect information from users, and perform other functions.

**Weblog**  A Web site that's published as a series of diary-style entries, usually with the most recent entry listed first. Weblogs, commonly called "blogs," are often used to link to interesting Web sites and share personal details of the publisher's life. Two examples: the author's site, Workbench, at `www.cadenhead.org/workbench`, and SportsFilter at `www.sportsfilter.com`.

**Web-safe colors**  The palette of 216 colors that are displayed correctly in a Web browser, regardless of the computer or operating system the visitor is using.

**Web server**  A server on the Internet that sends Web pages and other documents in response to requests by Web browsers. Everything you view on the World Wide Web is delivered by a Web server to your browser. *See also* server.

**Web site**  A group of related Web pages. When you are creating related Web pages in a program such as FrontPage Express, you should make an effort to link all the pages as a site.

**Web site address**  *See* uniform resource locator.

**Webs**  A Web site. This term was used frequently in earlier versions of FrontPage but is not being used in the 2003 version.

**whitespace**  The amount of empty space on a Web page that contains no text, images, or other elements. A reasonable amount of whitespace is essential for good design, readability, and an uncluttered look.

**Windows SharePoint Services**  *See* extended server.

**wizard**  A program that divides a task into a series of simple questions, making it easier to complete the task. Most software developed by Microsoft includes an installation wizard that simplifies the process of setting up the program on your computer.

**workgroup**  A group of people who work together, or groups of people who share the same FrontPage Web access privileges.

**World Wide Web**  A giant network of Web pages, hypertext documents that consist of text, images, interactive programs, and other content which can be presented by Web browsers and other software.

**WYSIWYG**   "What you see is what you get," an expression describing publishing software that displays a page exactly as it will appear when it is published.

**XML**   *See* Extensible Markup Language.

**ZIP**   A popular file-compression format for Windows.

# INDEX

## A

aboutme.htm element, 84
Access database, 276-277
AccessFP FrontPage
  Resource Centre Web site,
  365
accessibility, 43
access_log, 226-228
Acme Internet Web site, 365
Active Server Pages (ASP),
  188, 267
Adbility Web site, 311
Add browser dialog box, 209
Add button, 288
Add Choice dialog box, 288
Add File button, 268
Add Link button, 178
adding
    animated GIF files to Web
      pages, 153-154
    banners to Web pages,
      178-179
    captions to graphics, 43-45
    check boxes to forms, 286-
      287

clip art to Web pages, 45-
  47
components to Web sites,
  168-169
    Expedia travel site, 171
    MSNBC news, 169-
      170
data views to Web pages,
  337-339
databases to Web sites,
  268-269
DHTML effects to Web
  pages, 157-158
drop-down boxes to forms,
  287-289
elements to forms, 282-
  283
feedback pages to sites,
  124
forms to Web pages, 280-
  282
frames page to Web sites,
  347-348
frames to Web pages,
  inline frames, 358

graphics to forms, 290-291

graphics to Web pages, 38-39

  alignment, 41-42

  sizes, 47-49

  wrapping style, 40-41

hit counters to Web pages, 235

HTML to Web pages, 311-313

hyperlinks to graphics, 42-43

hyperlinks to Web pages, 22-24

Java applets to Web pages, 163-165

labels to forms, 285

layout tables to Web pages, 55-58

  edits, 58-60

link bars to Web pages, 172-173

  hyperlinks, 175-176

  Navigational view, 173-175

  sequence setup, 178

  text, 174

lists to Web pages, 24-25

marquees to Web pages, 152-153

MSN Search Web component to Web pages, 247-248

new pages to Web sites, 70-71

option buttons to forms, 286-287

pages to feedback pages, Form Page Wizard, 130

pushbuttons to forms, 289-290

questions to feedback pages, Form Page Wizard, 133-135

search engines to Web sites, 242-243

search form components to Web pages, 246-247

shared borders to Web sites, 83-84

site maps to Web pages, 248-250

tables to Web pages, 26-29

  borders, 29

  cell padding, 30

  cell spacing, 30

  columns, 31

  data, 30-31

  rows, 31

  sizes, 32

  text, 27

text areas to forms, 284

text boxes to forms, 282-284

text to graphics, 141-143

text to Web pages, 12-16

transitions to Web pages, 155

transparency to graphics, 144

video to Web pages, 160-161

Web pages to frames, 348-349

**agent_log, 226-229**

**alignment, graphics, 41-42**

**Altavista Web site, 212**

**Amazon.com Web site, 311**

**Analog, 226**

**anchors, 304**

**animated GIF graphics, 153-154**

**animated graphics, 93**

**animating text, 151-153**

**animation, GIF format, 36-37**

**applets (Java), adding to Web pages, 163-165**

**articles, 261-263**

**ASP (Active Server Pages), 188, 267**

**At-FrontPage Web site, 366**

**Authoring tab, 205-207**

**autostretch, 56**

## B

**Back/Next bars, 177**

**Back/Next buttons, 177**

**banners, adding to Web pages, 178-179**

**blinking text, 201**

**Blogger Web site, 223**

**blogs.** *See* **Web logs**

**Bobby Web site, 45**

**<body> tag, 306**

**borders**

  shared, 82-84

  tables, 29

**Browse button, 209**

**Browser Compatibility dialog box, 203**

**browsers, Web**

  testing themes in Web pages, 94

  Web page compatibility, 200

    previewing pages, 208-209

    server software, 202-203

    target audience, 203-205

technology restrictions, 205-207

text blinking, 201

Web users, 201-202

World Wide Web Consortium standards, 200

**Browsers Compatibility dialog box, 205**

**bugs, responding to feedback pages, 129**

**buttons**

Add, 288

Add File, 268

Add Link, 178

Back/Next, 177

Browse, 209

Change, 203

Chart, 233

Check, 205

Code, 220, 304

Colors, 96

Create Database, 276

Create New Folder, 79

Crop, 140

Edit, 147

Edit Query, 271

Format, 321

Formatting toolbar, 327

Former Painter, 160

Graphics, 100-101

Insert Hyperlink, 290

More Options, 272

options, forms, 286-287

Preview in Browser, 94, 209

Remove Effect, 158-159

Reports, 217, 233

Reset, 245, 280

Search, 248

Set Transparent Color, 144

Split, 328

Start Search, 245

Submit, 280, 290

Text, 99, 142

## C

**captions, adding to graphics, 43-45**

**cell padding, tables, 30**

**Cell Properties dialog box, 32**

**cell spacing, tables, 30**

**cells, layout tables, 61-63**

**CGI program (Common Gateway Interface program), 296-297**

**Change button, 203**

**Character Spacing tab, 323**

**Chart button, 233**

**check boxes, 286-287**

**Check button, 205**

**Chris's FrontPage Info Web site, 364**

**circle transitions, 155**

**clip art**

adding to Web pages, 45-47

locating, 50

**Clip Art Library, 154**

**closing tags, 303**

**code (HTML), adding to Web pages, 220-221**

**Code button, 220, 304**

**collapsible lists, 25-26**

**collapsible outlines, 25-26**

**color, 16-18, 96-98**

**Color button, 96**

**columns, 31, 58**

**comma-separated values (CSV), 291**

**commands**

Group Box, 286

tags, 321-322

Tools menu, Web Settings, 257

**Comment dialog box, 82**

**comments, 81-82, 124**

**Commission Junction Web site, 311**

**Common Gateway Interface (CGI) programs, 296-297**

**compatibility, browsers with Web pages, 200**

previewing pages, 208-209

server software, 202-203

target audience, 203-205

technology restrictions, 205-207

text blinking, 201

Web users, 201-202

World Wide Web Consortium standards, 200

**components, 85**

adding to Web sites, 168-169

Expedia travel site, 171

MSNBC news, 169-170

timestamp components, 86-87

**configuring**

frames, 346

lists, 25

**Confirm Delete dialog box, 87**

**confirmation pages, 297**

**Confirmation tab, 297**

**copying Web pages, 243-244**

**Corporate Presence Wizard,
107**
   choosing Web site pages,
      116-118
   creating corporate Web
      sites, 115-116
**Create Database button, 276**
**Create New Folder button,
79**
**creating**
   circle transitions, 155
   confirmation pages, 297
   corporate Web sites, 115-
      116
   discussion groups, 254-
      256
   dynamic Web templates,
      179-182
   feedback pages
      Form Page Wizard,
         129-130
      input types, 130-132
      prompts, 132
      variables, 132
   frames, 346-347
   headings, 14-16
   hyperlinks for target
      frames, 350-351
   link bars, 173
   lists, 24-25
      collapsible, 26
   mouseover graphics, 158
   page transitions, 154-155
   photo galleries, 145-148
   Random transitions, 155-
      156
   site maps, 248-250
   style sheets, 318
   tables, 26-27
   text hyperlinks, 23

   Web pages, 7
      from templates, 9-10
      user interfaces, 8-9
   Web sites, 67-69
      new sites, 78-79
      wizards, 106-107
**cropping graphics, 140-141**
**CSS, 315-317, 325**
   themes, 93
   viewing, 324
   viewing Web pages, 318
**.css filename extension, 318**
**CSV (comma-separated val-
ues), 291**
**Custom Query dialog box,
271**
**Custom tab, 98**
**Customer Support Web site
templates, 78**
**Customize dialog box, 91,
96**
**Customize Theme dialog
box, 98-102**
**customizing**
   search results page, 245-
      246
   themes on Web sites, 95-
      96
      color schemes, 96-98
      fonts, 98-100
      graphic fonts, 100-101
      graphics, 100
   Web sites, 80
      private subfolders, 80-
         81

**D**

**data**
   adding to tables, 30-31
   saving to databases, 275-
      277
**data views, 336-337**
   adding to Web pages, 337-
      339
   editing, 339-340
   filter records, 340
   formatting, 340-341
**Database Column Value
dialog box, 274**
**Database Interface Wizard,
107**
**Database Results Wizard,
269, 276**
**databases, 266**
   adding to Web sites, 268-
      269
   event databases, 266
   form data, saving, 275-277
   records, 266
      displaying, 269-275
      editing, 273
      fields, 266
      tables, 266-267
   requirements, 267
   tables, 266-267
**Date and Time dialog box,
86**
**default target frames, 352**
**deleting.** *See also* **removing**
   files from Web sites, 72-74
   published files, 192
   themes on Web sites, 102
   Web sites, 72-74
**description parameter, 215-
216**

**descriptions, adding to Web sites, 215-216**

**designing themes for Web sites, 90**

**DHTML (Dynamic HTML), 156-158**

**DHTML Effects toolbar, 157**

**dialog boxes.** *See also* **wizards**

  Add browser, 209

  Add Choice, 288

  Browser Compatibility, 203-205

  Cell Properties, 32

  Comment, 82

  Confirm Delete, 87

  Custom Query, 271

  Customize, 91, 96

  Customize Theme, 98-102

  Database Column Value, 274

  Date and Time, 86

  Drop-Down Box Properties, 288

  Edit Browser List, 209

  Edit Hyperlink, 24, 351

  Edit Picture, 147

  Editable Regions, 181

  Flash Properties, 162-163

  Font, 18

  Form Properties, 128, 275, 292-297

  HTML Markup, 220

  Import, 71, 159, 268

  Import List, 268

  Insert Hyperlink, 23, 174, 350

  Insert Table, 29

  Insert Web Component, 152, 168, 173, 220, 235, 247

  Java Applet, 163

  Link Bar Properties, 173, 177

  Link Style, 326

  List Properties, 25

  Marquee Properties, 152

  Modify Style, 321

  New Folder, 79, 116

  New From Existing Page, 243

  New Link Bar, 177

  New Publish Location, 110

  New Web Site Location, 68, 79, 108

  Open Site, 217, 276

  Optimize HTML, 309

  Page Banner Properties, 179

  Page Properties, 11, 215, 306

  Page Templates, 71, 242, 347

  Page Transitions, 155

  Paragraph, 323

  Photo Gallery Properties, 146

  Picture, 39, 290

  Picture File Type, 49

  Picture Properties, 40

  Remote Web Site Properties, 191

  Save As, 11

  Save Embedded Files, 49

  Saving Results, 126-128, 292

  Saving Theme, 102

  Search Form Properties, 245-247

  Set Attribute Value, 164

  Shared Borders, 83

  Style, 320-322

  Table of Contents Properties, 249-250

  Table Properties, 61

  Text Box Properties, 283

  Top 10 List Properties, 236

  Video, 160

  Web Site Templates, 106-107, 116, 223, 254

**directories**

  Web, submitting Web sites to, 213-216

  Web Presence Providers, 189-190

**discussion groups**

  Discussion Web Wizard, 254-256

  editing Web pages, 262

  layouts, 260

    framing, 261-262

  membership policies, 258-259

  Microsoft FrontPage Client Newsgroup, 366

  naming, 256-257

  naming Web pages, 262

  posting, 258

  reviewing articles, 263

  search results, 259-260

  table of contents, 259

  Usenet, 366

**Discussion Web Site Wizard, 107**

**Discussion Web Wizard, 254-262**

**Discussion Web Wizard icon, 255**

**discussion Webs, articles, 261.** *See also* **discussion groups**

**displaying**
database records, 269-275
discussion Web articles,
261
lists, 25
XML, data views, 336-337
**Disturbing Search Requests
Web sites, 230**
**Dmoz (Open Directory pro-
ject), 214-215**
**Dmoz Web site, 214**
**domain names, 189-190**
**dragging Web pages in
Navigation view, 175**
**Drop-Down Box Properties
dialog box, 288**
**drop-down boxes, adding to
forms, 287-289**
**Dynamic HTML (DHTML),
156-158**
**dynamic Web templates,
179-182**

**E**

**Edit Browser List dialog
box, 209**
**Edit button, 147**
**Edit Hyperlink dialog box,
24, 351**
**Edit Picture dialog box, 147**
**Edit Query button, 271**
**editable regions, 180.** *See
also* **editing**
**Editable Regions dialog
box, 181**
**editing**
banners, 179
comments, 82

data views, 339-340
database records, 273
discussion group Web
pages, 262
drop-down boxes in forms,
288
dynamic Web templates,
editable regions, 180-182
feedback pages, 124-125
framed Web pages, 350
graphics, 137-139
layout tables, 58-60
Personal Web site tem-
plates, 84-85
photos, Photo Gallery,
147-148
search form component,
245-246
shared borders, 82
style sheets, 319-320
target frames, 350
text, 322-324
text areas in forms, 284
timestamp components,
86-87
usage reports, 232
Web pages, 243-244
XML files, 333
**elements**
forms, 280-283
Personal Web site tem-
plates, 84
**email**
form responses, sending,
294-295
feedback pages, 127-129
**Email Results tab, 128, 294**
**Empty Web site templates,
78**
**error_log, 227-231**
**event databases, 266**

**Expedia travel site, adding
to Web pages, 171**
**Express service (Yahoo!
Directory), 214**
**Express Web site, 214**
**extended servers, 188-190**
**Extensible Markup
Language (XML), 332**
displaying, data views,
336-337
forms, saving as, 334-335
**extensions.** *See* **filename
extensions**

**F**

**favorite.htm element, 84**
**features, Web hosting ser-
vices, 188-190**
**Feedback Form icon, 124**
**feedback pages, 123**
adding
pages, Form Page
Wizard, 130
questions, Form Page
Wizard, 133-135
to sites, 124
creating, Form Page
Wizard, 129-130
editing, 124-125
responding to feedback,
128-129
saving, 125-127
setting up
Form Page Wizard, 130
input types, 130-132
prompts, 132
variables, 132
spam, 124

**feedback.htm element, 84**
**fields, 266**
**File System, 109-110**
**File Transfer Protocol (FTP), 109-110, 190**
**filename extensions**
.css filename, 318
.gif filename, 154
server, 125
**files**
copied from computers to Web servers, 195-196
deleting from Web sites, 72-74
form responses, saving to, 291-293
GIF, 36
adding to Web pages, 153-154
importing from Web sites, 113-114
importing to Web sites, 71-72
log files, 226
access_log, 226-228
agent_log, 226-230
error_log, 227-231
referer_log, 227
published, deleting, 192
saving feedback pages to, 126-127
XML, 332-333
**filter records, data views, 340**
**Flash, 161-163**
**Flash Properties dialog box, 162-163**
**Font dialog box, 18**
**Font tab, 100-101**
**fonts**
customizing themes on Web sites, 98-101

styles, 322-323
Web pages, 16-18
**Form Page Wizard, 129-130**
adding pages to sites, 130
adding questions to, 133-135
setting up forms, 130-132
**Form properties dialog box, 128, 275, 292-297**
**Form toolbar, 282**
**Format button, 321**
**Format Painter, 159-160**
**formatting**
data views, 340-341
database placeholders, 274-275
HTML, 306
options, 309-310
layout table cells, 61-63
**Formatting toolbar, 12**
buttons, 14, 327
fonts, 17-18
HTML tag options, 327-328
**Former Painter button, 160**
**forms, 123**
adding to Web pages, 280-282
check boxes, adding to, 286-287
drop-down boxes, adding to, 287-289
elements, adding to, 282-283
feedback pages, 123
adding pages, 130
adding questions, 133-135
adding to sites, 124
creating, 129-130
editing, 124-125
email, 127

input types, 130-132
prompts, 132
responding to feedback, 128-129
saving, 125-127
setting up, 130
spam, 124
variables, 132
graphics, adding to, 290-291
labels, adding to, 285
option buttons, adding to, 286-287
pushbuttons, adding to, 289-290
responses, 291
saving to files, 291-293
sending to CGI programs, 296-297
sending to email addresses, 294-295
sending via email, 294
submission, discussion groups, 255-256
text areas, adding to, 284
text boxes, adding to, 282-284
XML, saving, 334-335
**frame pages, saving, 354-355**
**framed Web pages, editing, 350**
**frames**
adding to Web sites, 347-348
alternatives to, 352-354
configuring, 346
creating, 346-347
inline, 357-358
modifying, 355-356
sizing, 356-357
target, 346, 350

defaults, 352

hyperlinks, 347

hyperlinks, creating, 350-351

hyperlinks, editing, 350

Web pages, adding to, 348-349

**Frames Pages tab, 347**

**framing, discussion groups, 261-262**

**From Existing Page hyperlink, 243**

**FrontLook Web site, 219**

**FrontPage Developer Resources Web site, 366**

**FrontPage Internet resources, 363**

**FrontPage Server Extensions, 108, 188**

importing subsites, 109-110

**FrontPage Technical Support Web site, 364**

**FrontPage Tools Web site, 178**

**FrontPage Web site, 364**

**FrontPage World Web site, 365**

**FTP (File Transfer Protocol), 109-110, 190**

# G

**.gif filename extension, 154**

**GIF files, 36**

adding to Web pages, 153

.gif filename extension, 154

**GIF format (Graphics Interchange Format), 36-37**

**Google AdSense Web site, 311**

**Google Groups Web site, 366**

**Google Images Web site, 43**

**Google Site Search Web site, 311**

**Google Web site, 10, 212, 218**

**graphics, 36**

adding to forms, 290-291

adding to Web pages, 38-39

alignment, 41-42

sizes, 47-49

wrapping style, 40-41

animated, themes in Web sites, 93

animated GIF files, adding to Web pages, 153-154

cropping, 140-141

customizing themes on Web sites, 100-101

deleting files from Web sites, 72-74

editing, 137-139

GIF files, 36

GIF format, 36-37

importing files to Web sites, 71-72

JPEG format, 36-37

mouseover, 158-159

original, 159

PNG format, 36-38

saving Web pages, 49-50

shaping, 138

sizing, 138-140

swap, 159

text, adding to, 141

imagemaps, 142-143

transparency, 143-144

**Graphics button, 100-101**

**Graphics Interchange Format (GIF format), 36-37**

**graphics programs, Macromedia, 161-163**

**Group Box command, 286**

**group boxes, form labels, 285**

# H

**<head> tag, 306**

**headings, 14-16**

**hit counters, 234-235**

**hosting Web sites, 187-190**

**<hr> tag, 303**

**<html> tag, 306**

**HTML (Hypertext Markup Language), 301-302**

Dynamic, 156

formatting, 306

formatting options, 309-310

optimizing, 309-310

round-trip HTML, 308-309

Web pages, adding, 311-313

**HTML code, adding to Web pages, 220-221**

**HTML markup, 307**

**HTML Markup dialog box, 220**

**HTML tags, 302-304**

Formatting toolbar options, 327-328

Styles list box, 320-322
types, 327
**http (HyperText Transfer Protocol), 109**
importing subsites, 111
importing Web sites, 112-113
**http referrer, 217-218**
**hyperlinks, 21.** *See also* **linking; links; text hyperlinks**
adding to graphics, 42-43
adding to Web pages, 22-24
From Existing Page, 243
link bars, 175-176
linking to Web sites, 216-218
More Page Templates, 242
Usage Data link, 217, 233
UsTop Referrer link, 217
Web Package Solutions, 223
**Hyperlinks to Add to the Page panel, 175-176**
**Hypertext Markup Language.** *See* **HTML**
**HyperText Transfer Protocol (http).** *See* **http**

**I**

**icons**
Discussion Web Wizard, 255
Feedback Form, 124
Normal Style Sheet, 318
Search Page, 242
**imagemaps, 142-143**
**Import dialog box, 71, 159, 268**

**Import List dialog box, 268**
**Import Web Site Wizard, 107-111**
importing site files, 113-114
levels, 112
**importing**
files to Web sites, 71-72
subsites, 110-111
Web sites
HTTP, 112-113
methods, 108-111
site files, 113-114
wizards, 107-108
Word documents to Web sites, 74-75
**index.htm element, 84**
**Inktomi and Fast Web site, 213**
**inline frames, 357-358**
**input types (forms), 130-131**
adding questions to forms, 133-135
prompts, 130-132
variables, 132
**Insert Hyperlink button, 290**
**Insert Hyperlink dialog box, 23, 174, 350**
**Insert Table dialog box, 29**
**Insert Web Component dialog box, 152, 168, 220, 235, 247**
**Insert Web Components dialog box, 173**
**interest.htm element, 84**
**interfaces, Web pages, 8-9**
**Internet resources, FrontPage, 363**
**invisible tables, 54**

**J-K**

**jaggies, 37**
**Java applet, adding to Web pages, 163-165**
**Java Applet dialog box, 163**
**Java Web site, 165**
**JavaScript, 93**
Photo Gallery, 148
**Joint Photographic Experts Group format (JPEG format), 36**
**JPEG format (Joint Photographic Experts Group), 36-37**

**L**

**labels, adding to forms, 285**
**languages, scripting, 93**
**Layout tab, 148**
**layout tables, 53-54**
adding/removing columns/rows, 58
creating, 55-58
editing, 58-60
formatting cells, 61-62
removing margins, 61
**layouts, discussion groups, 260-262**
**levels (Import Web Site Wizard), 112**
**Link Bar Properties dialog box, 173, 177**
**link bars, 172**
adding to Web pages, 172-173
hyperlinks, 175-176
Navigation view, 173-175

sequence setup, 178
text, 174
Back/Next bars, 177
Back/Next buttons, 177
creating, 173
**link lists, 218**
**Link Style Sheet dialog box, 326**
**linking.** *See also* **hyperlinks; links**
styles to Web pages, 326
Web sites, 216-218
**links, 218.** *See also* **hyperlinks; linking**
**List Properties dialog box, 25**
**lists, 21**
adding to Web pages, 24-25
collapsible, 25-26
configuring, 25
creating, 24-25
displaying, 25
links, 218
log files, 226
access_log, 226-228
agent_log, 226-229
error_log, 227-231
referer_log, 227-230
numbered/unnumbered, 24
**LiveJournal Web site, 223**
**locations, publishing Web sites, 190**
**log files, 226**
access_log, 226-228
agent_log, 226-229
error_log, 227-231
referer_log, 227-230
**logs, Web logs, 221-223**

**M**

**Macromedia graphic programs, 161-163**
**Macromedia Web site, 165**
**maps**
components, adding to Web pages, 171
site, adding to Web pages, 248-250
**margins, removing from layout tables, 61**
**Marquee Properties dialog box, 152**
**marquees, 151-153**
**<meta> tag, 306**
**metatags, 215**
**Microsoft FrontPage Client Newsgroup discussion group, 366**
**Microsoft FrontPage Web site, 364**
**Microsoft Internet Explorer Web site, 208**
**Microsoft Virtual Web site, 208**
**Microsoft Web Presence Providers Web site, 365**
**Microsoft Web site, 179, 366**
**Microsoft's Design Gallery Live Web site, 50**
**Modify Style dialog box, 321**
**More Options button, 272**
**More Page Templates hyperlink, 242**
**mouseover graphics, creating, 158-159**
**Mozilla Web site, 208**

**MSN Search Web component, 247-248**
**MSNBC news, adding components to Web pages, 169-170**

**N**

**naming**
discussion group Web pages, 262
discussion groups, 256-257
Web pages, 11
**Navigation view (link bars), 173-175**
**NCSA Common Log Format, 227**
**Netscape Navigator Web site, 208**
**New Folder dialog box, 79, 116**
**New From Existing Page dialog box, 243**
**New Link Bar dialog box, 177**
**New Publish Location dialog box, 110**
**New Web Site Location dialog box, 68, 79, 108**
**Normal Style Sheet icon, 318**
**numbered lists, 24**

## O

One-Page Web site templates, 78
Open Directory Project (Dmoz), 214-215
Open Site dialog box, 217, 276
opening Web pages, 12
opening tag, 303
Opera Web site, 208
Optimize HTML dialog box, 309
optimizing, 309-310
option buttons, adding to forms, 286-287
original graphic, 159
Outfront Templates and Tools Web site, 365

## P-Q

&lt;p&gt; tag, 306
packages, 223
padding, 62
Page Banner Properties dialog box, 179
page hit reports, 232
Page Properties dialog box, 11, 215, 306
Page Templates dialog box, 71, 242, 347
page transitions, creating, 154-155
Page Transitions dialog box, 155
Paragraph dialog box, 323
parameters, 215-216

passwords, 111
Personal Web site templates, 78
    editing, 84-85
    elements, 84
    saving site changes, 87
    timestamp components, 86-87
photo galleries, creating, 145-148
Photo Galleries Properties dialog box, 146
Photo Gallery, 145
    editing photos, 147-148
    JavaScript, 148
photo.htm element, 84
photos, editing (Photo Gallery), 147-148
Picture dialog box, 39, 290
Picture File Type dialog box, 49
Picture Properties dialog box, 40
Picture tab, 101
Pictures toolbar, 137-138
Pixel theme, 91
placeholders, databases, 273-275
PNG format (Portable Network Graphics format), 36-38
policies, discussion group memberships, 258-259
Portable Network Graphics format (PNG format), 36-38
posting discussion groups, 258
Preview in Browser button, 94, 209

previewing Web pages, 208-209
privacy, Web site customization, 80-81
programs, CGI program, 296-297
Project Web site templates, 78
prompts (forms), 130-132
publishing Web sites, 190-193
    common problems, 193-194
    exclusive files, 194
    extended servers, 190
    file deletion, 192
    FTP servers, 190
    locations, 190
    synchronizing files, 194-196
pushbuttons, adding to forms, 289-290

## R

Radio Userland Web site, 223
Random transitions, creating, 155-156
records, 266
    databases
        displaying, 269-275
        editing, 273
    displaying, 339-340
    fields, 266-267
    filter records, data views, 340
    sorting, 341
referer_log, 227-230

referring links, 218
Referring URLs report,
    217-218
regions, editable, 180. *See
    also* editing
Remote Web Site Properties
    dialog box, 191
Remove Effect button, 158-
    159
removing. *See also* deleting
    DHTML effects to Web
        pages, 158
    margins from tables, 61
    shared borders to Web
        sites, 83-84
    themes from Web sites, 95
    transitions from Web
        pages, 155
reports
    page hit reports, 232
    Referring URLs, 217-218
    Total Bytes Downloaded
        report, 234
    traffic reports, 234
    usage (Web sites), 226-
        227
        hit counters, 234-235
        log files, 226-231
        Top 10 List Web com-
            ponents, 235-236
        viewing, 231-234
Reports button, 217, 233
requirements
    databases, 267
    extended server hosting,
        189
    search form component,
        242
resampling graphics, 47-49
Reset button, 245, 280
resizing graphics, 47

resources, Internet
    (FrontPage), 363
Resources Web ring, 219
responding to feedback
    pages, email, 128-129
responses, forms, 291
    saving to files, 291-293
    sending to CGI programs,
        296-297
    sending to email address-
        es, 294-295
    sending via email, 294
restrictions, Web site tech-
    nology, 205-207
results, searches (discussion
    groups), 259-260
reviewing discussion group
    articles, 263
rings, Web, 219
round-trip HTML, 308-309
rows, tables, 31, 58


S

Safari Web site, 208
Sams Publishing Web site,
    22, 304, 364
Save As dialog box, 11
Save Embedded Files dialog
    box, 49
saving, 275
    database form data, 275-
        277
    feedback pages, 125
        email, 127
        file storage, 126-127
    form responses to files,
        291-293
    forms as XML, 334-335

frame pages, 354-355
imported Web sites, 111-
    112
personal Web site changes,
    87
themes on Web sites, 102
Web pages, 10-11
Web pages with graphics,
    49-50
Web sites, 111-112
Saving Results dialog box,
    126-128, 292
Saving Theme dialog box,
    102
scores, search results page,
    244
scripting languages, 93
scripting, turning off, 94
scrolling marquees, 151-153
Search button, 248
search engines, 212
    adding to Web sites, 242-
        243
        comments, 244
        duplicate Web pages,
            243-244
        edits, 243-244
    search results page, 244
        customizing, 245-246
        scores, 244
    submitting Web sites, 212-
        213
search form component, 243
    adding to Web pages, 246-
        247
    editing, 245-246
    limiting searches, 246
    modifying, 245
        word indexes, 246
    MSN searches, 247-248
    requirements, 242

**Search Form properties dialog box, 245-247**
**Search Page icon, 242**
**Search Page template, 242**
**search results, discussion groups, 259-260**
**Search Results tab, 245-246**
**selecting**
    corporate Web site pages, 116-118
    files to be published, 194
    themes for Web sites, 90-91
**sending form responses**
    to CGI programs, 296-297
    to email addresses, 294-295
    via email, 294
**server extensions, 125**
**Server Extensions**
    databases, 267
    search form component, 242
**server software, 202-203**
**servers**
    extended, 188-190
    files copied from computers to, 195-196
**Set Attribute Value dialog box, 164**
**Set Transparent Color button, 144**
**shaping graphics, 138**
**shared borders, 82-84**
**Shared Borders dialog box, 83**
**SharePoint services, 108, 188**
**SharePoint Team Web site templates, 78**
**Shockwave, 161-163**

**site maps, adding to Web pages, 248-250**
**sites, Web sites.** *See* **Web sites**
**sizing**
    frames, 356-357
    graphics, 47-49, 138-140
    tables in Web pages, 32
**software**
    graphics, 161-163
    Web sites, 202-203
        target audience, 203-205
        technology restrictions, 205-207
**sorting records, 341**
**spam, 124**
**spammers, 124**
**special effects, DHTML, 157-158**
**Split button, 328**
**standards, World Wide Web Consortium, 200**
**Start Search button, 245**
**storing.** *See* **saving**
**Style dialog box, 320-322**
**style sheets, 315-316**
    creating, 318
    editing, 319-320
    HTML tags, types, 327
    Web pages, linking, 326
**Style Sheets tab, 318**
**styles, 316**
    Web pages, 324-326
**Styles list box, HTML tags, 320-322**
**Submit button, 280, 290**
**subsites, importing, 109-111**
**swap graphic, 159**
**synchronizing files to be published, 194-196**

**T**

**table of contents, discussion groups, 259**
**Table of Contents component, 248-250**
**Table of Contents Properties dialog box, 249-250**
**Table Properties dialog box, 61**
**tables, 21, 266**
    adding to Web pages, 26-29
        borders, 29
        cell padding, 30
        cell spacing, 30
        columns, 31
        data, 30-31
        rows, 31
        sizes, 32
        text, 27
    borders, 29
    cell padding, 30
    cell spacing, 30
    columns, 31
    creating, 26-27
    data, adding to, 30-31
    layout, 53-54
        adding/removing columns/rows, 58
        autostretch, 56
        creating, 55-58
        editing, 58, 60
        formatting cells, 61-63
        invisible tables, 54
        removing margins, 61
    rows, adding to/removing from, 31

**tabs**
 Authoring, 205-207
 Character Spacing, 323
 Confirmation, 297
 Custom, 98
 Email Results, 128, 294
 Font, 100-101
 Frames Pages, 347
 Layout, 148
 Picture, 101
 Search Results, 245-246
 Style Sheets, 318
 Web Site, 70
**tags, 301**
 <body>, 306
 <head>, 306
 <hr>, 303
 <html>, 306
 <meta>, 306
 <p>, 306
 <title>, 306
 closing, 303
 commands, 321-322
 HTML, 302-304
  Styles list box, 320-322
  types, 327
 opening, 303
**target audience, Web sites, 203-205**
**target frame, 346-347**
**Target Frame button, 351**
**target frames, 350-352**
**technology, Web site restrictions, 205-207**
**templates, 77-78**
 creating from Web pages, 9-10
 dynamic Web, creating, 179-182
 Search Page, 242
 types, 78

**Teoma Web site, 212**
**testing**
 imported Web sites, 114
 themes using browsers, 94
**text**
 adding to graphics, 141
  imagemaps, 142-143
 adding to Web pages, 12-14
  color/font, 16-18
 animating, marquees, 151-153
 blinking, Web pages, 201
 DHTML, applying to, 156
 editing, 322
  font styles, 322-323
  paragraphs, 323-324
 link bars, 174
**text areas, adding to forms, 284**
**Text Box Properties dialog box, 283**
**text boxes, adding to forms, 282, 284**
**Text button, 99, 142**
**text headings, creating, 14-16**
**text hyperlinks, 22-23. See also hyperlinks**
**Theme pane, 91**
**themes, 89, 317**
 animated graphics, 93
 CSS, 93
 customizing on Web sites, 95-96
  color schemes, 96-98
  fonts, 98-100
  graphic fonts, 100-101
  graphics, 100
 deleting on Web sites, 102

 designing for Web sites, 90
 removing from Web sites, 95
 saving on Web sites, 102
 selecting for Web sites, 90-91
 testing on Web sites with browsers, 94
 viewing in Web sites, 91-93
**timestamp components, 86-87**
**<title> tag, 306**
**titles, 215**
 Web pages, 306
**toolbars**
 Back/Next, link bars, 177
 DHTML Effects, 157
 Form, 282
 Formatting, 12
  buttons, 14, 327
  fonts, 17-18
  HTML tag options, 327-328
 Pictures, 137-138
 Views, 69
**Tools menu, Web Settings command, 257**
**Top 10 List properties dialog box, 236**
**Top 10 List Web components, 235-236**
**Top Referrer hyperlink, 217**
**Total Bytes Downloaded report, 234**
**tracking Web site visits, 226**
 log files, 226-231
 usage reports, 226-227, 231-236
**traffic reports, 234**

transitions, 154-156
transparency, GIF format, 36-37
transparency (graphics), 143-144
types
    HTML tags, 327
    templates, 78

# U

unnumbered lists, 24
Usage Data hyperlink, 217, 233
usage reports (Web sites), 226-227
    hit counters, 234-235
    log files, 226-227
        access_log, 227-228
        agent_log, 228-229
        error_log, 230-231
        referer_log, 229-230
    Top 10 List Web components, 235-236
    viewing, 231-233
        edits, 232
        page hit reports, 232
        traffic reports, 234
Usenet discussion group, 366
user interfaces, Web pages, 8-9
usernames, 111
users, Web sites, 201
    server software, 202-203
    target audience, 203-205
    technology restrictions, 205-207

# V

variables (forms), 132
VBScript, 93
video, adding to Web pages, 160-161
Video dialog box, 160
viewing
    comments, 81-82
    CSS, 324
    text hyperlinks, 22
    themes in Web sites, 91-93
    usage reports, 231-233
        edits, 232
        hit counters, 234-235
        page hit reports, 232
        Top 10 List Web components, 235-236
        traffic reports, 234
    Web pages with CSS, 318
    Web Presence Providers directory, 189-190
    Web sites, 69-70
    XML files, 332
Views toolbar, 69
VMware Workstation Web site, 208

# W

Web browsers
    testing themes in Web pages, 94
    Web page compatibility, 200
        previewing pages, 208-209
        server software, 202-203

target audience, 203-205
    technology restrictions, 205-207
    text blinking, 201
    Web users, 201-202
    World Wide Web Consortium standards, 200
Web components, 85
Web directories, submitting Web sites, 213
    descriptions, 215-216
    Open Directory Project, 214-215
    parameters, 215-216
    Yahoo! Directory, 213-214
Web hosting, 187
    domain names, 189-190
    locating services, 188
        extended servers, 188-189
Web logs, 221
    packages, 223
    writing style, 221-223
Web Package Solutions hyperlink, 223
Web pages
    adding to frames, 348-349
    adding to Web sites, 70-71
    banners, adding to, 178-179
    browser compatibility, 200
        previewing pages, 208-209
        server software, 202-203
        target audience, 203-205

technology restrictions, 205-207
text blinking, 201
Web users, 201-202
World Wide Web Consortium standards, 200
choosing for corporate Web sites, 116-118
clip art, adding to, 45-47
confirmation pages, creating, 297
copying, 243-244
creating, 7
from templates, 9-10
user interfaces, 8-9
cropping graphics on, 140-141
CSS, viewing, 318
data views, 337-339
filter records, 340
formatting, 340-341
records, 339-340
discussion groups, 262-263
editing, 243-244
editing graphics on, 138-139
forms
adding, 280-282
check boxes, adding, 286-287
drop-down boxes, adding, 287-289
elements, adding, 282-283
graphics, adding, 290-291
labels, adding, 285
option buttons, adding, 286-287

pushbuttons, adding, 289-290
text areas, adding, 284
text boxes, adding, 282-284
frame pages, saving, 354-355
framed, editing, 350
frames, inline frames, 358
graphics, adding to, 38-39
alignment, 41-42
captions, 43-45
hyperlinks, 42-43
sizes, 47-49
wrapping style, 40-41
hit counters, adding to, 235
HTML markup, 307
HTML, adding to, 311-313
hyperlinks, adding to, 22-24
link bars, adding to, 172-173
Back/Next buttons/bars, 177
hyperlinks, 175-176
Navigation view, 173-175
sequence setup, 178
text, 174
lists, adding to, 24-25
metatags, 215
naming, 11
opening, 12
optimizing, 309-310
parameters, 215
saving, 10-11
saving with graphics, 49-50

search form component adding, 246-247
limiting searches, 246
MSN searches, 247-248
word indexes, 246
search results page, 244
customizing, 245-246
scores, 244
style sheets, linking, 326
styles, 324-326
CSS, 325
Table of Contents component, adding site maps, 248-250
tables, adding to, 26-29
borders, 29
cell padding, 30
cell spacing, 30
columns, 31
data, 30-31
rows, 31
sizes, 32
text, 27
text, adding to, 12-14
color/fonts, 16-18
titles, 215, 306
**Web Presence Providers directory, 189-190**
**Web rings, 218-219**
HTML code, adding, 220-221
**Web Settings command (Tools menu), 257**
**Web Site tab, 70**
**Web Site Templates dialog box, 106-107, 116, 223, 254**
**Web sites, 67**
AccessFP FrontPage Resource Centre, 365
Acme Internet, 365

Adbility, 311
All the Web, 212
Altavista, 212
Amazon.com, 311
At-FrontPage, 366
Blogger, 223
Bobby, 45
Chris's FrontPage Info, 364
Commission Junction, 311
components, adding to, 168-169
    Expedia travel site, 171
    MSNBC news, 169-170
corporate
    choosing pages for, 116-118
    creating, 115-116
creating, 67-69
    new sites, 78-79
creating with wizards, 106-107
customizing, 80
    private subfolders, 80-81
databases, adding, 268-269
deleting, 72-74
    hidden files/folders, 74
Disturbing Search Requests, 230
Dmoz, 214
Express, 214
files copied from computers to servers, 195-196
files, deleting from, 72-74
    hidden files/folders, 74
files, importing to, 71-72
frames, adding to, 347-348
FrontLook, 219

FrontPage, 364
FrontPage Developer Resources, 366
FrontPage Technical Support, 364
FrontPage Tools, 178
FrontPage World, 365
Google, 10, 212, 218
Google AdSense, 311
Google Groups, 366
Google Images, 43
Google Site Search, 311
importing
    HTTP, 112-113
    site files, 113-114
importing with wizards, 107-108
    methods, 108-111
Inktomi and Fast, 213
Java, 165
linking to, 216
    HTTP referrer, 217-218
    link lists, 218
LiveJournal, 223
Macromedia, 165
Microsoft, 179, 366
Microsoft FrontPage, 364
Microsoft Internet Explorer, 208
Microsoft Virtual, 208
Microsoft Web Presence Providers, 365
Microsoft's Design Gallery Live, 50
Mozilla, 208
Netscape Navigator, 208
new pages, adding to, 70-71
Opera, 208

Outfront Templates and Tools, 365
publishing, 190-193
    common problems, 193-194
    exclusive files, 194
    extended servers, 190
    file deletion, 192
    FTP servers, 190
    locations, 190
    synchronizing files, 194-196
RadioUserland, 223
Safari, 208
Sams Publishing, 22, 304, 364
saving with wizards, 111-112
search engines
    adding, 242-243
    comments, 244
    duplicate Web pages, 243-244
    editing, 243-244
search form component, 246
search results page, 244-246
submitting to search engines, 212-213
submitting to Web directories, 213
    descriptions, 215-216
    Open Directory Project, 214-215
    parameters, 215-216
    Yahoo! Directories, 213-214
testing imported sites, 114

testing themes with browsers, 94
themes, 89
  animated graphics, 93
  color, 96-98
  comparing with unthemed pages, 90
  customizing, 95-96
  deleting, 102
  designing, 90
  fonts, 98-100
  graphic fonts, 100-101
  graphics, 100
  removing, 95
  saving, 102
  selecting, 90-91
  viewing, 91-93
tracking visits, 226
  log files, 226-231
  usage reports, 226-227, 231-236
viewing, 69-70
VMware Workstation, 208
Web rings, 218-219
  HTML code, adding, 220-221
Weblogger.com, 223
WebRing, 219, 311
Word documents, converting to, 74-75
Workbench, 222
World Wide Web Consortium, 200
Yahoo! Directory, 213-214
**Web templates, dynamic, 179-182**
**Webalizer, 226**
**WebDAV, 109**
**Weblogger.com Web site, 223**
**WebRing, 219**

**WebRing Web site, 219, 311**
**WebTrends, 226**
**wizards, 105.** *See also* **dialog boxes**
  Corporate Presence, 107
    choosing Web site pages, 116-118
    creating corporate Web sites, 115-116
  Database Interface, 107
  Database Results, 269, 276
  Discussion Web, 254-262
  Discussion Web Site, 107
  Form Page, 129-130
    adding pages to sites, 130
    adding questions to, 133-135
    input types, 130-132
    prompts, 132
    setting up forms, 130
    variables, 132
  Import Web Site, 107-111
    importing site files, 113-114
  importing existing Web sites, 107-108
    methods, 108-111
  overview, 105-106
  saving existing Web sites, 111-112
  Web sites, creating, 106-107
**Word documents, converting to Web sites, 74-75**
**Workbench, 222-223**
**World Wide Web Consortium Web site, 200**
**wrapping graphics, 40-41**
**writing Web logs, 221-223**

## X-Z

**XML (Extensible Markup Language), 332**
  displaying, data views, 336-337
  files, 332-333
  forms, saving as, 334-335

**Yahoo! Directory, 213**
  Express service, 214
**Yahoo! Directory Web site, 213**